Migration, Mujercitas, and Medicine Men

Migration, Mujercitas, and Medicine Men

Living in Urban Mexico

Valentina Napolitano

UNIVERSITY OF CALIFORNIA

Berkeley / Los Angeles / London

A version of Chapter 3 appeared in *The Bulletin of Latin American Research* 17 (3) (1998).
A version of Chapter 5 appeared in *The Journal of the Royal Anthropological Institute* 3 (2) (1997) and was reprinted in *Across the Boundaries of Belief, Contemporary Issues in the Anthropology of Religion,* edited by M. Klass and M. Weisgrau (Boulder:Westview Press, 1999).

University of California Press
Berkeley and Los Angeles, California

University of California Press, Ltd.
London, England

Library of Congress Cataloging-in-Publication Data

Napolitano, Valentina.
   Migration, mujercitas, and medicine men : living in urban Mexico /
Valentina Napolitano.
      p.   cm.
   Includes bibliographical references and index.
   ISBN 0-520-23318-2 (cloth : alk. paper).—ISBN 0-520-23319-0 (paper :
alk. paper)
      1. Indians of Mexico—Urban residence—Mexico—Guadalajara.   2.
Guadalajara (Mexico)—Social conditions.   3. Rural-urban
migration—Mexico—Guadalajara.   I. Title.

F1219.1.G86 N66 2002
972'.35—dc21   2001008310

Manufactured in the United States of America
11   10   09   08   07   06   05   04   03   02
10   9   8   7   6   5   4   3   2   1

The paper used in this publication is both acid-free and totally chlorine-free (TCF). It meets the minimum requirements of ANSI/NISO Z39.48–1992 (R 1997) *(Permanence of Paper)*.

In memory of my mother, Mara (1929–1998)
Una donna vitale e coraggiosa
And to my beloved father, Picchio

Contents

Acknowledgments   ix

List of Abbreviations   xiii

Preface   xv

Introduction: Prisms of Belonging and Alternative
Modernities   1

1. Internationalizing Region, Expanding City, Neighborhoods
   in Transition   17

2. Migration, Space, and Belonging   39

3. Religious Discourses and the Politics of Modernity   69

4. Medical Pluralism: Medicina Popular and Medicina
   Alternativa   96

5. Becoming a Mujercita: Rituals, Fiestas, and Religious
   Discourses   128

6. Neither Married, Widowed, Single, or Divorced: Gender
   Negotiation, Compliance, and Resistance   156

Epilogue   181

Appendix A: Homeopathic Principles   189

Appendix B: Trees of Life and Death   191

Notes   195

Bibliography   217

Index   237

Acknowledgments

First I wish to thank people in the neighborhood of Polanco, especially Socorro Pérez Martinez and her family, including the newly arrived Dulce Citlali; Doña Mari and Don Donato Rubrica and their families and granddaughter Valentina; Alfredo López; Maru, Doña Cata, Don Roberto and Doña Mari; Martín and his family; Doña Tere and Doña Elsa; and many others I wish I had room to mention. My thanks to them all for allowing me to see the worlds in which we think we live as the multiple encounters of familial differences, and for reminding me to laugh at myself. Thanks also to Padre Nacho, who dealt with my otherness in an intelligent way. I also wish to thank the different Jesuits I met during my fieldwork. The dear friends of the Teopantli Kalpulli of San Isidro Mazatepec, who lifted my spirits and renewed my inner strength in moments of fatigue and isolation, also inhabit a special place in my heart. I am also grateful for the support of Lucy Herrada and her family, Hilda Gamez de Ortega, Mauricio Padilla Mirazo, and Luis Moreno.

I could not have found my intellectual and social bearings in sprawling Guadalajara without the crucial background preparation provided by Norman Long and the "Mexican group" at the University of Wageningen (Christopher and Elsa Martin, Magdalena Villareal, Gabriel Torres, and Humberto Gonzáles Chávez, among others). I am also grateful for the precious intellectual direction and timely support of colleagues at the Centro de Estudios Superiores de Antropología Social de Occidente in Guadalajara. I especially wish to thank Patricia Fortuny Loret de Mola and Renée de la Torre Castellanos for their comments at different stages of this book. Particularly warm thanks go to Guillermo de la Peña Topete, whose intellectual depth combined with a special human touch provided much needed direction. I also wish to thank colleagues at the School of Oriental and African Studies, University of London, who believed that having a Latin Americanist Ph.D. student with them was not such an odd rarity after all. I am especially thankful to Richard Fardon (for the diagrams on the board and much more), John Gledhill, Stephen Hughes-Jones, and Peter Worsley, who commented on and encouraged an early incarnation of this book. I also wish to remember the early inspiration of the late Michael Sallnow, who in my undergraduate study at the London School of Economics was the first to put rigor into my knowledge of Latin America. I would also like to acknowledge the support of James Dunkerly, Rachel Sieder, Victor Bulmer-Thomas, and Maxine Molyneaux at the Institute of Latin American Studies in London, and thanks also to Xochitl Leyva Solano, Kristin Norget, Barbara Placido, and Gustavo Nigenda. A special thank-you to Ajay Sehgal, whose brilliant intelligence and dedicated spirit sharpened, aided, and sensitized my understanding during a crucial period of fieldwork and life.

The final draft of this book was written during my appointment as a Research Officer at the Centre of Latin American Studies and Research Fellow at Clare Hall College, University of Cambridge. I am very grateful for the time I have spent at the Centre and the College, and for the intellectual and personal support I have been given, especially from Gillian Beer, David Lehmann, Keith and Clare Brewster, Goeffrey Kantaris, and Charles Jones, as well as the different generations of graduate students who have helped me to understand that research without teaching is like a battery without a flashlight. I am also in great debt to Clare Hariri, Julie Coimbra, and Anna Gray, whose efficiency made it possible for me to spend more of my time writing. My gratitude also goes to Dhoolika Raj, Ananya Kabir, and Sarah Radcliffe in Cambridge for their incisive and timely comments, and to Ann Varley, Margarita Velázquez, and Lesley Caldwell for their intellectual companionship and enduring friendship. I am also in great debt to the senior editor of the University of California Press, Naomi Schneider, who understood the potential of this book well before its current manifestation.

This book would never have been completed without the crucial research time spent at the Department of Anthropology, Culture, and History of Social Medicine at the University of California, San Francisco: special thanks to Philippe Bourgois, Christie and Elsa Kiefer, and

Margarita Loinaz. I am greatly indebted to Donald Moore in the anthropology department at the University of California, Berkeley for having opened up new windows of anthropological consciousness in my intellectual and human landscape.

Last but not least, my enduring thanks goes to my parents. My mother, Mara Marini Napolitano, who appears to me in many forms and continues to offer encouragement, felt that anthropology was good for me even if she could not figure out exactly what it was. She believed that I could do it well, with creativity and commitment, even though she did not live to witness this book's publication. And my father, Felice Napolitano, has supported me unstintingly in the path of fulfillment in life. This book is part of that process. I also thank my ever-present friend and sister, Antonella, with Barry Rosen. *Dulcis in fundo* to my life-partner, Ato Quayson, who has always encouraged me to see that the realms of intuition and life-flow are not antithetical but complementary to embodied analytical inquiry and enduring intellectual curiosity. His presence alone has taught me that this marriage is a powerful and vital one.

May you all be free from sorrow and live in peace.

Abbreviations

ACM	Acción Católica Mexicana
CCMG	Consejo de Colaboración Municipal de Guadalajara
CEBs	Comunidades Eclesiales de Base
CoReTT	Comisión Regularizadora para la Tenencia de la Tierra
CPS	Comité Popular del Sur
CROC	Confederación Revolucionaria de Obreros y Campesinos
CTM	Coordinación de Trabajadores Mexicanos
IMDEC	Instituto Mexicano de Desarollo Económico Comunitario
IMEPLAM	Instituto Mexicano para el Estudio de Plantas Medicinales
IMSS	Instituto Mexicano del Seguro Social
INEGI	Instituto Nacional Estadística Geográfica y Informática
ISSSTE	Instituto de Seguridad y Servicios Sociales de los Trabajadores del Estado
MFC	Movimiento Familiar Cristiano
MTH	Unidad de Investigación en Medicina Tradicional y Herbolaria del Instituto Mexicano del Seguro Social
MUP	Movimiento Urbano Popular
OCIP	Organización de Colonos Independientes de Polanco
PAN	Partido de Acción Nacional
PCM	Partido Comunista Mexicano
PRD	Partido Revolucionario Democrático
PRI	Partido de Revolución Institutional
PST	Partido Socialista de los Trabajadores
SEDOC	Servicios Educativos de Occidente
SSA	Secretaría de Salubridad y Asistencia

Preface

A book emerges out of and lives through a series of different incarnations. This one has taken a spatio-temporal frame of more than eleven years although it has had what I could define as a nonlinear history. In its different incarnations, many people have provided help and inspiration in different forms, and many of these human legacies have become stronger rather than weaker with time. I originally spent six months in Mexico in 1989 and nearly two years there between July 1990 and April 1992. I went back for several shorter visits of up to a month each in 1997, 1998, and 1999. For my longer fieldwork period I have to thank the University of London Scholarship Fund for its financial support, and also the University of Cambridge Travel Fund. My fascination with Mexico goes back to childhood, probably to when I was not even ten years old. While lying on my bed in the early morning (in my parents' flat in the heart of a quiet, middle-class northern Italian town), I recalled pictures and dream-images of Mexican open skies, gentle people and archaeological "ancestral" sites. Even now I cannot decipher the meaning and the biographical timing of those images, but I pay respect to a life that has given me the opportunity to discover that the call of dreams may indeed be a source of inspiration, but that the manifestation in life of a call of dreams requires a great deal of application, work, and the synergy of life contingencies.

While I was doing fieldwork, my physical appearance and the similarity between Italian and Spanish, led people to think at first that I was a "local" from a different class or another region. To begin with, I was often mistaken for a local middle-class student attending one of the City universities, and people in the barrios where I carried out fieldwork were rather suspicious of my daily presence. My Italian-ness, once revealed, often placed me in the position of "exotic outsider," and sometimes even helped open doors that otherwise would have remained closed. But I also encountered failures and roads that were closed to me. I learned through these experiences that both "opening" and "closure" can have equal analytical importance even if they carry an emotionally different quality. But my experience of otherness began much earlier (does it have a specific starting point?), even before I moved to England and embraced, more or less consciously, a British social anthropologist formation. I recall coming across ethnographies on southern Italy (where part of my family comes from) in my early years at University and thinking, when my anthropological knowledge was still at an embryonic stage, that we cannot separate the anthropological eye and pen from the subject gazed at, contacted, and described in a narrative, and that we have to inhabit this intersubjective space with an awareness of how uneasy, painful, or liberating it can be. It is the experience of a degree of alienation, and at the same time an unavoidable proximity, that makes the anthropological journey worth taking.

Introduction

Prisms of Belonging and Alternative Modernities

Let ethnography perform the theory.
Donald Moore

London 1989, pre-fieldwork: a teacher at University is asking me a question. What is there of "original" interest about the people and the city of Guadalajara, where I will soon begin fieldwork? These people seem to him like many others caught up in the process of Latin American urbanization: there are millions of them. My tentative response is that there are various aspects of their lives and constructions of selfhood that I could engage with and later write about. His response: there are many people in the world, but in order to "make" anthropology, we need to find special sociopolitical and cultural configurations.

Now, more than a decade later, I thank him for such a query. This book's focus is the possibility of reversing that same question. What happens if we let go of the fascination of doing research on what is novel and "particular"? Can particularity emerge instead from the everyday, ordinary life of a "place like many others"? These questions acquire a specific relevance in the context of Mexican anthropology's long-time focus on Indian-ness, ethnicity, rural societies, and, to a certain extent, the "marginal" urban poor.[1] The question is, where does this leave those who cannot claim those identities? One motivation for this study is the fact that anthropology needs to engage with these questions and not leave the study of urbanities to demographers and urban planners whose concerns may be complementary to, but which are often paradigmatically different from, those of anthropologists. Many readers may be aware of major and recent research on urban Latin America that has focused on demographic and gender changes, social movements, poverty issues, and the labor market; my wish here is to engage with some of these issues using an ethnographic and anthropological lens.

I have been helped in this interdisciplinary endeavor by current anthropological thinking. A major paradigm shift, and part of anthropological debate, involves letting go of the "representativeness" of unified social and cultural spheres (Marcus 1989). My early exposure to Durkenheimian collective representations and Geertzian "thick description" pushed me originally to frame the material of this book as an ethnography of a barrio. While writing, I came to realize that I was thinking in terms of actors with multiple voices and identities, of opposing and overlapping religious and medical discourses, of paradoxical tensions in the negotiation of womanhood and other gendered subjects. But I was still thinking that my material described a low-income neighborhood of Guadalajara, Mexico's second largest city, where I carried out my fieldwork.

It gradually became clear in this ethnographic journey that my material did not fit a paradigm of unified representativeness, which identifies group identity constituted by social and rational subjects within a specific cultural space and a bounded geographical place. In other words, I could not write a standard anthropology of a barrio. The material required a problematization of the relationship between identity, culture, and place (Gupta and Ferguson 1997: 13). Moving away from an idea of culture as an ordered domain shared by a group of people makes it possible to see culture as an open-ended and unfinished process which is contingent and political (Gupta and Ferguson 1997: 5). And we can also see place, such as a low-income Mexican neighborhood as unfinished, rather than given a priori to social relations. In this way, identity neither grows out of bounded communities, nor is it fully owned by collective or individual actors; rather, it is an ongoing process of "relations of difference."

The narrative of relations of difference that I present in this book emerged from the particular encounters I chose to pursue during my fieldwork. Other points of departure probably would have resulted in a different book. I invite the reader, then, to use the themes that emerge here as possible frameworks for considering other resonant conditions of urbanities in transformation. Processes of transformation run through, rather than being univocally representative of, an urban neighborhood—such as Lomas de Polanco, south of Guadalajara, where I did my fieldwork. Consequently, this book engages with a Mexican ethnographic and urban field that has emerged *through,* rather than being representative *of,* a barrio.

This book does not elaborate well-explored themes in Mexican anthropology such as political patronage, ethnicity, and Indian-ness, or the interface between gender and class in household reproduction. Instead the focus is on religious and medical discourses, selfhood and gender identity, and the dynamics of belonging and everyday life in a *colonia popular* (a primarily low-income and working-class neighborhood). Though this is not an ethnography of a slum area (Lomnitz 1977) or an ethnic minority ghetto (Bourgois 1995) (both long-time "exotic" others in urban anthropology), I aim to convey an emerging anthropological particularity through an ordinary urban place rather than assume its particularity prior to the ethnographic engagement. I hope in this way to allow what some anthropologists would call a disciplinary ordinariness to become anthropologically and interdisciplinarily interesting. Through an ethnographic engagement and journey I weave an anthropological theory that mainly questions what is ordinary, but also explores the relation between the ordinary and the exotic. First, however, let me map out the skeleton of this book, to weave into it, later, its conceptual cardiovascular connections.

The first chapter focuses on the microhistory of neighborhood formation within the wider context of the urbanization of the city of Guadalajara and the western region of Mexico. The neighborhood can be seen not just as a socioeconomic space but as a *spatial process:* it has become a *centro de la periferia* (center of the suburb) for a part of the southern, low-income area of the city because of its history of social mobilization, its image as part of the Guadalajaran urban landscape, and the changing nature of business and services provided. This chapter also explores how processes of acquisition and negotiation of legal and housing rights have influenced individual, family, and group identities. It also examines how differently positioned subjects and groups reveal different ways of conceptualizing a historical past of socio-religious mobilization that presently articulates the narrative of "personal" and "collective" aspects of identity in the urbanizing process.

Chapter 2 focuses on the process of migration, tying an analysis of urbanization and resettlement to a political economy of affects and belonging. To capture the complexity of migration, I present people's narratives about the home, the neighborhood, the city, and places of origin, and also describe ways in which these places and sites of affectivity are revisited. Migration emerges as a process of self-empowerment, or loss of power, and places become the symbols of the embodied phenomenology of space and time. But this phenomenology of belonging—by which I mean a somatic, cognitive, and affective experience of belonging—has a history of production and appropriation, related to histories of displacement and an acquisition of knowledge about the world (such as, for instance, equating the transition from rural to urban life to a passage from a state of unconsciousness into one of consciousness).

Chapter 3 addresses prisms of belonging in relation to the Catholic Church and focuses on the experience of the Comunidades Eclesiales de Base (CEBs, or Christian Base Communities), inspired by the theology of liberation, as well as on traditional Catholic groups. It analyzes the ways in which the Church is represented in terms of metaphors of the "new" and "traditional" Church in the eyes of some members and clergy. It is true that the so-called new Church—the CEBs—induces changes in matters of personal responsibility in one's own life and the life of the community; nevertheless, through analysis of the activity of some Jesuits and Diocesan priests, I argue that the new Church is similar to the traditional one. In the CEBs activities there is a subtle hierarchical control and distribution of knowledge between clerical agents, *promotores* (organizers/activists), and members. This suggests that a progressive social movement can actually be composed of subtle forms expressing conservative tendencies.

Chapter 4 draws attention to central issues concerning the growing phenomenon of medical pluralism and the diverse therapeutic practices that exist parallel to the national health care system. It particularly addresses notions of causality in relation to moral agency and beliefs. Medicina *popular* (popular, grass root health care), *curanderos* (healers), and homeopaths show distinct correlations between specific etiologies and ideas of sociability, of individual sin and redemption, as well as ideas about science and faith in the alternative medical field.

Chapter 5 discusses the *quinceañera* ritual that marks a girl's fifteenth birthday, and the role played by the time of *la ilusión* (in this case meaning dream and hope) which begins with this ritual. Dynamics of selfhood and womanhood emerge from a tension arising from specific Catholic discourses that privilege the communal celebration over individual participation, and emphasize the content rather than the form of the ritual. But for many girls, it is the performance of the *fiesta* that is important, involving as it does their process of individuation and their family's social empowerment. The sexual and bodily symbolism of the ritual does not fully explain the implications of the ritual for female and family identity. These aspects need to be understood within particular sets of family relationships which enhance specific female images, family respectability and status differentiation within the neighborhood.

The final chapter focuses on young women's transition from *la ilusión* to adulthood (often associated with marriage), and analyzes the multi-layered subjectivity of female experience and its contradictory nature in negotiating gender identity. For many women, traditional gender identity rests in motherhood, in experiences of self-abnegation, in service, and in providing a link for family relationships to unfold rather than stressing autonomy and individual agency. However, tensions arise between the multiplicity of perceptions of gender and the fixity of their representation. While female identity is still predominantly based on physical proximity and caring for others, the interpretation of traditional gender roles and the boundaries of motherhood and wifehood are shifting in the face of ongoing, open-ended challenges and a "void of knowledge" of available alternatives. It is also possible that contradictions between gender images and the meanings of engendered and embodied life experiences manifest as life-crises, gossip, and illness. The experience of the embodiment of gender then is central to an understanding of the phenomenology of everyday life.

But how does this ethnography perform the theory I am attempting to exemplify? First, it engages with the analysis of self and group identity, with a theory of the subject which has problematized the category of experience and its fundamentals (Scott 1992; Butler 1992), and with the ways in which both of these debates contribute to ethnographic understanding of urban Mexico. Second, it does this through an ongoing reconceptualization of an anthropology of belonging, localism, place, and urban identity (Hannerz 1996; Ferguson 1999) via the introduction of what I will call "prisms of belonging." Finally, the ethnographic insights run *through* a low-income neighborhood, showing ways in which modernity and tradition are constructed relationally by situated agents. In this the ethnography contributes to the debate and understanding of alternative, or vernacular, modernity. But let me address each of these points in turn.

I first wish to emphasize that the rest of this introduction is dedicated to these conceptual points and their relation to Mexican urban anthropology and this ethnography. This theoretical overview section is intended to point out the implications that this ethnography has for a wider anthropological debate.[2] It also contextualizes my work within existing anthropological production on urban Mexico.

Unfolding a Three-fold Path

THREAD I: THE PROBLEMATIZATION
OF SELF AND EXPERIENCE

We have learned through feminist thinking that experience cannot be taken at face value, and that "it is not individuals who have experiences, but subjects who are constituted through experience" (Scott 1992: 26). We have learned to distinguish between selves and subjects.[3] Consequently, what were once defined as collective selves, such as "women" or the "urban poor," were then studied as subjects because they are not givens; rather, they are produced through a historical process (Talpade Mohanty 1992: 84). Ascribed categories such as gender have been reconceptualized as performative processes—in the making and always open-ended—with potential for reversal. Difference is always related to what is made meaningful and embodied in a local context.

This antinormative and antifoundationalist stance—counterpoised to an existing idea of an essentialized self—is clearly an important critique of past debates in urban Mexican anthropology about a rural and urban divide, and a "Culture and Personality" approach. Although the "Culture and Personality" theory (Lewis 1959, 1961,1966) and ideas about an "urban-rural continuum" (Redfield 1947) have been out of anthropological fashion for some time, they continued to influence many North American ethnographic accounts of Mexico up to the late 1970s (Díaz 1966; Díaz Guerrero 1975; Romanucci-Ross 1973; Fromm and Maccoby 1970; Foster 1979; Kemper 1977).[4] These works were inspired by functionalist and modernist evolutionary paradigms that translated concepts of human and cultural adaptation, and which, as I explain later, clearly left unproblematized the categories of the person and of experience. The studies of Foster (1979) and Kemper (1977), for instance, focused on migration and treated identity formation in a functionalist way—as a process of modernization that involves changing traditional attitudes and lifestyles considered "backward" to a modern "forwardness" exemplified by increasing prestige and economic improvement. It is clear that these studies assumed ahistorical psychological characteristics and existential and ethnocentric universals as constitutive of individual and collective identities (Needham 1981). In other words, these authors considered human nature and the meaning of personhood to be universal and ahistorical concepts.

By the late 1970s, these studies were being challenged by historical materialist approaches.[5] In fact, Mexican urban anthropologists moved away from questions of adaptation and began studying such concepts as formality and informality, and urban space as a locus of production and consumption (Edel and Hellman 1988). Anthropological analyses of urban Mexico began to emphasize structures of production and reproduction—analyzing the "life of the poor" in its diversified forms of strategic adaptation to economic shortages and the effects of the early 1980s oil crisis (e.g., Lomnitz 1977; Hirabayashi 1983; Higgins 1983; González de la Rocha 1994; Roberts 1986; Selby 1987; Selby et al. 1990). Parallel studies engaged with debunking stereotypical "Culture and Personality" ideas of pathological and self-inflicted marginality, and focused on specific sociopolitical resistance to incorporation into the national system (Vélez-Ibañez 1983; Logan 1984). Others used a historical structural analysis to comprehend migration and the process of identity, pointing out in some cases the limitations of this approach in understanding of micro-levels of identity formation (Arizpe 1978: 50). They all pointed out that poor people, migrants, and those in the urban working class were more active agents than previously thought.

Yet some questions are still open. How are the subject and the collective constructed through the urban process? Which processes of historical and political negotiations inform the subject's belonging and group affiliation within the urban space of a colonia popular? And finally, how does the subject use cultural processes such as symbols and rituals to interpret everyday life? Some recent Mexican ethnographies have addressed these issues in part by situating the gendered self/subject in a process of historical and social transformation (Behar 1993; Gutmann 1996); they have also stressed the processes of translation, and the "will to identity" (Gutmann 1996: 245)[6] that motivates people in working-class neighborhoods.[7] The will of individuals or social groups cannot fully explain events, which result in part from unintended consequences of agents' actions (Ortner 1984: 157). An example of this can be seen in the effects of specific Jesuits' actions on grassroot evangelist movements in Guadalajara, which I discuss in Chapter 3. A prolonged history of evangelical activism by Jesuits and evangelization based on fostering lay leadership has in some cases divided Christian Base Communities and decreased their aggregate power, the opposite of what the Jesuits had intended.

In a colonia popular, taking people's ideas about shame, guilt, and goodness into account can contribute to an understanding of identity when combined with analyses of personal failure (such as pregnancy out of wedlock) and notions of responsibility and worthiness that emerge out of religious discourses, family relations, and family differentiations. In other words, the phenomenology of affects is connected to difference in-the-making; sentiments and psychological characters emerge out of negotiations of power and distinction in everyday life. It is clear, then, that a focus on the subject emerging from a normative process has made anthropologists aware not only of psychological traits and class position as the essentialization of an urban culture, but also of the relationships of power and domination on which these essentializations are based (Gledhill 1994: 68). Focusing on people exclusively as subjects was not, however, adequate for writing parts of this book, such as when I wanted to describe aspects of belonging and cognitive transformation in processes of migration. To understand modernity, I needed to focus on politics with regard to practices, knowledge acquisition, and the withholding and transmissions that shape the identity of subjects as well as phenomenological processes of self-transformation.

Questions of self-transformation emerged, for instance, when I had to confront what exists beyond or before language, such as in chapter 6, when I discuss the condition of "not knowing" of womanhood in transformation. That is to say, the gap between the unknown (a desire to be different without yet knowing how) and the known (the available social positioning) is a place of anxiety and uneasiness that becomes part of the process of transformation. I needed a language of a phenomenological self to account for the instances when language breaks down and transformations take place. La mujer sufrida (the suffering woman) is not just a well-known cultural and Marian representation of Mexican womanhood, it is a phenomenological, open-ended process of social and moral incorporation and exclusion. Suffering, when it takes the form of pain, can be both the disruption of a capacity for communicating, or the engendering of it and the possibility for a new form of communication (Scarry 1985; Das 1995). Suffering and pain can mark exclusion, rejection, and the impossibility of incorporation, but they can also be read as a passage toward inclusion in a specific moral community (Das 1995: 181–182).

Nonetheless personal transformations are not enough to capture urban identity. They have to be understood as emerging from the interplay of complex social and economic processes. For example, internal migration and the urbanization of western Mexico were related to decreasing returns of agricultural labor and the crumbling of a state-subsidized agricultural economy. The creation of new urban labor markets in the 1970s–80s, fostered by an increasing number of multinational industries, in the region of Guadalajara has been translated for many people into a shift from a subsistence ranch economy to a dependence on wage labor. Therefore, narratives of longing and belonging need to be read as part of the lived experience of these structural shifts, as well as of the policies of urban settlement pursued from the 1960s up to the 1990s in Guadalajara and throughout the state of Jalisco.

THREAD 2: PRISMS OF BELONGING

The second anthropological debate that runs through this book concerns migration and the sense of belonging in an urban space. These domains emerge in the everyday life of the colonia popular in acts of translation that are not only cognitive, but also embodied. Certain acts embody the tensions and narratives of people recalling, imagining, and experiencing rural life, the home, the neighborhood of Polanco, and the urban world of Guadalajara. The recollection and imagery involved are very much in the present, and not constructed in the form of historical, unilinear rural-urban development that characterized much of the Culture and Personality, structuralist, and functionalist studies. Memories of rural and urban living instead are sites of differentiation, with the people expressing them looked up to or down upon in different contexts. *El rancho* and *el pueblo* point to axes of difference and evoke oppositional, but also complementary, imagery used in strategically different ways. They produce a dynamic of affectivity, embodiment, and interpretative processes that shape the performing of selfhood — part of it being negotiation of one's relationships and statuses.

To capture the various resonances of people's experience, I have developed a concept of "prisms of belonging." These exist at the interface of cognition, history, and memory, and are expressed in the ways people talk about and experience spaces such as the home, the neighborhood, the city, and places of origin, as well as in the ways these places are "revisited." They are important because under different circumstances, people express different situated selves. The purpose of prisms of belonging is to indicate the heterogeneous perceptions, feelings, desires, contradictions, and images that shape experiences of space and time. Prisms of belonging have a three-dimensional nature: they are spatial and temporal; they combine cognitive-emotional experiences, memory, and history; and they link self-understanding to the process of migration and urbanization. They have a history of production and appropriation and are read generationally: they are produced by migrant subjects, but urban living and new generations take over their reproduction. Especially in relation to dynamics of religious affiliation and belonging, prisms of belonging are not only the experience itself but also the contested interpretations through which experience is categorized. Prisms have a refractive and, to some extent, elusive nature: what we can see through them depends on the angle we are looking through. And as part of a process of vernacular modernity, the angle of vision, the point of perspective, is important (Rofel 1999: 18).

Prisms of belonging are particularly useful in understanding how migration can be described as both an experience of self-empowerment and a loss of power, and how places can become the symbols of embodied experiences of living, thinking, and feeling. Migration and settlement in Polanco seems, for many, to have been a process of acquiring knowledge about the world, and — for those involved in grassroot religious or health movements — a passage from a state of unconsciousness to consciousness. At the base of different representations of places and spaces, there is an urge (as well as a pressure) to belong. In this context, the recalling and reenactment of boundaries — of self, of the private and public spheres, of individual and family, past and present — may not be so clear-cut, because they are continuously reshaped in particular contexts and within specific life strategies.

A focus on prisms of belonging also helps to understand grassroot expressions of new and traditional Catholic churches. The tension between the two, which is a tension of modernity, is also part of the particular history of urbanity. A discursive analysis of grassroot religious formations as a discursive analysis of the struggle of grassroots formations to appropriate notions of "change," the "new," and the "traditional" — so typical not only of Latin American but other developing social landscapes — reveals a struggle among narratives of belonging. People and groups express and experience affects, rejection, passions, and indifference as different forms of church activism develop, and as various types of evangelization promote different, but also overlapping, ideas of personhood, the relation between human and divine agencies, and society at large. The reading of these differences and overlaps is one of the tensions of modernity in Mexican Catholicism. It is both an impulse toward a narrative of socio-religious subjects inscribed in a process of citizenship, and a practice of Catholic identity (as I explain in Chapter 3) that has been historically formed as a counter-state and counter-secular narrative in Mexican history.

The concept of prisms of belonging reflects the fragmented and refractive nature of experience and allows us to reinstate experience as a category of analysis without essentializing it, viewing it through an understanding of its sociopolitical genesis, its historical reproduction and appropriation, as well as its phenomenological location. It also addresses an anthropological tension between interpretative and antifoundationalist approaches,[8] while not allowing either political, economic, or phenomenological perspectives to predominate. Instead, these different angles of analysis are predominant in some parts of the book, but backgrounded in others.

An anthropological perspective on an urban reality provides an excess of material that is "vulnerable" to rethinking (Gupta 1998: 30); once again, this perspective's ethnographic strength is not in seeking an overarching explanatory frame—a unified thesis—but in listening to and learning from the interplay of different thematic configurations. It is exactly this analytical perspective on emerging thematic configurations and their theoretical genealogies which provides the groundwork for an anthropology *through* the barrio.

The thematic clusters that emerge in this book should not be confined to the specificity of their location and production. Their emergence in threads of analytical inquiry suggests a particular engagement in the study of urban Mexico: a continuum between realms of socioeconomic studies, political economy, and interpretative and phenomenological analyses. In other words, the well-documented transformation of the market labor economy and household production and reproduction in urban Mexico and the Guadalajara region (e.g., González de la Rocha 1994, 1999; Escobar Latapí et al. 1987; Murphy and Stepick 1991) needs to be understood with close attention to the anxiety of the transformation of the subject, and the uneasiness of intimacy of the self as part of a process of social transformation. Let the ethnography perform the theory by engaging us with insightful articulations of different, but related, thematic clusters.

THREAD 3: VERNACULAR MODERNITIES

The third main thread that runs through this book is an articulation of modernity and tradition that embraces the study of vernacular modernities: the ways in which modernity—as the linear project of development, scientific inquiry, and progress—has been embraced but also resisted outside of the dominant centers of power. What has emerged from this process of resistance and reshaping is not only preserved tradition, but a local reshaping of modernity. Modernity includes an attitude about the present and one's place in it, and vernacular (or alternative) modernities evolve around the destabilization of universal idioms, the historicization of the context of exactly this present and of oneself in it (Parameshwar Gaonkar 1999: 14). Alternative modernities are, then, about grassroot interpretations which subtly displace dominant and national narratives.

Recent ethnographies have fruitfully engaged with the study of vernacular modernities (Coronil 1997; Donham 1999; Ferguson 1999; Malkki 1995; Appadurai 1996). They have paid attention to facets of the discourse of modernity: to the conflation of nature's and citizens' fertility and their incorporation into a historical narrative of a nation-state (Coronil 1997); to the nondelivery of modernity and an anthropology of decline (Ferguson 1999); to different domains of experience in exile and resettlements which can or cannot produce new narratives of communities (Malkki 1995). These studies have also made clear that processes of social modernization are not equivalent to processes of cultural modernity. The same impetus to economic, technological, or industrial growth, or to participatory citizenship democracy and human rights advocacy, can be culturally interpreted and reshaped in various ways.

Three themes in this debate are directly relevant to the Mexican urban narratives discussed in this book. First, modernization and urbanization are not linear and teleological processual movements. There are possibilities of regression, and always multiple and contested interpretations. This book's discussion of grassroot religious movements, the plurality of medical etiologies, and narratives of health and disease describes an overlap in a struggle of representativeness of *el pueblo* (meaning "the village" but also "the people") and a claim for authority, which is conferred by holding knowledge. Different interpretations of modernity coexist and overlap rather than being mutually exclusive, and the particular interpolations of these coexisting phenomena and interpretations voice the specificity of a vernacular modernity.

The growing phenomenon of alternative medicines and *medicina popular* embraces some of these specificities. These expressions of modernity can create conditions of empowerment, as with women in self-help groups, but they also reproduce existing biomedical hierarchical power structures, as with homeopaths who prefer to be associated with medical doctors rather than curanderos.

Second, if modernity originated as a project of incorporation in a dominant and hierarchical mode, its appropriation in subaltern sites and through subaltern angles of vision requires a focus on incorporations as well as resistances of the local in the nation-state, and the subject in a mode of citizenship. What emerges through the neighborhood of Polanco is that the process of appropriation is very much open-ended, and it generates anxiety and suffering as well as relocation and empowerment. It is open-ended because, to a certain extent, modernity has failed to deliver what it promised. One example is the failure of a national health system to provide effective coverage for those who are entitled to it. However, the lack of funds and the poor management of national health-care needs to be understood within recent Mexican history. In the late 1980s and early 1990s, during the presidency of Carlos Salinas de Gortari (1988–1993), technocratic efficiency and faith in democratization centered on a strong presidential figure were recurrent images in the national discourse. Salinas personally embodied a dream of national modernity. However, under the succeeding presidency of Ernesto Zedillo (1994–1999), that dream and reality became increasingly different.

During the late 1980s and first half of the 1990s, the time period at the center of this book, Mexican society went through important changes. In 1994, at the end of his term, Salinas left office with the country pursuing increased modernization and efficiency. A technocrat trained at Harvard, Salinas had begun his presidency with a public policy program, PRONASOL (Programa Nacional de Solidaridad, or National Solidarity Program), that sponsored a wide range of projects with the political aim of visibly targeting the exclusion of the poor from national economic growth.[9] Salinas pushed an agenda of modernization through large-scale privatization of state-owned companies, while fostering presidentialism and an image of the state as a good provider for the urban (and rural) poor.[10] However, his main objective in dealing with internal tensions was a *concertación* (internal co-optation and homogenization of difference and oppositional political forces, rather than mutual agreement by different political parties, as has been the case of *la concertación* in post-dictatorship Chile) and subsequent neutralization of different local and regional sociopolitical forces within centralized national plans (Harvey 1993). He was able, throughout his presidency, to subdue social tensions with the promise of an existing (but in reality not well-established) national economic competitiveness and stability, which was built on the image of a perfect marriage between democratic consolidation and neoliberal reforms.

However, modernization without real democracy has its toll.[11] Throughout Salinas's presidency and partly during President Zedillo's term, a de facto withdrawal of the state's food, health, and educational programs (also imposed on the Mexican government by international monetary fund rescue plans) has weakened the safety net that had existed for a good part of the Mexican low-income population. As a reaction, grassroot movements have grown, becoming central in negotiating with federal and municipal powers for services and resources. In some cases the sociopolitical action of these groups has challenged patron-client relations and the government policy of *concertación*. It remains unclear whether, in the long term, they will succeed in altering those mechanisms.[12]

With the election in 2000 of a new president, Vicente Fox (the Partido de Acción Nacional candidate for the right-center coalition Alianza para el Cambio), a new and interesting phase has opened in Mexican democracy and civil society. It is still early to assess where Fox's new government is leading Mexican society and economy with its combination of technical and managerial aspirations and a strong Catholic and conservative impulse. Nonetheless, internal divisions within the Alianza para el Cambio in both the senate and the national assembly are already emerging. Two example are the government's negotiations with the Zapatistas over the COCOPA law (Comisión de Concordia y Pacificación), which deals with the rights and culture of indigenous people, and a proposed financial reform (at the time this book was going to press) that would raise taxes on medicine, basic foodstuffs, and books.[13]

However, this book is not meant to directly address the debate about the transformation and democratization of Mexican politics in the last decade. Other works have done this (e.g., Rodríguez 1997). I only wish to point out that the ideal of modernization of the state needs to be read through local cultural practices of modernity. A focus on these everyday cultural and social practices (which inform the imagining of the national and the global) unveils how the work of imagination and the politics of affects are fundamental to understanding national projects of modernity (Appadurai 1996: 9). Analyses of issues related to modernity, in particular socioeconomic systems, are further understood via a focus on everyday life formation and representations, and their relation to the work of imagination.

Finally, vernacular modernities are about the transfer of knowledge between different actors, and the appropriation—as well as the circulation—of knowledge becomes important terrain for understanding how modernity and its failure are reinscribed, reimagined, and reproduced. By claiming knowledge, people are claiming agency, and this transfer produces patterns of emergence and residual cultural processes. I refer here directly to the work of Raymond Williams, who argues that the novel elements of a culture are not always the emergent ones, which are defined as a set of "new" values, meaning, and types of social relations (Williams 1977: 123). What is novel in sociocultural formation is not always oppositional to dominant culture and discourses. It can be instead defined as the residual, which becomes visible because of the default process of the dominant discourse. The residual and the emergent are further stages of sociocultural differentiation, that, Williams argues, give important clues about the nature of the dominant. The crucial points are that the process of generally emergent, that is repeated and continuously renewed, is often confused, in a process of negotiated incorporation to the dominant, with the "locally residual" (Williams 1977: 125). Secondly the emergent is often visible at a pre-emergent level that generates tensions and is actively endorsed, but not fully articulated in its expression.[14] Transfer (and withdrawal) of knowledge from the perspective of vernacular modernities opens the question of what is considered emergent and residual, and by whom and in what circumstances.

The articulation between residual, emergent, and dominant forms may wax and wane, but its impact on consciousness and forms of urban movements spills beyond the temporal frame of their life cycles, well into longer lasting configurations of civil society and its transformation. And I now invite the reader into an ethnographic journey in which these forms help to modulate our perspectives of urban Mexico.

A Note on Methodology

My fieldwork was structured around informal and repeated interviews, mainly in the neighborhood of Polanco, which is in Guadalajara in the Mexican state of Jalisco. I also spent time in bordering areas and some informants' villages of origin. I followed people and families in Los Altos de Jalisco, Zacatecas, and villages south of Lake Chapala. I did not produce and implement surveys; instead, I conducted unstructured interviews, taped when I could but otherwise recorded by hand during or immediately after. For this I got the nickname of la mujer de la libreta (Notebook Woman).

I also interviewed several Jesuits and Diocesans in Guadalajara, and

I attended meetings with them as well as with Church and medicina popular activists in different parts of the city. Between 1990 and 1992 I spent twenty months in participant observation of different household activities, public-space interactions, and medical practices. I returned in spring 1997 and again in summer 1999 and early 2001. Those were extremely important visits, during which I saw the effects of the 1994 economic crisis and the continuous diversification of the neighborhood. I was really surprised, on one hand, by the presence of new bank branches and, on the other, by the increasing economic hardship for many families I knew.

When I arrived in 1990 I was asked to help with a sociological survey of one of the parishes, but I declined. I was afraid to be seen as a Church activist, which would have precluded access to other groups. I now regret that move, not only because of the misunderstanding that arose (one of the priests proved somehow hostile to my presence), but also because I was not aware that presumed anthropological neutrality is already in itself a clear political position. Nevertheless, I did become engaged in group activities involved in researching the history of negotiations for legalizing land ownership in the neighborhood, and I conducted archival work in the municipal and the Jesuit libraries in Guadalajara.

I also had in-depth conversations with various members of a group of families and helped them out, whenever I could, with some of the problems of daily encounters. I often encouraged people to talk about what they dreamt (literally, as well as what they aspired to), about their intimate lives, and I often assumed the role of daughter as a means of showing respect and putting myself in a position of learning. In translating people's quotes from Spanish into English, I maintained a colloquial style. For confidentiality, I have changed people's names.

During my second and third fieldwork periods, I distributed early drafts of this work to people, talking about it and receiving important feedback. That experience has made me even more aware that not only the act of writing, but also the text itself, is a process.

CHAPTER I

Internationalizing Region, Expanding City, Neighborhoods in Transition

When there is nothing on earth that forgetfulness does not fade, memory alter, and when no one knows what sort of image the future may translate it into.

Jorge Luis Borges, "Mutation," *The Aleph*

I have been asked more than a few times why I initially chose to carry out my fieldwork in the Guadalajara area and, in particular, the neighborhood of Lomas de Polanco (hereafter referred to as Polanco). I was drawn to the dusty streets with bending trees, fighting for life, and the patchy colorful houses that reminded me of Burano Island in Venice. And at first I imagined Polanco to be an island in a tight archipelago of the economic, social and spatial matrices of Greater Guadalajara.

The colonia is actually south of the city, close to the old industrial area. Its architectural development is varied, and houses have one, two, or, rarely, three floors. The older houses were constructed with *adobes* (sun-dried bricks), the new ones are made of *ladrillos* (factory-made bricks). Some houses are well decorated both inside and outside and even have car space, but others may not even have had a sewer system or running water until very recently. It is common to encounter *viviendas* where unrelated nuclear families live in separate rooms, often sharing the bathroom, courtyard, and wash basin, but always having separate cooking facilities. The visual impact of the place is multicolored and variegated, as many house extensions on the ground floor have been built using materials and techniques that don't match the originals, to

MAP 1. Mexico, with locations of major cities (courtesy of Ann Varley and Allan Gilbert, from Gilbert and Varley 1991)

accommodate a new business or provide a home for newly married offspring.

Later I realized that the appearances of the houses tended to show a division between those *que la han hecho* (who have it made) and those who don't, and I discovered that Polanco had a well-known history of grassroot movements and politico-religious organizations. By accident, I found myself in an interesting space of urban history, in a neighborhood in transition, part of an expanding city that was playing a major role in the internationalization of a regional economy.

While my initial selection of Polanco arose from contingent personal choices, I soon discovered that it was intersected by wider urban unfoldings. In this chapter, I sketch the metropolitan and regional space through which the voices and events I narrate and discuss in this book have emerged. Urban anthropology involves listening to the voices emerging from socioeconomic processes and specific urban histories, and then weaving their connections into an ethnographic narrative.

As in other metropolitan areas of Latin America, urbanization takes

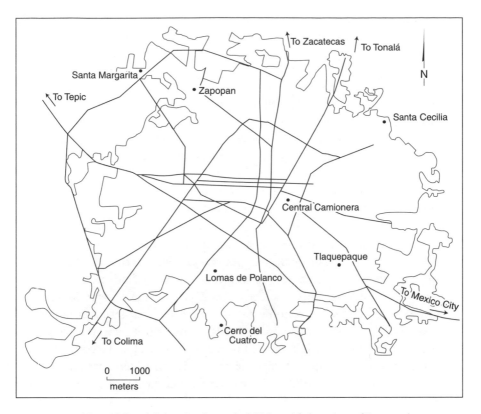

MAP 2. Map of Guadalajara in the early 1990s, with location of Lomas de Polanco (courtesy of Ann Varley and Allan Gilbert, from Gilbert and Varley 1991)

place through the constant redefinition of identity and space in the context of social contrast, reference, and belonging (De la Peña and De la Torre 1996: 251). To grasp the fluidity of urban complexity, we need to disentangle intertwined phenomena (e.g., economic transformations, land regularization, development of social movements) and see how they form the plot onto which identity unfolds. The colonia is a space of articulation between individual and familial dynamics and civil society. It is important to point out that a colonia popular is originally a low-income, working-class neighborhood. Its degree of economic homogeneity might vary over time, but the Spanish term *popular* refers always to its class composition.

The identities and participation of citizens in Guadalajaran civil society cannot be understood without examining histories of the colonias populares. Guadalajara's demographic expansion has not developed via land invasions, as did other major Mexican cities such as Monterrey (Bennett 1995: 14–15) or Mexico City (Lomnitz 1977); consequently, settlers in peripheral urbanizing areas did not have prior bonds of action and identity to tie them together.[1] Guadalajara's demographic expansion has been shaped by a form of human settlement and subsequent regularization of land and house ownership that have required collective action by civil and religious neighborhood organizations (De la Peña and De la Torre 1990)—hence the need to understand the social organizations of the barrio and its localism in Guadalajara.

The neighborhood of Polanco is a typical colonia popular being transformed from a very poor, underprivileged neighborhood to a suburban center. This transition is embedded in the microhistory of its social mobilization and the socioeconomic dynamic of its population. Collective action has made the neighborhood a famous case study of the opposition of small plot owners to a combination of private interests and public requirements (Sanchez Van Dyck de Levy 1979; Morfín Otero 1979). But socioeconomic factors must be taken into account in analyzing the decreased response to calls for mobilization in the 1990s. The dynamic of this neighborhood thus has to be read in the context of expansion of the metropolitan zone of Guadalajara (hereafter referred to as Greater Guadalajara) and the internationalization of Jalisco's regional economy.

Guadalajara, an Expanding Metropolitan Area

Settled in 1532, Guadalajara has been a major administrative center since early Spanish colonization, but its exponential urbanization is a relatively new phenomenon that can be traced to the period between 1940 and the 1980s (Vázquez 1990: 52). The city has been distinguished by religious and economic conservatism;[2] however, this economic tendency has been challenged in the last fifteen years by the expansion of multinational activities in the industrial area south of the city. The growing investment of foreign and multinational capital has internationalized both the city's and the regional economy, but this has not improved the well-being of many traditional labor sectors (Torres Montes de Oca 1997: 77).

Since the mid-sixteenth century, Guadalajara has been a center of ecclesiastic and government power, and as it became an increasingly important economic and political hub, much of the indigenous population was displaced into outlying areas. Nevertheless, the indigenous population of Greater Guadalajara was significant well into the nineteenth century, even if the city's population is still largely mestizo.[3] During the seventeenth century Guadalajara was considered second to Mexico City, Puebla, and the mining towns in the central region of Guanajuato and Zacatecas (Berthe 1970), but in 1708 it became the regional capital. Soon after, the 'Real Consulado, which administered all of the Spanish Crown's business and trade activities in western Mexico, was transferred to the city. Since the eighteenth century, the local and regional economy has been based on agriculture and the production of nondurable goods such as textiles, shoes, and food products (De la Peña 1986).

Guadalajara's real economic and social growth began in the nineteenth century. After Mexico won independence in 1821, small-scale industries were developed, many of them by migrants from Europe. The Guadalajara region's economic expansion was facilitated by construction of a new railway in the early twentieth century that also provided a link to the Pacific area and intensified trade with the United States (De la Peña and Escobar Latapí 1986). The population in rural Jalisco and Guadalajara at this time included merchants, shopkeepers, bureaucrats working for the government, church, and military, and *rancheros* (cattleholders) who had taken over parts of the large haciendas that were split up and redistributed after the revolution. Ranchero culture (discussed in Chapter 2) is still central to Jalisco's regional identity.

Migration to and within the Guadalajara region has been strictly connected to land tenancy. During the dictatorship of Porfirio Díaz (1877–1911) economic policy resulted in increased migration in west-central Mexico,[4] and the establishment of communal landownership under the *ejido* system during the presidency of Lázaro Cárdenas (1934–1940) did little to improve conditions in the long run.[5]

Guadalajara is now the largest urban center in western Mexico, which includes the states of Jalisco, Colima, Aguascalientes, Nayarit, Michoacán, and Zacatecas. Since 1940 Guadalajara's population has doubled every ten years, reaching two and a half million in 1980 (Arias 1985) and (according to a 1991 census by Instituto Nacional Estadística Geográfica y Informática [INEGI]) exceeding three million in 1990.[6] In 2000, an informal estimate placed the population at more than four million.

Guadalajara is divided into four sectors that were, and to a certain extent still are, class centered. Those of the middle and upper classes tend to live in Hidalgo and Juárez (the northwest and southwest sectors, respectively), while lower-class families live either in the city's center, the northeast sector of Libertad, or the southeast sector of Reforma. However, new low-income settlement areas have developed outside the ring roads, especially west of Greater Guadalajara,[7] and the upper and middle classes are expanding toward Zapopan, making Guadalajara less of a spatially, east/west "divided city,'" as Walton (1977) described it more than two decades ago.

From the 1940s to the mid-1980s Guadalajara attracted large numbers of migrants with the prospect of work in both formal and informal sectors (Escobar Latapí and De la Peña 1990). Monterrey has been characterized by entrepreneurial high-risk industrial investments for a long time, but only relatively recently have Guadalajara and the Jalisco region acquired an important role in the multinational economy (Arroyo Alejandre and De León 1997). The production of multinational companies such as Kodak, Hewlett-Packard, Motorola and IBM[8] rests on a network of *maquiladoras* in nearby municipal areas, which expanded in the 1980s as a result of surplus labor, infrastructure improvements, and government support (Duran and Partida 1990).[9] The major focus of multinational production has become the electrical/electronic industry, which in Jalisco accounts for one of the two major exports, the other being beer (Medina Ortega 1997). This concentration of technological industries in Guadalajara at the turn of the twenty-first century has earned it recognition as "the Silicon Valley of Mexico."

Since the mid-1990s, the internationalization of Jalisco's economy has produced increasingly radical changes, and a renewed crisis for the low-income population. Economic restructuring has been geared toward deindustrialization and has favored the services and the presence of partnership with North American capital, and increasing dependence on the fate of the technological market industry. Guadalajara has long been a center of small and mid-level industries, but this still large sector of the economy has struggled to be competitive in an international market, with the consequent increase of labor layoffs. The integration between this type of industry and multinational production is problematic, requiring conversion of labor skills and a shift from small-scale to large enterprise relations of production. It also requires new strategies for organizing production and distribution, and a renewed integration of this metropolitan area into the regional economy.

"Aquí me quedo" (Here I stay): Urbanization and Migration in Greater Guadalajara

The high rate of migration to Guadalajara that began in the 1940s and lasted until the early 1980s resulted from factors such as the substitution of cash crops for staple crops, the official freezing of prices for basic agricultural products, increased rural unemployment, and the concentration of services and commercial activities in Guadalajara (Gallegos Ramírez 1990).[10]

Since the early 1960s, entire families began moving to Guadalajara, and not always because of poverty. In fact, those who decided to migrate often had more resources and were more open to taking risks than their village-mates who decided to stay. As Rouse (1992, 1995) has argued in the case of transnational migration to California, the whole dynamic of production and reproduction of migrant circuits—as a flow of people, goods, labor and social capital between home and migrant communities—needs to be taken into account to understand reasons for migrating.[11] To understand migration only, or mainly, in terms of push and pull factors is a reductionist way of explaining a more complex phenomenon that involves the increase of social capital in the ongoing exchange of resources and people between migrants' places of origin and their destinations.[12]

Until the late 1980s, urbanization of Greater Guadalajara was spurred primarily by migration from the countryside, and privileged spatial expansion rather than increased population density (De la Peña et al. 1992). It has also been characterized by private appropriation of land and ongoing land speculation. In the late 1980s and 1990s, people were moving from already urbanized areas to newly urbanizing areas, many of them leaving extended households already settled in Greater Guadalajara (Soria Romo 1991), coming to the Jalisco region from Mexico City and less traditional areas of migration such as the Pacific Regions (Velazquez and Papail 1997: 25). The urban journey of many people living in colonias such as Polanco began when they arrived with relatives or friends and rented in older central areas of Guadalajara. After they saved enough money to buy a piece of land, they moved to peripheral and urbanizing areas. But a piece of land bought in the colonias might have had problematic strings attached.

Urbanization of Greater Guadalajara has evolved around connivance between the private and the public sectors, and the breaking of local planning laws to the detriment of low-income settlers (Varley 1989). Its course can be divided into three periods (De la Peña 1989). From the early 1930s to the mid-1940s, the sale of land was done privately and not regulated by the government. The following period of urbanization—which lasted until the mid-1960s—still revolved around private land trading, but state control manifested itself through the formation of *fraccionamientos populares,* the result of a government law in 1953 that allowed plots of land to be sold for construction. More than two hundred fraccionamientos populares were created in Guadalajara during the 1950s and 1960s (De la Peña 1989: 9), and the law specified that, through a plan of the *ayuntamiento* (municipality), major services would be installed before the transfer of individual plots.[13] The cost of basic infrastructure was to be the responsibility of the *fraccionador* (the person managing or owning the land), who would include it in the cost of each plot. However, this procedure was not followed in many cases in Greater Guadalajara (Vázquez 1990: 125–126). As already mentioned, the fraccionamiento was often an end-goal in the urban journey for the migrants who rented, or lived, with relatives in other parts of the city before buying. But many migrants who bought land from fraccionadores found themselves caught in the sticky web of speculation.

The third period of urbanization, from the mid-1960s to mid-1990s, has been focused on *asentamientos* (townships). When the land assigned for fraccionamientos populares had been sold, urbanization of Greater Guadalajara expanded into ejido land. Since legally the city was not supposed to provide services until land was regularized, the status of such land has been a crucial dispute in many asentamientos. On the other hand, middle- and higher-income settlements in Guadalajara have received services before being legalized; hence regularization can be a matter of who says what is irregular, not the actual status of the land (Varley 1989), and relates to how people, especially public officials, see the land and the acquisition of ownership according to the meanings and metaphors attached to specific urbanizing land (Ward 1999). One political strategy used by public bodies to marginalize new settlers in low-income areas is to label a settlement illegal, which is also a reason to withhold services. Most of those moving to new asentamientos are recent migrants from outside the region and families who have been forced out of the rental market in older Guadalajara's neighborhoods and have reduced buying power in the housing market (Soria Romo 1991). In contrast, most people living in fraccionamientos populares such as Polanco settled there in the 1960s and 1970s.

Patterns of urbanization and urban livelihood have been affected by recurrent economic crises in Mexico. The 1982 debt crisis reduced the real purchasing power of wages rather than the number of jobs available in the market and caused a polarization in working conditions (Escobar Latapí 1988: 19). The economic crisis touched many facets of life among the urban poor: consumption dropped and productive activities whose end products were acquired in the market (such as ready-to-eat food), began to be carried out within the household. The education of young people, especially girls, was sacrificed if working mothers were unable to manage childcare and housekeeping as well. Although many colonias populares experienced relative economic improvement between the late 1980s and mid-1990s (during Salinas's presidential sexennium), the devaluation of the peso in 1994 worsened the situation again, especially for those relying on factory work and wages. The cost of living steadily increased while the wage power did not, and by the end of the 1990s, people were experiencing profound crises and anxieties because of unemployment or underemployment.

Vicente Fox's neoliberal policy is intended to strengthen the economy by containing income taxes, and to facilitate major investments while addressing poverty and wealth redistribution. Once again hopes are pinned on the so-called trickle-down effect, but whether or not that will occur remains to be seen. In recent years Mexico has become, more and more, a nation where members of a small elite class have greatly increased their wealth while a large part of the population has not seen substantial and sustainable benefits of economic growth.

In periods of crisis, the stage of household life corresponding to the extended family (for example, when a young couple lives virilocally) expands, though this does not mean that reciprocity and mutual help increase within and between households. Instead, the opposite seems more likely to be the case, as there is a cost of social networks and reciprocity between households that translates in increasing family nuclearization and social atomization (González de la Rocha 1999). The increased informality, flexibility, and insecurity of the job market as well as low wage returns in formal employment affect most of the low-income population in Guadalajara, as in other parts of Mexico. The promise of a much brighter future for this population is still remote.

La lucha popular: Glorious Pasts, Present Reassessments, and New Directions

Social movements have played an important role in defining citizenship in Mexico (Foweraker and Craig 1990), and their presence in urban contexts sheds much light on the expressive, identity nature of community organizations (Escobar and Alvarez 1992; Foweraker 1995). Whether or not their reproduction goes beyond achieving proposed goals such as land tenure and housing, obtaining services, or pursuing women's political action and larger social goals (Stephen 1997) is a matter of debate. Yet there is no doubt that social movements have a central role in the creation of heterogeneous, negotiated, and diversified urban identities. This heterogeneity can be seen in Guadalajara's Movimiento Popular Urbano (Urban Popular Movement), from its beginning in the early 1970s to the present. This movement has developed in four distinct stages characterized by different priorities, leading activist groups, and forms of community organization (Regalado Santillán 1995).

During the first stage (1971–1981) the MPU's actions were strictly connected to activities of the Comunidades Eclesiales de Base, evangelical groups inspired by liberation theology.[14] In 1981–1984 political, grassroot non-party forces first appeared, working in parallel to mobilization of the Comunidades. The third stage (1985–1987) saw the reinforcement of a political agenda in the social movements within the colonias populares, but it was partly characterized by a top-down activist approach led by the Jesuits and laymen trained by them, and therefore counted on a reduced grassroot base. The fourth phase (1987–1993) indicates an important consolidation as grassroot social organizations began to develop around the issue of housing claims and different inter-neighborhood associations began to form. During this phase, demands for better housing and a higher standard of living were not confined to isolated neighborhoods but gained support from the wider public. People were beginning to recognize the failure of Greater Guadalajara's municipalities to provide and implement appropriate plans for urban development, and hence to guarantee appropriate land and infrastructure for popular housing (Regalado Santillán 1995: 222).[15]

The fifth (and current) stage, which began around 1994, has seen urban popular mobilization around issues of electoral transparency, political change, and human rights. The initial landmark event of this stage was a civil disaster in Guadalajara on April 22, 1992 (Ramírez Saíz and Santillán 1995). An explosion in a central barrio killed more than two hundred people and destroyed hundreds of homes. It was caused by leakage of highly flammable hydrocarbon (an organic compound derived from petroleum) into the sewage system, which, days before the explosion, was reported by residents to the municipal authorities. Authorities dismissed the warning and took no preventive measures, and for a while, they attempted to cover their own and Petrolio Mexicano's (PEMEX's) responsibility. The other landmark event marking the fifth phase was the beginning of the Zapatista rebellion in Chiapas in 1994. These two incidences—the disaster and the uprising—brought to the forefront of Guadalajara (and Mexican) civil society questions of political and administrative transparency and defense of indigenous/human rights.

The phases of mobilization in Polanco have followed the general pattern. The *colonos* (the people living in the colonia) have played an important role in the development of civil society in Guadalajara through defending their rights via creation and participation in urban movements such as the Comité Popular de Sur (central to the Movimiento Urbano Popular) and religious groups such as the CEBs (organized by the Jesuits and their affiliated centers (Servicios Educativos de Occidente [SEDOC] and the Instituto Mexicano de Desarollo Económico Comunitario [IMDEC]). Also important have been their links with opposition political parties (including the Partido de los Trabajadores [PT]). The Comité Popular, in particular—born out of the organization of colonos of Polanco in 1973—has, together with the movement Inter-colonias, constituted the formative backbone of the Movimiento Urbano Popular.[16] The colonos' involvement in these movements was part of a process of negotiation with municipal and regional powers. The municipality, on its side, has contested the ownership of parcels of ejido land through the Comisión Regularizadora para la Tenencia de la Tierra (CoReTT)—a national organization with an independent budget, established by presidential act in 1973, which can either repossess land or legally recognize tenancy.[17]

Polanco is a fraccionamiento popular inhabited since 1953, but its status as such was recognized only in 1959, and covered only 106 hectares. In a fraccionamiento popular the regular *lote* (basic lot) should be at least ninety square meters. In Polanco, most lots are eighty square meters (eight-by-ten meters or four-by-twenty meters), and paired houses built on split lots are common. The colonia has two Catholic parishes: Santa Magdalena and the Anunciación. The population consists mainly of so-called old and intermediate migrants who moved here during the rapid urbanization that took place between the 1960s and early 1980s. A 1979 study by SEDOC (Servicios Educativos Deocuidente, a Jesuit organization) indicated that 82 percent of the inhabitants came from outside Greater Guadalajara, and the average family included six individuals (SEDOC 1981); the study mentioned that 55 percent of heads of households were from the region of Jalisco. Another 20 percent were born in Guadalajara, and 20 percent came from the regions of Michoacán, Zacatecas, Nayarit, and Colima. The population in the early 1990s was estimated in the parish census to be about twenty thousand.

Population data also show that the life-cycle of the family in Polanco is in a stage of consolidation (González de la Rocha 1994), with adult offspring relieving the head of the household and taking on part of the economic burden and forming new, separate households. According to the SEDOC and parish censuses of mid-1985 and 1989, 44 percent of Polanco's workers were employed in factories, 30 percent were employed in private-sector businesses such as building construction and transportation (informal systems of public transport such as collective minivans), and only 7 percent worked in retail sales and street-vending. At that time ratio of male to female factory workers was one to three; other working women were employed as *sirvientas* (housemaids) in middle-class colonias in the western part of town.

These are suggestive data, and I would like to leave them as such. I have already mentioned that during my fieldwork, I did not use survey methods, nor was I primarily interested in analyzing the neighborhood's class and labor composition. However, secondary sources reveal that the colonia has been composed primarily of a low-income population. I use the term "low-income" throughout the book to address a socioeconomic condition that is not homogenous, but internally diversified. For instance, there are differences between those who are employed in the formal economy and entitled to national health insurance (see Chapter 4) and those earning contractual wages, or those who are house or shop owners, and those who are house tenants, or those who are investing social capital in the education and upper mobility of offspring and those who are not. Nonetheless, I have identified Polanco as being a socioeconomic space in the making, dominantly low-income—a condition characterized by economic conservatism, an investment in basic family necessities rather than increasing personal expenditure, the need for social networks to pull together resources in times of hardship, and generally speaking, a careful mastery of household expenditures. Therefore, I use the term low-income to address socioeconomic generalities as well as diversified impulses in the population.

The disputes around landownership and provision of services in Polanco have made the neighborhood's history a prominent example of the process of urbanization in Guadalajara, so I describe it with its specific singularities, but also as an example of other, similar cases. Urbanization of the Polanco colonia is particularly interesting for three reasons

(Morfin Otero 1979). First, the land on which Polanco was built was—and still is, at least in part—ejido land. Second, the relation between the colonos, fraccionador, and public authorities has been representative of the type of connivance between political and economic powers that has also taken place in other colonias of Greater Guadalajara. Third, as mentioned above, the Movimiento Popular in Polanco was born out of a struggle for installation of a better sewage system, and the movement was coordinated by the Jesuits through the CEBs.[18] This combination of factors has made Polanco a key example in the history of urban movements in Guadalajara.

Now I will describe some of the microhistory of Polanco, to give the reader a sense of the negotiations that have taken place in the lengthy process of land regularization. By presidential decree, between 1927 and 1934 the ejidos of Santa María Tequepexpan and El Polanco were divided and distributed to *campesinos* (farmers). The actual colonia of Polanco extended into the ejido of Santa María de Tequepexpan, but in the mid-1950s, Jaime Alberto González—the owner of Guadalajara's newspaper *El Diario* managed—in an allegedly unclear and apparently fraudulent way—to acquire the property, which was then transformed into a fraccionamiento popular (Sanchez Van Dyck de Levy 1979). Although it appeared that González legally acquired part of this land from an obscure owner and received another part as a donation, the description of the land in the municipal legal document did not correspond to what was then sold as the fraccionamiento Polanco (Morfin Otero 1979). In 1959, to defend himself from possible accusations of fraud, González the fraccionador created a society called Fraccionadora Polanco de Guadalajara. Once the fraccionadora began to sell lots, González claimed the right to install basic services from the ayuntamiento of Guadalajara, even though he was selling properties that he did not legally own.

Although González should have installed services at his own expense, he instead passed those charges on to people buying lots. The first settlers had to wait until 1961 for the street grid plan and the water system to be installed, and another year to have the electricity connected, the cobbled pavement completed, and the central park laid out. In 1961 after rumors began circulating that the fraccionador had committed fraud, González changed the name of the society. He continued selling lots, however, because no legal action was taken against him or the fraccionadora. The situation was aggravated a few years later when the municipality wanted to charge the colonos again for installing the drainage system.

In 1974 the settlers of Polanco submitted their first request to the federal justice for *amparo* of the land in the ejido of El Polanco—a ju-dicial process guaranteed to individuals by the Constitution to defend their rights in situations involving state institutions. The legal judgment did not solve the issue of ownership of the ejido lands, and at the same time, CoReTT threatened to intervene to sort out the legacy of the land ownership. CoReTT could have expropriated the lots from colonos who believed that they had bought and owned the plots legally.[19] As an op-tion, CoReTT wanted to resell the lots (which were by then already improved) at the current market price, not for what they would have cost when the colonos first took possession.

Authorities tried to portray this land dispute as an invasion by the colonos and not as a fraud committed by the fraccionador.[20] To focus on fraud would divert attention from the biases of the public structures involved in the process of urbanization. Thus, from 1974 to the mid-1990s, Polanco was a theatre for lots of pushing and pulling between the fraccionadora, the public works department, the municipality, and colonos over legalization of land rights. Two main groups have been involved in defending the rights of Polanco's inhabitants. The Comité de Vecinos, which has the support of the Casa del Pueblo (the leading neighborhood organization representative of the Partido de Revolución Institutional [PRI]), has always supported the municipality, using strat-egies of dividing the population through backing up individual claims in obtaining small reductions or better payment conditions. Represen-tative PRI institutions such as the Casa del Pueblo have always fought to control representation of the colonos in the negotiations with mu-nicipal authorities.

In this way the colonia of Polanco, like others in urban Mexico, has become a focus for ways of incorporating residents in wider urban in-stitutions—as well as ways of excluding them (Vélez-Ibáñez 1983)—and an arena for the control of the mediation of rights and services. In fact, one group of residents (groupo de representantes), the second major group involved in the negotiations, found direct channels for negotiat-ing with public institutions such as the municipality and the Consejo de Colaboración Municipal de Guadalajara (CCMG) (a governmental ad-visory group) beyond the watchful eyes of the Casa del Pueblo—an action of disarticulation of the negotiations from traditional PRI grass-root constituencies that resulted in increased popular protests to back up colonos' demands.

What do these experiences suggest in terms of community identity? Three main dynamics emerge that are common to other parts of urban

Mexico. The first is the complex interplay between connivance and co-optation between municipal, federal, and national bodies, and private enterprises and popular movements. Legalizing landownership and creating better housing are important arenas for negotiation of citizens' rights and the consolidation and redefinition of group identity. In Guadalajara's case, the formation of fraccionamientos populares has shaped neighborhoods that are different from the human settlements created by land invasion. Second, the neighborhood has to be understood as a space of negotiation, shaped by tensions of incorporation and exclusion within the wider urban metropolitan space. Therefore, the space of the neighborhood is central to understanding the articulation of the urban in its multiple levels, as well as the actors involved. Third, processes of legal urbanization and land invasion and subsequent regularization, typical of this and other Latin American cases, should be understood as an interplay of different progressive or conservative religious, lay, and political forces.

Many land invasions and occupations, and subsequent urban settlements, in different parts of Latin America may appear similar, but they invariably lead to different struggles regarding land ownership, adequate housing, and sociopolitical mobilization. Collective identity cannot be explained when the social movements' actions are not examined as part of the larger context in which that identity takes shape (Stephen 1997: 284). Generality and specificity in those processes have to be part of analytical inquiry. These points are further illustrated by the history of the *movimiento para el alcantarillado* (movement for the sewage system) that developed in Polanco. This confrontation between different agencies was resolved in favor of the colonos, and the conflict's history is defined by activists in the colonia as "a glorious past." This popular mobilization in Guadalajara affected the way urban space was symbolically conceptualized and experienced not only in Polanco, but in other urban areas as well.

The history of this urban movement can be divided into three periods. The first stage—the first six months or so of 1975—was a time of preparation and reflection within the recently formed CEBs inspired by Jesuits.[21] These groups were formed mainly by couples who met to reflect on the application of the Bible to everyday problems (discussed in detail in Chapter 3). At that time neighborhood sanitation was very poor because Guadalajara's trash dump was situated on the Cerro del Cuatro, the hill south of Polanco. During the rainy season (May to October), water and garbage slid down the hill, repeatedly flooding Polanco.

In 1975 Governor Alberto Orozco Romero announced a plan to install a drainage system, but the colonos discovered that they would have to bear the full cost. Moreover, the attorney of the fraccionador, González, had begun repossessing the houses of those who were falling behind with their payments (Morfín Otero 1979). In October 1975 the Grupo de Representantes was formed to organize popular resistance. Important goals included finalizing an agreement that residents would pay only 25 percent of the installation charge and drawing attention to the fraccionador's incompetence and his financial responsibility for the installation.[22] The municipality attempted to break the group's solidarity by seeking support from other groups such as the Comité de Vecinos. This committee claimed to have already achieved the best option by having negotiated a reduced installation fee from the CCMG. In reality the proposed fee was reduced by only 21 percent (Morfín Otero 1979).

In March 1976 the colonos received the first bill for the drainage system, and the Grupo de Representantes decided to risk the legal consequences of asking people to protest the unjust charges. At the same time some of the colonos organized themselves and succeeded in defending the families being threatened with eviction because of late payments.[23] The tug-of-war between the municipality, the representative of the colonos, and the fraccionador ended after more than three thousand people gathered for a protest in front of the government palace. Bowing to public pressure, the municipality agreed that the colonos would have to pay only a quarter of the cost determined by the CCMG, and the drainage system was installed in 1978.

Regarding the issue of land ownership, in 1984 Governor Enrique Albares Castillo signed a document recognizing that fraud had taken place, and that the fraccionador had taken illegal actions in Polanco. This action failed to stop the land tenancy commission from threatening to evict residents from parts of Polanco and Santa María Tequepexpan in 1986 and 1987, but fortunately the evictions never took place. Nevertheless, by the late 1990s the situation was still not completely resolved. In 1995 it seemed that one part of Polanco was still ejidal, and that the tenancy commission could have intervened only in that area. The Grupo de Escrituración of the Organización de Colonos Independientes de Polanco (OCIP), formed in 1990, was still defending residents against such interventions. The organization provided a cultural center and a meeting place, as well as an archive of the history of Polanco. For a while it also hosted an independent radio station, "Radio Pueblo." However, tenancy commission's intervention has become less likely because of support for a constitutional change to article 27 that would repeal the inalienability status of ejido land.

It is clear that the mobilization of residents to address the drainage issue was a critical experience in relations between the government and civil society in Guadalajara. It was one of the initial mobilizations of the Movimiento Urbano Popular (MUP), the network of organizations that emerged before and after April 22, 1992. The achievements of the Grupo de Representantes became central to the formation of the Comité Popular del Sur (CPS), and also the MUP. The Polanco residents negotiated for a reduced charge for the drainage system without mediation by established local groups such as the Coordinación de Trabajadores Mexicanos (CTM), the network through which power usually was allocated in the Mexican system (at least until the PRI's power monopoly was weakened by the 2000 general elections). And this was achieved despite the municipality's efforts to weaken the movement by exacerbating its inner divisions and offering bribes to some individuals (Vélez-Ibañez 1983).

Polanco's grassroot organization nevertheless suffered from the same problems that have affected the CPS and, in the late 1980s and 1990s, the MUP.[24] One problem is internal disagreements about decision making and establishing alliances with emerging or already established political groups. A second problem is that these groups pursued defensive political action rather than proposing new plans to shape urbanization in deprived urban areas (Ramírez Saíz 1992: 190, 191). In this way, the experience of social movements in Guadalajara is different from those in other areas such as Mexico City or Chiapas. A combination of factors, including religious and political conservatism and the failure to organize people around issues of ethnicity and identity, has resulted in less citizen participation in urban popular movements (Regalado Santillán 1995: 232). However, since the 1988 presidential campaign of Cuahutemoc Cárdenas and the creation of the Frente Democratico Nacional, the Movimiento Urbano Popular has broadened its political action, fostering more alliances and privileging social mobilization over specific political affiliations.

In the late 1990s, those who had been or still were involved in social mobilization complained that participation in Polanco had decreased considerably since the mid-1980s. Many groups were having trouble understanding the changes that different colonias were experiencing, and finding the right words to motivate residents. Promoting solidarity among the underprivileged to fight for improved living conditions is not as successful a strategy as it was in the 1970s, even though Polanco's streets weren't all paved and the neighborhood lacked a complete drainage system until work was done between 1996 and 1998.

Colonos identify different causes for this apathy. On one hand, the population involved with the Catholic Church had been confused by frictions generated between the different policies of the priests in charge of the main parishes and the Jesuits in Polanco. Those tensions reflect major internal divisions between the diocesan and the Jesuit order (see Chapter 3). On the other hand, people's priorities have changed, the neighborhood is experiencing relative forms of gentrification, and the message and proposals of groups such as the OCIP have had difficulty adjusting to those changes.

As already mentioned, by the end of the 1990s, changes in the social mobilization in Polanco and Greater Guadalajara show a greater concern with the wider issue of legitimate elections, free of fraud, and the defense of human rights. The Parish of the Anunciación, for instance, has been involved in training observers for local, regional and national elections, and there is a growing awareness of the socioeconomic exclusion of indigenous groups in other parts of Mexico. There is a tendency to delocalize issues of urban mobilization, turning attention away from specific service or house-ownership issues and redirecting it toward major issues at the core of Mexican civil society.

The Centralization of the Suburb

It is clear that Polanco, like other colonias in Guadalajara, is becoming a differentiated world where some people are better off than others. In the 1970s social mobilization in Polanco evolved around metaphors of fighting for democracy and against poverty, but in the late 1980s and 1990s, people expressed reluctance to engage in similar struggles. Many people still feel they are poor, especially with the renewed crisis of underemployment and inefficiency of public and welfare services. For some people the struggle is a personal one, while others perceive it as a struggle of the community (see Chapter 3). Religious choices in Guadalajara are also changing, with a constantly diminishing interest in liberation theology and increased interest in charismatic and evangelical forms of Christianity, as well as in right-leaning Catholic organizations (De la Torre 1998).

In Chapter 2 I will describe how, until the mid-1980s, Polanco had a high crime rate and was the scene of serious confrontations between

youth gangs, smugglers, and often corrupt police. Confrontations between citizens and government are now more common in the southern
suburbs, on the Cerro del Cuatro. Thus the major task faced by those
still active in Polanco's social movement is finding a political discourse
that will renew their impact on the rest of the colonia. In the 1970s
Polanco became famous for its movimiento popular organized through
the activities of the Comunidades Eclesiales de Base; in the 1980s and
1990s, its importance has grown as a center for business and commerce.
The expansion of diversified services has made Polanco popular among
those living in nearby neighborhoods and those in the expanding asentamientos in the Cerro del Cuatro area. Censuses have shown a slight
decrease in the estimated population, which combined with the above-
mentioned phenomena, an increase in property values, and transformation of some dwellings into business properties constitutes what I
call a centralization of the suburb.

A major phenomenon that had important repercussions on the colonia's economy and everyday life was the creation of a *tianguis* (street
market) in 1985. It takes place twice weekly and has expanded visibly
along the central street. As a union stronghold of the Confederación
Revolucionaria de Obreros y Campesinos (CROC), any decisions about
setting up stalls and running the market must be approved by the president of the tianguis. This expansion of the market has had important
consequences for the neighborhood. The quantity of merchandise and
the competitive prices have attracted shoppers from many colonias populares in the southern part of Guadalajara. While in the colonia for the
market, they also take advantage of other services, such as medical and
dental care. Preexisting businesses, however, have suffered from expansion of the tianguis. Those who have good stalls in the market or those
who have well-furnished retail shops in the main street are doing good
business.[25] Those who tend to suffer from the competition are permanent stall-holders who sell food, clothes, and goods at higher prices than
found at the tianguis, and the traders in the permanent covered market.

Another major consequence of the introduction of the street market
has been an increase in property values. The main street has become a
very profitable business center, and since the late 1980s, domestic resi-
dences on this street have become more rare, and the price of these
properties has shot up. The urban structure of Polanco has consequently
changed, with the central street becoming a space for trade rather than
a place for living. In 1997–1998 banks such as Banca Promex, Bital, and
Caja del Sol also opened branches here.

In conclusion, in the 1990s a new phenomenon in the urban space

FIGURE 1. The main street of Polanco in 1999. Note the recently opened bank branch and paved street, which contribute to the changing aesthetic of the center of a periphery. (Photograph by the author.)

appeared. The expansion of Guadalajara into outlying areas has led to the conversion of a relatively old suburb into a center for new suburbs. The increased informality of the market is one component of the process of centralization. Yet the socioeconomic situation in Polanco is still difficult for many. The consolidation stage in the family life cycle (González de la Rocha, 1994), increased property values, and the lively atmosphere of booming business are some of the characteristics changing Polanco's identity from that of a poor neighborhood into one that is more socioeconomically diversified. In different urban and urbanizing Mexican cases, as the case of Greater Guadalajara shows, many groups are still marginal to the system of service redistribution — they have to fight for urban services—but they are integrated into the lower end of the productive system (Gallegos Ramírez 1990). This type of marginality is still one of the key inspirations of popular/political movements such as the OCIP in Polanco and the MUP in Guadalajara, but people's perception of themselves as marginal is changing. Marginality is a relative phenomenon, and those perceptions, as well as structural, socioeconomic connotations, are fluid and changing. Consequently, groups that formerly succeeded in mobilizing residents through metaphors of marginality and empowerment of the poor have been revising and questioning their strategies and have become part of a national mobilization focused on civil society issues such as election fraud and human rights issues.

This transition is important and reveals the effects of past religious evangelization into present grassroot movements. The content and forms of current social mobilizations vary, but the importance of a civil forum of expression in Guadalajara is increasing. Even if the initial actions of the CEBs or the MUP could be considered, to a greater or lesser degree, as residual phenomena (Williams 1977), their impact in the long run is shaping a new and emerging activism in civil society. To recognize the threads that link past and residual urban mobilizations to present, emerging ones is central to understanding the formation of civil society in Guadalajara and the rest of urban Mexico.

The first migrants who settled in the fraccionamiento popular of Polanco had to put up with several hardships associated with establishing a new neighborhood: basic services were installed slowly and incompletely, and people had to fight for installation of an adequate drainage system and recognition of their rights to own land. The history of Polanco is thus a good example of how, in Guadalajara and other parts of Mexico, the rapid process of urbanization has been fertile ground for connivance between wealthy landowners and government agencies and officials. However, the children of the migrant settlers are now acquiring skills and education to which their parents did not have access, and some are demanding citizens' rights that their parents did not have or had to painfully acquire. Nonetheless, educational and social mobility is not uniform in Polanco, and many families still have to struggle with decreased buying power and are forced to rely on the female labor force to sustain household incomes (González de la Rocha 1994). Greater socioeconomic differentiation has been taking place since the mid-1980s, and the poorest and most unskilled members of the community—especially if they were renting—have slowly been pushed out of the neighborhood.

In Chapter 2 I introduce and discuss how the various prisms of belonging articulate representations and embodied experiences of this urban space. At this point, however, it is important to note that urban settlements such as colonias populares have emerged from a conflictive articulation between state regulatory presence, private enterprise, and citizens in negotiations concerning land, housing, and public services. Hence the urban space emerges out of this articulation between power relations and specific places with local histories. Stemming from a modernity project of Mexican economic progress as well as the current economic expansion and transformation of Greater Guadalajara, a specific urban space such as Polanco becomes morally tinted, as I explain in the next chapter—first peripheralized, and then centralized. Hence the narratives of residents and the private and public powers in this urban process about land regularization and housing not only constitute a place—Polanco—that is incorporated into the city, but suggest some of the complex layers of which the urban space is composed.

CHAPTER 2

Migration, Space, and Belonging

At times the mirror increases a thing's value, at times denies it.
Not everything that seems valuable above the mirror maintains
its force when mirrored. . . . The city exists and it has a
simple secret: it knows only departure, not returns.

Italo Calvino, Invisible Cities

Mi pueblo, levantado sobre la llanura. Lleno de árboles y de hojas,
como una alcancía donde hemos guardado nuestro recuerdos.
Sentirás que allí uno quisiera vivir para la eternidad.

My village, above the plains. Full of trees and leaves, like a
treasure box where we have kept our memories. You'll feel that
you could live there forever.

Juan Rulfo, Pedro Páramo

The migration experience and migrants representations of space and
time are parts of the learning processes. This learning is not only about
gains, but also about losses. In this chapter I explore the prisms of belonging that emerge in the relationship between urban and rural space
by capturing some of the heterogeneous perceptions, feelings, desires,
contradictions, and images that shape experiences of space and time both
at personal and family levels. Spaces are associated with particular ways
of being and moral beliefs, which shift in relation to the contexts in
which they are perceived. Ways of talking about experiences in different
geographical spaces illustrate the process through which people map
their world, and give insight into their self-perception (Lynch 1960).

Different images of the urban and the rural are present in the colonias populares, and representations of the rural are directly related to experiences in the changing dimensions of the urban.

Studies of migration to urban contexts in Latin America have focused for a long time either on structural or on psychological causality (Mahar 1992), while issues of self-awareness, worldviews, and the re-enactment of the past in the present in the migrants' experience have received much less attention.[1] Hence, in this chapter I analyze, within a context of migration, ways in which the space of the home, the city, and the colonia is represented as a known/unknown, secure/insecure space as perceived by the media and those living within or coming to the colonia. Diversification of the quality of space is present in the representations of places of family origin, which may be recalled with pride or with shame.

The process of representation and experience in the urban space may imply self- and family empowerment and expansion of knowledge, but also interruption in and loss of ontological security. The migrants' families' places of origin may assume different connotations for offspring generations; for those brought up there, such places may be associated with harsh conditions, social expulsion, or a nostalgic, "lost" past. For their children, these places may be associated with a more relaxed social environment for young people, and less rigid rules of courtship than found in the city. Some of the questions addressed in this chapter concern the visibility and invisibility of specific urban and rural dynamics that relate to selective memory and a hierarchy of representations, a hierarchy that is translated into a difference in social relations.

Lomnitz-Adler (1992) has argued that these processes of translation, as processes of internalization, are fundamental to understanding processes of identification within, and as a part of, different national and regional identities. Identity then emerges from a fracture between different internalized and objectified cultural forms.[2] Still, the process of internalization takes place within a system of power relations that is not exclusively coercive but also creative. Actors' creativity in shaping their own perceptions of the world is thus as important as their engagement with collective action. Furthermore, collective boundaries cannot be assumed to be homogeneously shared by the population, because past and present representations assume different and often contrasting forms.[3]

As previously discussed, the specificity of Guadalajara's urbanization shows the importance of relating a study of individual agency with an analysis of the central role that civic and religious neighborhood associations have played in the creation of community identity and civil society in Guadalajara (De la Peña and De la Torre 1996; De la Torre 1998). This creative dimension of power emerges also in the analysis of neighborhood organizations and the role of religious and lay leaders in defining the space of the barrio and the city of Guadalajara (De la Peña 1989; De la Peña and De la Torre 1990). The urban space becomes a space of articulation and conquest for multiple leaders, actors, and organizations.

The narrative expressions of the colonia, the city, and the rural space are part of the productions and appropriation of prisms of belonging, which are then important clues to the process of identity in contemporary urban Mexico.[4] The formation of these prisms both as cognitive maps and embodiments of experience is part of particular life histories and strategies.[5] From that angle, I will discuss the relation between prisms of belonging and localism. We now know that locality is primarily "relational and contextual" to other domains (Appadurai 1995: 204).[6] In other words, the local as such does not exist, but is a process that continuously refers to other scales of socioeconomic and political phenomena for its meanings.

The Importance of Belonging

Migration to Guadalajara and the colonia of Polanco needs to be read as part of this developing identity of urban space, and its effects on people's identities have to be analyzed in terms of belonging, experience of places, and processes of inclusion and exclusion. Since identity can also be in between places (but nonetheless always occurs in a specific place), it is important to focus on how the notion of belonging is strategically inserted into personal biographies at particular moments of collective formation and social differentiation.

Belonging to and identifying with a specific land are very important for people in Polanco, and this is easily discerned in everyday speech. Being "loose," or not belonging to a particular place, is defined as a negative characteristic. The term *vago* (which means "vagrant") is used to refer to young people who take drugs or are the source of trouble. They do *vagancias,* which are lawless things such us stealing car radios and smashing car windows. Attributes of wandering are commonly used to describe actions considered negative. The word *vago* is also used for children who act against their family's will, and for married people who do not fulfill the responsibilities of marriage. It is important to remember that the verb *estar casado* (to be married) comes from the root word *casa* (house). In the same sense, to be a good boy or girl (*ser un buen muchacho/a*) is the opposite of *ser vago,* with the notion of being good being closely related to traditional ideas of cooperating in the life of the household.

The goal of having a house of their own is fundamental for most families in low-income urban areas, and ownership is much preferred to renting. The impact of land and ownership disputes discussed in the previous chapter can be better understood through recognizing that people's perceptions of social and emotional stability are associated with their houses and the land on which are built. Landownership still has strong symbolic power in urban spaces, and negotiations in land disputes can be viewed also as a negotiation of, and resistance to, enforced deterritorialization of identity. The difficult process of acquiring land affects attitudes about owning a home. The acquisition of legal documents for the ownership of land makes people feel more relaxed about passing their houses on to their children. This loyalty to one's land and home does appear to be changing over generations. Clara, a middle-aged woman born in the rancho of El Murillo near Ameca, showed her concern about this change when her married daughter wanted to buy a flat in an estate block in a relatively more affluent area near Polanco: "They want to buy a flat in the area of Jardines de la Cruz, but what are they going to own . . . the air? It would be better if they bought a small piece of land in the Cerro [del Cuatro, a set of colonias near and on the top of a hill that still lack basic services] and built something there."

For Clara, the idea of upward mobility is related to the capacity to stop renting and own a house on a piece of land, even if it is in a worse area. For her children, though, and for other recently married couples, upward mobility is identified with living in better-off colonias, even if in a reduced space "in the air" such as blocks of flats, where communal space is more restricted and the living spaces are smaller. Such decisions by succeeding generations clearly indicate that for some, neighborhood location has become more important than the nature of the property.

When it comes to the internal space of a house, in Polanco, as in other colonia populares, people tend to ruralize the space of houses. The room at the entrance is usually the best decorated room in the house, or even the only decorated room, because it is what visitors see (but it can also be used as a bedroom at night). Often there are pictures on the wall of married couples, including the heads of the household and their married children, and Catholic images of the Virgin and saints. Also

FIGURE 2. Mauricio in the home of his aunt, Juanita, which is a good example of a certain style of home decorating that indicates a liking for the reproduction of natural motifs and the display of religious images. (Photograph by the author.)

common are images of landscapes, but these do not necessarily represent places of origin; instead they tend to be stereotypical postcard-type photos. In some houses the walls are entirely covered with different images, as if empty spaces were something to be covered up.

Mirroring the differences in decor found in working- and middle-class English households, poor households in Polanco use cheaper versions of the decorations used by those of the middle class: the difference is not in design and colors, but in material (Hunt 1989: 77). Poorer Mexican households display knicknacks, souvenirs, and cult figures made of plastic or other inexpensive materials. Plastic or paper flowers are common ornaments, but when the house is used for production, as in different forms of home-based cottage industry workshops (Miraftab 1994), the decoration is removed for the workday and put back into place in the evening.

When I asked people why they chose artificial decorations rather than real plants, I was told that "they look nicer, and more refined."[7] Real plants can nonetheless be found in the courtyard (*el corral*), which is often used for keeping animals such as rabbits, chickens, or pigs and

FIGURE 3. Houses in the colonia are reminiscent of the lifestyle and homes in the rancho, as in the display of pots and pans on the wall of Juanita's home. (Photograph by the author.)

also as working or storage space. However, the balance between the house and the corral is the opposite of that found in the countryside. In rural areas the corral is the center of activity (for raising animals, washing dishes, sitting and preparing corn, and so on), whereas in the city the most activities take place in the house itself.[8]

The kitchen, however, still recalls rural life. Although there is no firepit on which to place the *comal* (a circular plate of metal used to heat tortillas), the way in which the cutlery, pots, and pans are displayed on the wall in many houses is reminiscent of life in the rancho. Also hung on the wall is colorful pottery, often from the kilns of Tonalá and Tlaquepaque. The pleasure people get from displaying these items outweighs practicality, for Polanco is very dusty, and things need to be cleaned often.

Contrasting uses of the house itself have been captured in a comparative study of the use of domestic space by Mexican migrants in the United States and by villagers in rural Jalisco (Pader 1993). The use of domestic space in Mexico emphasizes interdependence, movement in space, "familism" (Pader 1993), and a lack of separation between the different parts of a house; it also reveals an orientation toward group rather than private, individual space, and "continual physical connections among household members" (Pader 1993: 126).

In Polanco, the existence of a separate space, such as a private room with separate bathroom or cooking facilities, is not common, even for recently married couples living in their parents' house (which can cause strain, however, for young married couples who are prevented from enjoying much intimacy away from the eyes of in-laws). Toilets often have curtains as doors, and relatives (normally of the same sex) tend to sleep in the same bed, even as adults. There is no division between adults' and children's spaces, and children play and move about as they please, resulting in a continuous cross-cutting between these two worlds. Adults do not seem particularly annoyed by children's noise, and children find their own entertainment without relying on adult encouragement.

Contrasting Images, Different Wavelengths

While most households in Polanco share a focus on the internal space of the house, a tension between security and risk taking emerges in the multiple mappings of space outside the home. Many people consider it unsafe to walk at night, especially through back streets and near Polanco's park, but during the day the colonia is felt to be a relatively secure place. In the morning, laborers leave early for shift jobs, as do students for the *preparatoria* (high school). Women sweep the street in front of their houses first thing in the morning because leaving the front doorstep dirty is considered the sign of a poorly kept house. A few older women and their younger helpers sell breakfast out of food stalls near the bus terminal. In general, women fill their mornings with activities considered to "make a woman": sweeping, washing the floor, preparing food. By mid-morning, the main street of Polanco is full of activity. This is a time when women can talk to "strange" men more easily, and there are stories and gossip about women falling in love with men whom they first glanced at on their way to the market. Long queues form for buying tortillas and *masa* (basic corn dough), which people complain are inferior to those produced in the rancho. Technological changes, whilst alleviating gender specific load became catalysts for despising of modernity.

Many women affirm that during the day Polanco feels similar to a pueblo, even if life is faster in the city. New business activities are set up in Polanco as fast as others close down, and they are often run from front doors or from converted front entrances, a sign of fragmentation of the market and increased competition. Many of these small businesses — selling sweets, homemade snacks, soft drinks, and so on — are carried out by women and in the ambiguous space of the threshold. As I will elaborate in Chapter 6, the ambiguity is related to the fact that women should cross the space in the colonia with a purpose: they should not simply hang around as men do. They can, however, interact from the house's threshold, making it possible to run a business without leaving home.

The location of these businesses indicates a transition from visibility to invisibility, allowing women and young household members to inhabit a space of consumption, labor production, and finally, household reproduction. The threshold is also an area that reflects Mexico's current economic crisis and people's lack of confidence in economic recovery. At the end of the 1980s, threshold businesses also sold goods such as small electronic equipment and baby toys, but in the mid- and late 1990s, they almost exclusively sold homemade food or relatively inexpensive sweets and snacks. This is because there is less capital available to purchase goods to sell.

The households in which women need to set up such small businesses are part of the lower end of the spectrum in the colonia's economic transformation. Conditions of visibility and invisibility in the urban space can be seen in the relation between the visible architectural space and the invisible exchanges, interactions, and networks it contains. In the urban space, then, the threshold of the house becomes a symbolic setting for back-and-forth shifts between visibility and invisibility. In terms of social relations, the threshold becomes a symbolic ground for the encounter of the visible activity of women's labor and the "invisible" activity of household reproduction.

After dusk the outdoor space is considered unsafe, and the only people on the central street are couples walking or eating at food stalls, and men going to their night shifts or the *cantinas* (bars). Some people still hold onto rural beliefs about the Devil catching those who are in the street at night, and in the urban context the Devil is symbolized by the vagos and drug-addicts who are blamed for creating an evil and disruptive side of the colonia.[9] Thus attributing social dysfunction to "bad," drug-addicted individuals or to migrant communities is not only typical of North American inner cities (see Bourgois 1995 for the Puerto Ricans' case in East Harlem, New York), but also of Mexican urban contexts. Yet the phenomenon of urban drug dealing is better understood as a result of specific urban economies and exploitative labor systems, rather than individual or community psychological dysfunction (Bourgois 1995: 322, 323).

Since the centralization of the periphery (discussed in the previous chapter as the conversion of an older peripheral neighborhood into a center for new ones) has been taking place, the *bandillerismo* phenomenon (and parallel police harassment) has shifted to more-peripheral colonias such as the Cerro del Cuatro.[10] Residents' perceptions of Polanco as an impoverished and violent place are slowly changing, but for a long time, Polanco was seen by many *tapatíos* (inhabitants of Guadalajara) as a prototype of a dangerous colonia. Polanco has been described variously in the local press as an island of solidarity, a place of struggle for urban rights, and even as a dangerous cluster of rebels ready to bring the Cuban revolution into Mexico. One reporter described a journey through the streets of Polanco and Santa Cecilia during which "he discovered a series of slogans on the walls, in which people are encouraged to rebel; other slogans attack the military force, the police and the government" (*Conciencia Pública* 4, March 1987).

The colonia has often been seen as an outstanding example in the urban periphery's deprivation and marginalization from civil society. Consider, for example, the following headline from *El Sol de Guadalajara* (August 9, 1991):

CALAMATOUS POLANCO
Abandoned for 35 years, with illegal use of land and unpaved streets,
Indifference toward "major floods,"
Murders anad ambushes committed nearly every day,
It is a free land for drug addicts and criminals.

But these images have not corresponded entirely to the people's perceptions of themselves.

Anthony Cohen has argued that the identity of a community is related to the experience of its boundaries in symbolic opposition to other-than-us, and that people's sense of self arises from the "contrivance of distinctive meaning within the community's social discourse." So, communities are mental constructs whose symbolic boundaries allow people to "think themselves into difference" (Cohen 1985: 117). In Polanco the nature of symbolic boundaries varies from actors to actors because those boundaries depend on actors' intentionality in expressing and stressing different images of the community, as well as the contexts in which those images are evoked.

People express both love for the colonia and shame. Living conditions have improved, but the colonia's appearance has not improved as much as that of other neighborhoods established about the same time or later. In some cases this "backwardness" is accepted with pride because Polanco has *pueblo* characteristics rather than the wealthier modern look of nearby neighborhoods. These colonias—where some of Polanco's women work as *sirvientas* (housemaids)—are portrayed as less friendly places, where neighbors know little about each other. Nevertheless, when comparing Polanco to a different "other," different characteristics are emphasized.

Some people perceive Polanco as a more alienated environment, even in comparison with poorer neighborhoods. One young teenager from a poor family complains that her friends in Polanco are often snobbish: "Young people are very presumptuous and snobbish here. For this reason I get along better with the people in Echeverria [a nearby colonia], because people there are simpler. They do not show off their clothes."

A similar attitude is expressed by some of the people who are more in need (often those in rented accommodations), who argue that people in Polanco used to be more helpful, but have become more self-oriented. Neighbors living in *vecinidades* normally do not share water or electricity if a family's services get cut off or if they do not have running water or electricity in the house. Relying on neighbors' help is often described as a thing of the past; now people are too caught up with their own lives to think about others. The rise in rental prices has also affected people's feelings about the communitarian and individualistic quality of the social space. Homeownership, home improvement, car ownership, and having adult children employed in stable wage labor are among the main characteristics associated with increased status and social capital.

Antithetical images of the colonia coexist with a sense of increased

FIGURE 4. An example of home improvements and the addition of an extension on the first floor. Often the extension is used to accommodate married offspring until they can afford to rent or buy their own homes. (Photograph by the author.)

selfishness, and the neighborhood space also can be perceived as a known, friendly environment. In some cases, people are supportive of needy neighbors, and activities such as the *posadas* (Christmas parties) include all the families living on the street, even if they have little to contribute. Neighbors also keep an eye on each other's property, and residents say they have established *confianza* (ties of trust) with their neighbors similar to those they formed in their pueblos.

A key to explaining these contrasting attitudes about the environment is the history of Polanco. In Chapter 3 I will discuss in detail how Polanco has been affected by strong development of the Comunidades Eclesiales de Base inspired by liberation theology, and grassroot mobilization between 1970 and the early 1990s.[11] This evangelization during neighborhood formation, and also during its consolidation as a colonia popular, may have been aided by people's sense of belonging more to their place of origin than Polanco, as well as their lack of initial ties with neighbors in urban areas.[12] A sense of a common identity has been created through group participation in the colonia's activities rather than through ties of kinship or common origin.

Perceptions and the viability of house and neighborhood space in

Polanco relate to boundaries of the self within the family and the community, and across genders. Ways in which domestic and neighborhood space are conceived cannot be separated from those who experience it and construct its boundaries symbolically in opposition to the space of others. Hence I now turn to how migrants and their offspring perceive the city as a whole, and how those boundaries are shaped.

Coming to the City: An Expansion of Knowledge

Jesús Martín Barbero has argued that in Latin American urbanization "the appearance of the masses meant that it was now impossible to continue maintaining the rigid hierarchical organization that constituted the society . . . for in the midst of the ignorance of the masses regarding the norms of the city and the way that their mere presence was challenging the order of this environment, there was a secret desire to get possession of the good life that the city represented" (Martín-Barbero 1993: 157, 158). Thus the study of mass urbanization through different subject positions sheds light on the changing nature of the urban, urban desires, and social environment.

Different subject positions unfold in people's changing imagery of the city and the role of this imagery in shaping identity. Notions of "expanding knowledge," of "hardening the heart," or of self-empowerment are important elements in understanding how experiences of migration shape people's mapping of the world, their experiences in it, and their self-consciousness. Physical occupation of a space/place does not necessarily bring a sense of belonging, which is a negotiated way of remembering and constructing a collective memory of place (Parkin 1998: ix). Belonging is also a phenomenological experience of the local that emerges through a tension between the ideals of the same particular (Schama 1995). Belonging evokes emotions and involves a longing for certain ties to specific places and social spaces (Lovell 1998).

The perceptions of migrants' children born or raised in Polanco are different from those of their parents brought up in the countryside. Nevertheless, the influence of their parents' rural background is still strong, often creating conflicts between generations, especially in terms of gender relations and religious beliefs. To explore how rural roots feed into urban culture, it is important to pay particular attention to those who personally experienced the rural in their childhood or adolescence.

The city of Guadalajara, with its multiple faces, represents one period in people's experience, but perception of the city is filtered through the experience of the pueblo and rancho. Many migrants' first experiences in the city involved moving from one colonia to another before they were able to settle in fraccionamientos. Some of them came from pueblos (villages with populations of a few hundred), while others came from ranchos, the clusters of isolated houses in the countryside. Pueblo means also population, so it defines both a geographic space and a human bond between people. I will discuss in the following chapter how the pueblo is articulated in Catholic religious discourses to claim an authenticity of representativeness. Moreover, I will see how a tension between pueblo and pueblos is a pull between universalism and particularism, part of a tension of modernity.

It has been argued that the process of the formation of the self is related to memory, cognition, and history, and also that it is shaped by whatever genre is used to recall and represent such memories (Tonkin 1992: 50). The understanding of the past, then, is closely connected to the process of recollection in a social context, because in that process the self is both the subject of the narrative and the agent-narrator. Thus memory is not only a mental act, but an act of encoding semantic, visual, verbal, bodily, and habitual experiences to construct a narrative (Connerton 1989).[13]

The experience of moving to the city is described through personal idiosyncratic memory. I encountered some resistance in getting people to talk about such experiences because their recollections stirred up intense emotions. But through co-experiencing such emotions, I was able to understand how they are a "means through which human bodies achieve a social ontology through which institutions are created" (Lyon and Barbalet 1994: 56). The prisms of belonging that emerge in this book connect memory, cognition, and history in a process of becoming that maintains axes of difference that are often painful to recall. It is coming into being through axes of difference that cut through, but also link up urban socioeconomic integration and self-understanding.

Migrating to the city may have been a shocking experience for many people, but also an enlightening one. In many cases the city is represented as having human qualities, as in Doña Chayo's observation that "if somebody is unprepared, the city eats a person from the countryside." She also sees the city as a morally dangerous place: "In the city there is not freedom but libertinism. In the rancho there are not bad people because everybody needs everybody else. One can leave the children free. There are no drugs, nor perdition, as in the city."

In this sense the pueblo and rancho are conceived of as secure places in contrast to urban deprivation, violence, and drug addiction. Although Doña Chayo is married, her husband is not a very good breadwinner and often drinks and gets into trouble. She is definitely the one in charge of the household and the upbringing of their six children. She defines herself as a *mujer corajuda,* or angry woman, and she often appears so when, with a high-pitched voice and piercing eyes, she speaks about how the neighbors look down on her sloppily dressed children, or criticize her for not being an "accommodating" woman. Her efforts are constantly directed toward smoothing family relations, managing relations with neighbors, and keeping her younger children out of trouble. Thus Doña Chayo's experience of the urban environment, especially for raising children, is one of potential violence, danger, and confrontation.

However, this contrast between the city and the pueblo/rancho does not always coincide with people's actual experience. I was surprised to find that people's reasons for moving to Guadalajara were only partially economic. Problematic family circumstances also pushed households to migrate. Difficult relations with extended family, and even the murder of close relatives, were often mentioned or hinted at as reasons for migrating. In some cases families had to flee from bloody revenge.[14] Nonetheless, to a certain extent, violence in the countryside is perceived as being different from urban violence because the latter occurs randomly and is often generated by unknown people who observe no code of honor.

The economic and social impact of drug smuggling, however, has changed countryside lifestyle dramatically in many of the places of origin of urban dwellers. Some areas, especially Los Altos de Jalisco and Zacatecas, have become centers for smuggling drugs to the United States, and they are also major centers for those wishing to migrate to the United States. The influx of drug money and remittances from migrants headed north has changed the economics of many villages. Nowadays, living conditions there are often superior to those of older migrants to Guadalajara as life styles increasingly follow U.S. patterns, referred to as *nortenización* (Alarcón 1988). Consequently, a growing number of people feel misplaced by the changes that their pueblos are undergoing, and also now feel worse off than some of those who remained in the village.

Migrants often deny their place of origin its distinctive history and evolution. Some people born in the rancho recall their past experiences in terms of a split, saying that "te recuerdas siempre lo bueno y no lo malo" (you always recall the good, not the bad). The longing to be there, a physical/magical space where life might come together and wounds could be healed, contrasts with the realization that the physical place itself does not have that intrinsic power.

For many people, the transition from a rural to an urban environment is perceived as a step from an unconscious to a conscious life, and is represented in terms of both self-empowerment and the loss of that power. The images are frequently contradictory. Raymond Williams (1973) points out that the invention of a tradition, of a "mythical" past, can increase social solidarity when class conflicts are present, and memory of that past becomes necessary for maintaining social solidarity. The urbanized and industrializing Guadalajara, with its low-income colonias, is becoming a space of increasing class and social capital differentiation. Reactions and resistance to these differentiations need to be understood in the context of different social actions and symbolic experience.[15]

Consider, for example, the case of Maximiliano, a worker in the Corona beer factory. He came from a rancho near Talpa in Zacatecas in the late 1970s. He used to be an *amansador* (horse tamer) and has had various jobs since he first came to work seasonally in Guadalajara at the age of fifteen. He describes his early life as that of a man of action who was not always well accepted in the rancho because of his tendency to be *"muy valiente"* (very brave) both in his work and with women. He ended up staying in Guadalajara after "winning" the love of a woman who later became his wife. Through his experiences in Guadalajara, he started to formulate his own taxonomy of the world, a world of possibilities for self-realization: "When I arrived here, I started to be in contact with many people, and I started to catalogue everything, and the different types of people. But in the city one feels that everyone is equal. With money, it is not possible to buy friendship. Everybody needs others, even millionaires—to have money is not everything."

From his male perspective, Maximiliano thinks that a changing view of the world is more characteristic of men, because they are "out there," looking for jobs and interacting with people. He believes this explains why many women end up with a "bad" man in the city, because they have not sufficiently developed a capacity for cataloguing people, and are thus unable to correctly interpret male intentions. Maximiliano's experience as a worker has been a fortunate one. He has been with Corona for many years, and feels that he has been treated well there, an experience that has contributed to his perception that men are more able to "master" urban space than women are. In this respect, the urban space acquires new communicative properties, which are perceived and experienced through gender-specific lenses.

The formulation of a new taxonomy through interaction in the city is also expressed in the words of Don Domingo, a man in his early sixties who was born in San Cristóbal de Chapala.[16] He left for Guadalajara at the age of fourteen to help his uncle build a small house, partly because he disliked working the land, but also because he had been interested since childhood in learning about construction. Now a semiretired whitewasher, he and his wife live in a house divided into two parts. One part is occupied by his only son, Gerónimo, who is married with five children, and the extended family is now actively involved in the CEBs.

Domingo's recollections of his youth are very sad. His family was extremely poor, his mother was always busy caring for their large family, and his father drank a lot. His father's neglect was so severe that most of his children died. Domingo recalls being very lonely, with no one to satisfy his basic needs and provide for his well-being. Nevertheless, his experience in Guadalajara as an adolescent was as hard as anything in the village, and shaped even more his *manera de ser* (way of being):

I stayed overnight in the yard sleeping like a small dog wrapped in newspaper, and that stays in one's memory. This is what is hard, the heart shuts, this is what happens. Other people are not able to understand that if someone who is hungry and in great need asks you for help, you do not see him because you went through the same type of experiences and nobody helped you, so you do not help others. So one tries to hold a straight life and does not admit mistakes.

The case of Domingo reveals a difficult area of inquiry: the use of language that is metaphorical and strategic, allowing him "to move from the abstract and inchoate of lived experience to the concrete and easily graspable" (Low 1994: 143). In other words, what is the relation between metaphorical language and "messy" experience? Recurrent dialogues with Domingo taught me that unspeakable suffering often results in, to use his phrase, a "shutting of the heart": a condition of closure imposed by the urban space on the human body. Through recounting a bodily experience shaped by the urban encounter, Domingo is communicating an evaluation of relations, and set of emotions, that shapes particular actions. As discussed in the introduction, emotions, moral evaluations, and reason integrate in everyday life, and this integration is fundamental to understanding the process of self-formation in social relations.

Domingo has long suffered from diabetes and nearly had to undergo a foot amputation (see Chapter 4). I noticed, however, that many times when visitors asked about his health, he would reply that he himself was well, but that his foot "was bad." He had endless discussions with his wife, who wants to reduce his sugar intake, and he would become quite angry when she tried to do that, convincing her, most of the time, to give up her fight. I noticed that the distance he perceived between "himself" and part of his body was a way to omit pain from his narrative in his relation to others — a "shutting off" that recalls his earlier experience.

Coming to the city and having to find some way to survive can also, however, help a person to learn about the world and assimilate experiences. As Domingo said, "In the village people do not analyze much because they do not know very much, and if they do not know, they start to fall behind once, twice. But in the city one learns to catalogue people by the simple fact of looking at them." Bodily experiences and memories of feelings thus shape perceptions of the city. Domingo's experience is a case of ontological insecurity in which the framework of basic trust in others has been weakened, and anxiety increased (Giddens 1991b: 46). For Domingo, reference points in his life — fundamental to his key experiences and expressed in his self-narrative — have been shaken by coming to the city. In such cases, the construction of a narrative of the self is fundamental to forming a sense of that self (Taylor 1989: 47). However, the city also brought Domingo in contact with multiple worlds: he knows people of different classes and status, and has broadened his perspective through the CEBs. But the experience of the city has also re-created the sense of fragmentation and isolation that he experienced early on in life. These two aspects represent layers of his narrative: one a memory of expansion, new connections, and exploration of human relations, the other — mentioned much later and with reluctance — related to feelings and experiences of body, closure, pain, and fragmentation. It is in the nature of these passages, in the memory of loss, that we are given a glimpse of how a life history becomes a life strategy. Migration to the city may be an experience of taxonomic and consciousness expansion, but it may also become, for the same actor, a memory of bodily and emotional disjunction.

The experiences of Maximiliano and Domingo indicate that prisms of belonging emerge out of tensions between conscious and unconscious sources, and from a desire to deny places of origin their distinctive force and the legacy they can offer individual histories. Experience of the city can also inhibit self-empowerment because it confronts a person with the limitations of urban life. In the rancho, many people did not feel the sense of powerlessness they experienced after moving to Guadalajara. By virtue of being oriented toward a self-sufficient economy, life in the rancho could often provide for basic needs, but once migrants came to the city, they usually needed to find wage work to satisfy their families' basic needs. Cyclical labor rhythms, then, have been transformed into daily wage labor and dependence on the market.

One testimonial of this labor change was offered by Eleonora, who in the late 1960s, at the age of thirteen, moved to Guadalajara from a rancho in Michoacán. After a series of various jobs she found work in a maquiladora that produces electronic equipment, forcing her to leave much of the housework to her daughter living at home. Because her father killed someone in a so-called honor dispute, the family was forced to flee the rancho. Eleonora has often felt overwhelmed by the subsequent changes in her life and has had to struggle to find her way through:

You leave the village because people throw you out, because people are very united, so if you have done something . . . you cannot stay there any more. . . . When I arrived in the city, I was sad to have to buy small amounts of food every day because there was no money. In my house, in the rancho we had more than enough. The world closed for me and that made me sad. Life in the rancho is nice because one has all that one needs.

Her experience of "flexibility of the market"—the result of changing jobs more than once—in an internationalizing economy of the Guadalajara region and the insecurity of the workplace is interpreted as the harshness of the urban space and problematized as a family history. Her story appears to me as a reading of the political economy through a language of honor and shame. Moreover, since time and space are characterized by given modes of production, the globalizing economy—experienced as highly structured factory work—requires a reconstruction of the local and a deferred fulfillment of desire in the present urban condition.

The experience of coming to the town can also be an experience of self-reflexivity, a perception of one's own self, that was not present in the countryside. According to Doña Marisol, Domingo's wife, "There is more spiritual tranquility. What needs to be done is done with pleasure, and it is not felt to be difficult. But the happiness in the rancho is a dumb happiness. . . . One lives day by day, in God's will, without ideals. I did not think there. . . . There one is not oneself."

Rural life is thus portrayed as a place where things are hard, but where there is little feeling of sadness; sadness arises with growing self-awareness and a perception of the contrasts between different possible ways of being. In Doña Marisol's experience and narrative of the self, intersubjectivity existed prior to subjectivity, and this supports the view that "discovering the 'other' in an emotional and cognitive way is of key importance in the initial development of self-awareness as such" (Giddens 1991a: 51). Moreover, it indicates again that urban migration is linked to self-awareness and a redefinition of the boundaries of the self. Doña Marisol, a very intelligent woman in her early seventies, has also been involved in the CEBs, as well as in the *grupo de salud* (see Chapter 4), so her experiences of social and religious mobilization in the city are also part of these changes in self-awareness and boundaries of the self.

Representations of places of origin, then, are shaped by experiences in the city in many ways, with places of origin tending to become part of a "fixed" and contrasting temporal past. Recalling the past in a dimension "beyond time" is to use the past as a resource to legitimize the present and turn it from an unknown into a familiar form (Cohen 1985: 99). For people in Polanco, the familiar form of the present is not the result of a linear progression from the past, but is more a composite form of gain and loss, of awareness, and of continuity with, and opposition to, the past. It is an emergence of identity. Modernist and reductionist approaches that rest on a contrast between backwardness and progress underestimate how social and physical experiences in the city create a body of knowledge at cognitive and affective levels that shapes representations of past and present, as well as lead to acquisition or loss of personal and family empowerment. To understand this process of self-identity further, it is necessary to illustrate what it means for some people "to be" from a certain place.

"Soy de rancho": (I am from the ranch)

Expressions of ranchero culture originated in western Mexico and were presented in famous literary productions and in the traditional music of the Mariachis. These have become stereotypical symbols of "Mexican-ness" (both within and outside Mexico).[17] Distinctive elements of ranchero identity thus belong to wider regional and national scenarios. In the colonia of Polanco, however, people use notions of el rancho to express varied and contrasting qualities of human interaction, and to represent either a sense of common roots in contrast to the fragmentation of the city, or a negative distinctiveness in contrast to the homogeneity of urban life.

Ranchero life centered on the breeding of animals, subsistence agriculture, and handcraft production in scattered settlements, with a strong form of family organization (González 1979). The fundamental traits of rancheros trace back to Spanish colonial times rather than indigenous origins; in the stratified ranchero society, private ownership of land is privileged over communal ownership, and isolation and competition are emphasized (Barragán López 1990). Social stratification favors the formation of political oligarchy as well as intense rivalries and frequent antagonism, and the nuclear family is the primary unit of social organization, with virilocal residence and family principles based on traditional Catholic values. Within the family, males are considered superior to women, relationships imply love and respect, and male siblings share equally in inheritance (De la Peña 1984).

These ranchero characteristics have been challenged by closer contact with urban populations and changes in the livestock industry. But according to González (1979: 107), during the latter part of the nineteenth century the rancheros who lived in the area around San Juan de Gracia (in Michoacán, south of Lake Chapala) "had a poor but not sad life. Their ideal was the simple man. Sweat, strength, braveness and astuteness were regarded as worthy qualities. Physical strength, agility, ability to horse ride, and audacity were the worthiest qualities: in other words what embodied primitive life."

Many rancheros now decide to leave their land because they feel isolated and lack the services that would allow them to develop a viable trade in cattle and farming products (Barragán López 1990). Some who have migrated seasonally to the United States and have successfully raised money to invest in breeding activities have instead acquired new land and turned their ranchos into small haciendas—a larger piece of land used for farming and breeding. They are now often better off than people in the villages, who describe them as hard workers but also as behaving roughly, especially toward women.

"Soy de rancho" now refers to specific socioeconomic factors and identifies not only a place of origin but also a particular way of conducting oneself in relationships. People in Polanco use expressions such as "no soy ranchero" (I am not from the rancho) or "te dejaron como novia de rancho" (you have been left as a girlfriend of the rancho), both of which have negative connotations. The former implies a rejection of shyness or feeling out of place, while the latter refers to a person left waiting for someone who fails to show up, or more generally to someone who has been let down.

El Murillo offers a good example of life in the *ranchería*, which is a cluster of campesino houses originally developed around a hacienda, on which the campesinos would have been employed. When haciendas were replaced by ejido land tenancy, these clusters survived as small settlements (Pérez Martinez 1993: 14). A rancho is an even smaller and more isolated settlement. The ranchería, still smaller than a pueblo, often has no permanent community infrastructure such as schools and health community services.

El Murillo, which is north of Ameca, in the eastern part of Jalisco, is composed of forty-two houses spread around a bushy hill, and its inhabitants are, to a greater or lesser extent, related by kinship.[18] There are striking contrasts between the colors and materials of the houses—which make them blend in with the surrounding vegetation—and the massive courtyard antennas next to water wells dug by hand. The large courtyards are also where small animals are raised, and much of daily life takes place outdoors. Houses are often left unpainted inside. Men cultivate sugar and breed animals, while women get up before dawn to prepare tortillas, wash floors, sweep the courtyard, feed animals, fetch water, and wash clothes. When women rest, they meet to embroider, while men get together to drink and smoke. Women almost always wear a *mandil* (apron), taking it off only when they go to Ameca. Indoors the houses are neat and simple. In the bedroom there are many religious images on the walls, colorful embroidery, and dolls and small souvenirs. The bedroom's orderliness and the care with which things are kept make it appear like a small shrine. The bedroom, in contrast to the colonia in the city, where lack of space is greater and children are messy indoors, is not a viable space during the day: life takes place outdoors.

Young people who live in rancherías find them boring and complain about having to go to Ameca to enjoy themselves. However, for people like Chuita and Maru, the daughters of Doña Clara (mentioned earlier) who live in Polanco, the rancho is associated with the beauty of nature, natural food, and a much more soothing rhythm of life. Chuita noticed that on the ranchería, "La familia es muy fuerte, pero cada quien quiere jalar para su lado" (the family is strong, but everyone wants to have his own way). Family conflicts are common, and younger people sometimes find it difficult to understand and justify such disputes, in part because their experience of Guadalajara has made them more flexible and open to change.

Adults often dream of going back to the ranchería and retiring there, but younger people see it more as a place to spend vacation. For those who have grown up in the city, the division between work and leisure seems stronger than for their parents who have lived in the rancho. Young people often seek entertainment outside of home, while their parents' major entertainment (together with satellite television) tends to be associated with the celebration of religious festivities and life-cycle rituals: they are diversions which relate to a space of reproduction of kinship relations. The annual celebrations of the local patron saint, as in the ranchería of El Murillo, are rituals that create a social and family memory, and make group remembering possible (Connerton 1989: 39). The reenactment of communal memory in such socio-religious events develops both cognitive and affective memory, a memory renewed by the emergence of different social networks, such as those between the migrants who have left (especially for the United States) and those who have stayed (Massey 1987).

"Soy ranchero" is also identified with an inability to communicate, because rancheros are perceived as people who speak and behave differently than people brought up in the city. The case of Don Jesús Ortega illustrates the point. Born on a small rancho in Michoacán on the border with Jalisco and now in his seventies, he moved to Polanco thirty years ago because he did not like working the land. When he settled in the colonia, he started a successful shop on the main street selling electrical appliances, and his family is now well-off by Polanco standards. He is married with ten adult children, most of whom are professionals, and he affirms that he loves his children very much but does not know anything about their lives. He was brought up in the same way by his parents; they taught him to do his work without disclosing his feelings or daily plans. His wife is in charge of maintaining the family network, but he does not talk much to her either. (Nevertheless, it was she who held the marriage together when he used to drink a lot and spend money on other women.) For Don Jesús it is as unnatural to talk about himself and his activities as it is to ask about the activities of other family members. Still, he says he understands the personal needs of his children better than his wife does, and he respects their privacy to a greater extent; keeping to oneself is a common characteristic of people of the rancho, but does not imply any less love for family.

Don Jesús has observed many changes since he left the rancho:

Life in the rancho is very different. People do not work so much as in the past. There are machines. Now in half a day it is possible to sow what we used to sow in a month. . . . Now people dress better. In the past the differences were very noticeable. People have changed mentally too. In the past, parents and the priest kept people in fear, but now people are more aware.

In fact, "soy de rancho" meant, and still means, to hold to a strong popular and traditional religiosity. God punishes and rewards, allowing human action but also holding some responsibility for it: "I have faith that God will forgive me for all the bad things I have done, because he gave me the faculty to do so. Otherwise he would not have given me the faculty to do those things. If it was not wanted, I would have not done anything. If God does not allow, one cannot do it."

Like many people from the rancho, Don Jesús believes that ultimately human will cannot change divine destiny. His perception is that death is felt as closer to life in the rancho than in the city because human power is experienced as more subordinated to nature. After thirty years in Polanco, he still wakes up at 5 A.M. and goes to sleep after dusk, and wears the typical ranchero's hat. When asked if he feels like he's from Polanco, he denies it. His restlessness, like that of other older people I came to know well (including Doña Marisol), was expressed in various forms, from jerkily getting up and going in and out of the house, to playing with small wood carvings while talking and needing to get away from crowded places. Restlessness seems to go hand in hand with feelings of being confined in the urban space. Young people talk about older people who have lived much of their life in the ranchos as physically restless, a characteristic probably related to the fact that the rancho is a self-sufficient economy. People there are used to the constant activity required to prepare and produce many of their necessities.

For people in Polanco, being from the rancho is associated with states of culture and nature that contrast with those of the colonia. The rancho is recalled as a more natural, emotional, and passionate place where people are less sophisticated:

In the rancho people are different. They are more reserved and less intelligent. If they heard news of a war coming, they would have a more emotional reaction. When, for instance, there was the possibility of a war with the Cuba of Fidel Castro, the people in the rancho locked themselves in, and when people of the government came, they did not open their houses, thinking they were people sent by Fidel. (Soledad, coordinator of the *grupo de salud* [see Chapters 4 and 6])

The rancho is a place where women were (and, in some cases, still are) stolen away from their families and forced to marry. It is a place where people do not show affection, except between a mother and child, and bodily distance, especially between father and children, is strongly emphasized.[19] Yet it is also associated with the element of culture, whereas the colonia and the town are associated with the animal side of human nature because they are places of violence and deprivation. The rancho is also thought of as a place where social codes and the law of honor are respected, and where the unpredictable and disruptive elements of human cohabitation (such as urban violence) are weaker.

All of these beliefs illustrate the contradictory nature of the prisms of belonging: the diversification and shifting nature of the quality of space as expressed and perceived by different actors. The experience and appropriation of ranchero imagery, as well as its changes, in a colonia popular have to be examined in light of the city's changing dimensions. Media communication, use of idiomatic language, and changing economies in rural and urban communities are some of the interrelated elements that reveal the often contradictory nature of the prisms of belonging. Likewise the rural, the urban, and the tensions between them emerge as operative categories, rather than a priori classifications, that through changing generational perspectives get inscribed into everyday life formation.

"Soy de pueblo" (I am from the village)

In many respects, the perception that people in Polanco have about the pueblo is similar to the idea of the rancho: it symbolizes certain qualities of life that have been lost in the colonia. It represents a restful space apart from the hard life of the city. However, at the same time the pueblo represents conditions of economic hardship and social pressure to conform.

The expression "mi pueblo" does not always refer to a particular village of origin but is a general term referring to place of origin. Many people talk about their pueblos—which may by now be small towns—but they rarely go back, and their memories often arouse nostalgia and a strong sense of being from there rather than the city. Nostalgia is a state of mind that relates to both public and subjective experiences of time, and this state of mind is experienced as a feeling of dissatisfaction with the present and a lack of belief in so-called progress (Chase and Shaw 1989). People also feel nostalgia because they lack faith in any future utopia: in Polanco, belief in the utopia proposed by the CEBs has been abating, while churches such as Jehovah's Witnesses, or especially movements such as that of the Catholic charismatics, have become more popular (De la Torre 1998). Nostalgia seems more common in older people who have not been involved in movements that propose some form of collective utopia; in contrast, younger people often appear joyful in describing their perceptions of the village of origin.

One reason that people born in Guadalajara like to go back to the pueblo of their parents is that social exchanges between sexes is easier there. The physical layout of pueblos facilitates socializing because there is always a center square where young people meet and where couples take their weekend strolls. In many villages, such as in San Cristóbal of Lake Chapala or Totatiche in the region of Los Altos de Jalisco, during weekends groups of girls walk arm in arm, circling the square. While they go in one direction, the boys walk in the opposite one, and a ritual exchange of looks and smiles takes place without anyone actually talking. A boy may throw flowers or sweets at a girl to show his interest, and she can then either ignore him or react to his bid for her attention. Although this traditional courtship still goes on in the pueblos, the city has no safe central, public space for such interactions.

While the pueblo is perceived as a safer place, the colonia is perceived by parents as a dangerous place to let girls walk around and display themselves to boys. Many parents would like their daughters to marry somebody from their village, believing that a person's origin guarantees many of his qualities. People from one's own village are respected as having specific traits that are often alien to those in nearby villages, particularism being, as González suggests, a strong component in the *identidad pueblerina* (González 1979). So, just as the ranchos are perceived as places of hard work and family conflicts, the pueblos are seen as joyful places offering respite from the city, where "la gente es muy fiestera" (people like to have parties). *Bandas* and *conjuntos* (different types of musical groups) play for weddings, confirmations, quinceañeras (girls' fifteenth birthday celebrations, discussed in Chapter 5), and religious festivities held for migrants to the north who come back to visit. In the pueblo, the potentially disruptive anonymous element of the city gives way to a feeling of familiarity with the land, the people, and their way of life. People in a pueblo greet one another in the street, and there is a sense of respect for strangers; in the colonia, elders who have come from the rancho or the pueblo still do not address an unfamiliar person as *tú* but instead use the polite form, *usted*. A sense of respect and hierarchy is associated with a way of relating to people in the pueblo, and rules of acceptable behavior appear to be stricter.

The village of San Cristóbal, where Don Domingo was born, is on the edge of Lake Chapala and has become a major resort for rich *tapatios* (those from Guadalajara) and retired North Americans. Still, because the village is on the less developed side of the lake, many people leave to seek work in Guadalajara, and some have migrated to the United States.

Although San Cristóbal is considered backward by people in surrounding villages (as well as by the local priest), many former residents who now live in Guadalajara miss the peace, security, and friendliness of the village. The village's reputation for backwardness is linked in part to its indigenous roots.[20] Also, the people in San Cristóbal are not very concerned with improving their standard of living; in fact, those who have set up the most prosperous businesses have come from other villages. In San Cristóbal, young people go to work in Guadalajara, either commuting daily or spending the week there and returning home for the weekend.

Ana, Don Domingo's niece, has been training in a nursing school in Guadalajara and is largely self-supporting. She had to fight with her father to be allowed to go to school, because he wanted her to find a husband and stay at home in the village. In her first years at school, she felt different from her classmates; she was shy and reserved, had a different look, and was innocently trusting. Now, however, Ana feels out of place in San Cristóbal: she is twenty-six, does not have a boyfriend, and feels that "me estoy quedando" (literally, "I have been left behind," meaning nobody will marry her). Her experience in the city has changed her way of looking at men: she realizes that many men do not have honorable intentions, and she now perceives them in a different way than she did when she lived in the village.

Ana's experience could be read as similar to that of Maximiliano, but her gender position is different. Her "cataloging" arises from her sense of being left behind and from a place of partial discomfort. When Ana is back in the pueblo, she is confronted with her family's poor economic situation and the lack of progress in constructing their house. Her blame is implicitly directed against her mother, who is not a good "saver" in comparison to her sister-in-law, who lives next door and is excellent at saving and generating income. Her perception is that her family "has not made it," and she feels embarrassed to show her poor household to friends who come from Guadalajara. Ana sees the pueblo as a place where life is calmer, where things are known, and where she too is known, but where people check on their neighbors constantly. Since she has been living in the city, the village has become associated with pressure toward conformity and visibility of her family's failure. In the village, those who are different must deal with social isolation and (in the case of a Domingo freemason cousin) the allocation of religious blame.

Ana's experience of the relationship between rural and urban experiences is shared by many in Polanco who were brought up in the pueblo. They feel a sense of security and easiness in the pueblo, but at the same time they perceive greater social control, and contradictory images of the village as a place of love and hate crop up frequently. The pueblo, then, is a place for encountering one's self, a place to rest—as is the rancho—but it is also a place that has driven families away and is a source of separations and crises. Perceptions and experiences of space and places thus are shaped by gender positions and positions of subalternity. However, subjects are often engaged in shaping opportunities to redefine their relationships to space and particular spaces.

Some of these redefinitions emerge in the ethnographic encounter, in the narration of both life histories that unfold as life strategies, and the difficulties that arise in holding different, often antithetical images of oneself while occupying distinct and coexisting places. My ethnographic experience with people in Polanco, especially in light of my own experience as an Italian migrant to Britain, is about a mutual acknowledgement and recognition (often partial or tentative) of the uneasiness and persistence of these constant redefinitions.

Prisms of Belonging and Localism

The tensions between urban and rural emerge as operative categories and embodied experiences that are continuously reinscribed in urban everyday life formation. Media communication, rites of passage (discussed in Chapter 5), and the use of language highlight the contradictory as well as the performative nature of prisms of belonging. In a way, then, prisms of belonging articulate a process of localism.

James Ferguson (1999) has discussed localism as an urban style that signifies micro-political attachments to rural allies. Ferguson analyzes the condition of contemporary decline of the modernity project in Zambia, related to the decline of the Copperbelt mining towns in the north of the country. Through this ethnography he argues that localism and cosmopolitanism are both urban styles of performance of difference, rather than beliefs of a particular age or class or group, and that these styles inscribe distinctions in social relations through the use of specific clothes, ways of talking or drinking, and listening to music. Localism in its positive attribution is about the achievement of a stylistic competence, but in the case of cosmopolitan style (a display of the mastery of a worldly cultural element, such as elements of American street fashion and fashionable garments), the distinction can easily cross over to a dangerous condition of excess, especially for women. Therefore, both localisms and cosmopolitanism are about the insertion of a hierarchy between the displayers (or consumers) of a cultural style and the witnesses of that display, and about the reproduction of particular social ties for economic and social capital.

Localism, in my view, is rightly related to cultural styles of display and communication, and is about the inscription of difference in social and gender relations; however, prisms of belonging capture another area of localism that concerns the embodiment of experience and the reading of internalization and externalization of operative categories in the migration process via particular life histories and life strategies. A focus of identity within a theory of performing subjects should not ignore the complexity of the phenomenological experience that informs that same performance. Prisms of belonging also try to capture the self that is revealed. Thus localism in a condition of migration needs to be further explored via the production and appropriation of prisms of belonging to reveal subtle ways in which self-consciousness and interpretation connect processes of cultural display, performance, and mastery to the embodiment of experience.

Through the concept of prisms of belonging, I have argued that a phenomenological account of expansion or contraction of knowledge and operative category of experience are important to understanding the process of urban/rural identity. As illustrated in this chapter, the colonia and the city are perceived as known or unknown spaces, while representing in the life of the people a possibility of self-empowerment, self-reflection, or loss of power over the course of one's life. Those realities and possibilities can also be read as an expression of what Lomnitz-Adler calls "intimate cultures" in an urban space: cultures which do not correspond to reified bounded groups, but are formed through links of cultural understanding (Lomnitz-Adler 1992: 33) while producing or reproducing hegemonic relations.

The rancho and the pueblo represent spaces that allow people opportunities for finding themselves and overcoming a sense of separation. At the same time, they can represent an inability to know about the world and people's actions in it. There is pride (in the sense of integrity and value) as well as shame (in the sense of a failure to live up to an urban image of the self, as in the case of Ana) in being from the rancho or the pueblo. The pride related to the rancho and pueblo is connected to their symbolic lack of change over time, while pride in Polanco is associated with its capacity for change. In fact, residents now believe Polanco is becoming a safer place, with less violence and fewer trouble-makers than in the past.

Belonging to a particular household, neighborhood, village, or ran-cho is fundamental to how people perceive those places. In this sense, time, space, and memory are interwoven in prisms of belonging because the tradition of the past can be re-created and transformed in the urban present. In fact, narratives concerning symbolic representations of space and belonging contain multiple and coexisting images of the urban and the rural. The different images and experiences that people embrace of city, colonia, pueblo, and rancho, and their changes over time, raise the issue as to whether individual voices may represent a communal identity.

While recalling a communitarian self school of thought, which seeks identity in the tension between individual and society, I could argue that the formation of a community's identity is a relational process that takes place through the experience of its borders, and that the experience and awareness of borders through confrontation with the other shapes that identity. However, on one hand, community identity is not equiv-alent to communal identity: conformity cannot be mistaken for unifor-mity (Cohen 1993b: 208). So the voices of the various actors narrated in this chapter reveal different ways of imagining and representing the past, both rural and urban; they cannot be taken as homogenous rep-resentations, but are instead "interpretative resources" (Cohen 1993b), even though cross-generational perspectives and experiences consis-tently challenge and inscribe those tensions in everyday life formation.

On the other hand, though, as discussed in the following chapters, as interpretative resources produce representations, they are often con-tested, in some cases withheld, or claimed as authentic in others. And this process not only creates differentiation in social relations and among social groups, but, as discussed in Chapter 6, it produces differentiation within the same gender subject.

Moreover, it becomes clear how locality unfolds at the level of lived and embodied experience. The flexibility and insecurity of the labor mar-ket and the changing media images of a neighborhood are articulated in the prisms of belonging—in a language of perceptions, emotions, and representations that may be made visible or kept invisible. Personal idiosyncratic experiences are not determined by, but shape the heterogeneity of, and co-arise with, collective representations, but the embodiment of these collective representations in everyday practice are also sites of differentiation of social relations. Thus prisms of belonging also reveal processes of self-consciousness that seem to arise, particularly, through moments of ontological insecurity, confrontation and negotiation with different others, and with an other within oneself.

CHAPTER 3

Religious Discourses and the Politics of Modernity

Aun falta más. La visión de Dios. La luz suave de su cielo infinito.
El gozo de los querubines y el canto de los serafines. La alegría de
los ojos de Dios, última y fugaz visión de los condenados a la
pena eterna. Y no sólo eso, sino todo conjugado con un dolor terrenal.

But there is more. The vision of God. The soft light of his
infinite sky. The rejoicing of the cherubims and the singing of
the seraphims. The joy of the eyes of God—the last and
fleeting vision of those who are condemned to eternal suffering.
And this is not all, but it is married to earthly pain.

Juan Rulfo, Pedro Páramo

This chapter continues to focus on self-consciousness, representations,
and embodiment of migrant and urbanization experiences via a close
examination of the micro-politics of negotiation of knowledge that creates axes of belonging, affiliation, inclusion, and exclusion. I analyze here
the ways in which the Catholic Church is represented in terms of metaphors of "new" and "traditional" by lay members and the clergy, and
how the creation of a "popular subject" (as its empowerment via the
experience of community organization within popular religion [Levine
1992, 1993a]) is part of a narrative of identity.[1]

The analysis is centered both on the grassroot movement of the Comunidades Eclesiales de Base and on traditional Catholic groups. The
CEBs are devoted to biblical interpretation organized at the street level,
based on residential vicinity and local knowledge, and are inspired by

principles of liberation theology.[2] They are the praxis of this theology, and therefore—like any form of implementation of theological and theoretical principles—they have multiple forms of expression that may not always coincide with the radical theological message. The Company of Jesus, a Jesuit order, also has played a central role both in this theological formulation and its implementation through the Comunidades.[3]

Although it is true that the new Church—the Comunidades—induces changes in matters of personal responsibility in one's own life and the life of the community, through the analysis of the activities of some Jesuits and Diocesan priests I draw parallels and note similarities between the new and the traditional Church. I also explore emergent and residual formations that unveil the tensions of modernity in Catholic evangelization. On one hand, there is a clear emergent formation related to the process of modernity and citizenship: the Comunidades have been engaged in a project of transformation of believers into social (empowered) subjects and citizenship. On the other is the traditional Mexican Catholic Church, which has historically defined itself (since the revolution and its liberal, French Revolution-inspired egalitarian ideals) through an anti-state posture. In fact, the activism of the Comunidades, as that of other religious movements, has to be understood within the wider context of coexisting discourses internal to the Catholic Church.[4]

In the Comunidades' activities there is a subtle hierarchical control and distribution of knowledge between clerical agents, *promotores* (organizers/activists), and members. This suggests that a progressive social movement can actually be composed of subtle forms of conservative tendencies and residual formations. In this respect the line between emergent and residual formation becomes blurred. A vernacular modernity is composed of both emergent and residual forces, an open-ended negotiation of capacities for the production of similarities and differences, but what is interesting is how those tendencies are configured and how they mutually interact. This chapter is a micro-political examination of these configurations.

In a Catholic religious terrain that articulates a politics of modernity as well as of anti-modernity,[5] processes of identity and belonging emerge through overlapping discourses and conditions of tension, negotiation, and negation. Conflicting attributions of authenticity and representativeness are ways to understand the processual experience of identity. The heterogeneity and the competition not only between Catholic and Protestant evangelical movements (Burdick 1993), but also within the Catholic Church itself, give important insights into identity formation and the construction of knowledge. The new and the traditional practices of evangelization within the Mexican Catholic Church represent different fields of religious identities insofar as they postulate different relations and balances of power between clergy, lay, and divine agents as well as notions of change and religious commitment. Those practices of evangelization have legacies in partly different constructions of personhood: on one hand, a project of social accountability and striving for social entitlements, and on the other, a religious practice based on a close parallel between a father/child and divine/human agencies relationship, and a focus on sensory religious experience.

New and Traditional Priesthoods

In order to discuss the tensions of modernity embraced in the negotiation between the new and traditional churches, and to highlight their different types of evangelization, I first examine the life histories of two Diocesan priests: Padre Nemo (who was in charge of the Parish of the Anunciación until 1997) and his predecessor, Padre Francisco, because their personalities, orientations, and actions explicitly embody these two tendencies within the Catholic Church. The two priests differ in many respects, but they also share a position of exclusivity. The experiences of Padre Nemo and Padre Francisco in the Parish of the Anunciación raise issues about identity in the religious community in Polanco, and highlight tensions and the convergence between the experience of the Comunidades and traditional groups.

Before introducing some of the dynamics of these processes, I want to briefly outline the appearance of the two parishes to give a pictorial feeling to the histories of lay participation and clerical action in Polanco. Santa Magdalena is a large church at the east end of the colonia. It looks finished and decorated, and it has a large annex at the back where different activities take place: catechism, choral singing, theatrical productions (there is a theater that was once used by the Jesuits for meetings of the popular movement), and youth group meetings. The two priests in charge were the main priest, Padre Rodolfo, and an assistant priest, Padre Jorge. Padre Rodolfo is a very clever man from a middle-class background. His style of religious leadership differs from that of his predecessors in that he supports the Comunidades but wants to avoid confrontation with the religious hierarchy of Guadalajara. He has changed the political orientation of the parish, which was once similar to that of the Jesuits.

The Church of the Anunciación, in contrast to Santa Magdalena, is hidden from view. In the late 1980s, access was via a side street and through a gate that looks like one of the doors of Polanco's many workshops. The Anunciación was originally a dependent chapel of Santa Magdalena but gained recognition as a separate church in 1988. Construction started in the early 1980s, but as of the early 1990s there was still much to be done. During my last visit in 1999 the church's main body had been completed, including a large wall-panel sculpture of the Stations of the Cross by the local young artist Alfredo López (which had became a debated media case in Guadalajara for its representation of a completely naked Christ).

During the period of intense social mobilization in Polanco (the late 1970s to late 1980s), more than sixty adult and twenty youth groups of Comunidades met once a week, coordinated by Jesuits who worked actively in the parish of Santa Magdalena. The Jesuits, rather than the clergy of Santa Magdalena, were the organizers of the Comunidades. By the mid-1990s the situation was different. The Comunidades were present in both parishes and organized by the parish priests, following a common plan ordained at the level of the diocese. By then some of the people involved in the Comunidades associated with the Church of the Anunciación were different from those who had participated when the Jesuits were actively involved.

Padre Nemo arrived at the Parish of the Anunciación in March 1988. He was assigned to Polanco by Cardinal Posada Ocampo,[6] who knew that Polanco had already reached its peak in the grassroot organization of the new Church movement. The cardinal thought that once Padre Nemo arrived, he would probably find it difficult to organize the Comunidades and their movement during the mobilization's contraction in the neighborhood.

Padre Nemo came from a poor farming and woodworking family in Cocula, Jalisco. He entered the seminary when he was fourteen and felt he was entering a big family: "Since I was a child, I've realized that the life of the priest could be oriented toward the pueblo. . . . There was much missing in my pueblo. There was lack of services. It was like an abandoned pueblo."

The stress on solidarity with the campesinos is a constant theme in Padre Nemo's account. He portrays them as the good and exploited people, in contrast to the rich, "those of the government." Padre Nemo's ideal vision of religious hierarchy is one of service, not of power. In his view, the Comunidades are not a movement of the Church; they are the *Church in movement*. The Comunidades are not only a way of organizing social and religious life: they are a way of being. The Comunidades are portrayed in his words as an "innate" property of social, spiritual, and religious beings. He offers two explanations for why the Comunidades are in crisis in Polanco: the hostile attitude of the former priest, Padre Francisco, toward the Comunidades, and the rising interest in the charismatic movement, which used to hold regular meetings in the parish before the arrival of Padre Nemo, neither of which implies any self-criticism of how he has organized the Comunidades in Polanco.

Padre Nemo, like the Jesuits, believes that the Comunidades are the model for all the other movements within the Church, to the extent that the solid establishment of the Comunidades in the parish is seen as prior to any development of evangelization groups. However, he sees the other movements as potential threats to the Comunidades given the hostile period the Comunidades underwent during Padre Francisco's time. Padre Francisco openly supported these traditional groups, while for Padre Nemo, the fact that some people simultaneously belong to the Comunidades and these groups is explained by the Comunidades' embryonic state. He realizes that in Polanco the Comunidades are not yet able to fulfill the need for mysticism and prayer (which infuse many practices of the traditional Catholic Church), but his language reveals how Comunidades tend to associate a traditional type of religiosity with the superstitious, fatalistic view of religion, in contrast to a "true" religion grounded in consciousness and social action. This raises crucial issues within the Comunidades of how to integrate popular religion and transform it from "manipulated consciousness and ritual distraction" (Lehmann 1990: 128) into a true language of the people at the grassroot level.

Padre Nemo acknowledges that there is a dependency on clerical agents for the organization and maintenance of the Comunidades. This has been noticed as one of the major problems in the Comunidades' practice (Levine 1993a: 179). Also, parishioners complain that Padre Nemo does not visit people in their homes and that he is never actually in the church because he is constantly attending meetings outside the parish. Some parishioners also express disapproval that Padre Nemo had not been putting enough effort into the construction of the church, something Padre Francisco is remembered as having been very interested in.

Padre Francisco was born in Guadalajara and grew up in a large lower-middle-class family (a higher socioeconomic level than that of Padre Nemo's family). He was in Polanco from 1980 to 1988, and he was drawn to clerical life by contact with Salesian priests and "the necessity for something transcendental — because life is short — and to have a long-lasting plan in life . . . and the necessity to be in a place where one is needed."

During his time in Polanco, Padre Francisco focused much of his effort on church construction, and after mass he would stand at the door and ask for charitable donations to further that cause. At that time the church was the center of activities, but after he left, some parishioners not inclined to the work of the Comunidades noted the emptiness of the building.

Padre Francisco argues that construction of the church created a sense of unity. He had a good relationship with Cardinal Posada, although he did not get along with the Jesuits. Later, when Padre Nemo arrived, the group that had collaborated closely with Padre Francisco drastically decreased its participation in parish activities and never really joined the work of the Comunidades.

Padre Francisco's main critique of the Jesuits is that they wanted to do everything in their own way: "It is like having a parish within another parish. It is like having more than one head." He argues that he is not against *el cambio* (change), but that people in Polanco were not mature enough for it. He defines Polanco as a poor neighborhood, composed of people of the pueblos, a "noble and humble, less-problematic people." The problem for Padre Nemo, according to Padre Francisco, is that he failed to understand this human nature fully:

One needs to go one step at a time. Padre Nemo does not realize how people are. The people are from the countryside. They are humble, they do not know about Nicaragua. Their problem is their child who is drug addicted. . . . Their problem is in everyday life. They can just manage that. There is no need to discuss this and that . . . so they can live quietly and at ease.

Padre Francisco's attitude about people in colonias populares is centered on the necessities of everyday interaction, and on the narrow perspective these necessities impose on people's lives. They can act only for, and as part of the satisfaction of, their basic everyday needs, but not as a conscious part of a wider socio-structural reality. However, Padre Francisco is conscious of the differences between his conception of the Church and the one held by the Comunidades and Padre Nemo. He is aware of multiple religious identities focused on different balances between sacred/profane, and mystical/mundane, but for him, these tensions within the Catholic Church seem to create confusion rather than pluralism: "We, the priests, are responsible for inspiring different mentalities. . . . They [members of the Comunidades] are too concerned with what is here and now, and we are said to be too concerned with the hereafter."

Both Padre Nemo's and Padre Francisco's visions of the Church hinge upon a long-standing Catholic idea of the separation between the flesh and the soul, the manifest versus the non-manifest, the mystical versus the mundane. Nevertheless, while Padre Nemo seeks to bring these elements together—challenging the Church's hierarchical power structure—Padre Francisco sees the maintenance of these divisions as a core element of Church institutional reproduction.

Padre Francisco represents the "father": the direct bridge between laypersons and the religious hierarchy. The pyramidal hierarchy and the notion of religious intermediaries are key points in this view. Moreover, the priest personifies a conception of Church as a sacred physical space. Padre Francisco's preoccupation with finishing construction of the church for the Parish of the Anunciación suggests that the physical building is the heart of religious life and that it acts as a centripetal force in bonding people together. Padre Nemo's ideal, in contrast, rejects the figure of the priest as being the supreme mediator between God and the faithful. He believes priests should be there to counsel and to serve, but not to pronounce authoritatively as to what is or is not authentic knowledge. His goal is to transform a vertical Church based on hierarchy into a horizontal Church of the people. The guiding principle of the Comunidades—exemplified by Padre Nemo's action—is the need to move away from the actual building to create a sacred space within the neighborhood. The Church in this case becomes a "centrifugal" Church that moves from the church building to the people, rather than bringing the people to the church.

This metaphor of the movement of the Church is very important within the Comunidades, and it embraces a theological statement. Elio, one of the oldest coordinators in the Anunciación, worked for a long time with the Jesuits but then stopped participating because of personal disagreements. He later came back to work in the Comunidades formed in the Anunciación. In one coordinators' meeting, he said, "Those of the traditional Church want to know God, but this is impossible. It is only possible to encounter him in the service of others." Elio suggests that God cannot be known, only experienced. To "encounter" suggests movement, so humans can approach God through movement, through "action." God is in the life of every person—in doing, not only in knowing—and the realm of God includes the process of building a liberated society, not just the end result (which is unknown) (Lehmann 1990: 126). Thus God must be approached through a third element outside one's own self; that is, through social experience. In the Comunidades, God is conceived of in three-dimensional terms, and the devil (*el diablo*) represents the denial of that three-dimensionality.

The conception of el diablo within the Comunidades is different than that of the traditional Church. The devil is part of a discourse related to human suffering and to the definition and boundaries of human and non-human agents (Parkin 1985: 11, 12), and is part of both moral and ontological language (Pocock 1985). In the case of the Comunidades, the devil is associated with the other and is thought to be outside of the community; the devil also is linked to notions of capitalist exploitation and individualism versus brotherhood and solidarity, and to a form of thinking: an attitude toward life based on egoism or selfishness.

In their rhetoric, both priests use the word "pueblo," but with different and overlapping meanings. Padre Francisco refers to the pueblo as a sum of those from different pueblos, or villages of origin. The pueblo has childlike qualities: it is innocent, simple, and vulnerable, and needs to be held by its hand. It is also close to nature. It represents other people's pasts, and all those elements are lost as people get closer to so-called civilization. In this way evangelization is promoting a father/child relationship. The pueblo may have a popular type of knowledge, but its ignorance prevents it from improving its socioeconomic situation.

For Padre Nemo, the pueblo is more a structural category defined in opposition to the ruling class that exploits it. Differences and idiosyncrasies between pueblos are blended into a single pueblo, with specific local communities merging into a general brotherhood. The pueblo thus becomes an agent in itself: it takes responsibilities, fights, responds, and creates. But there is a tension between the idea of a composite pueblo and that of pueblos as specific villages of origin. As discussed in the previous chapter, being from the pueblo has contradictory meanings that are positive, ambiguous, or negative depending on the contextual moment of recall, and its representation is also used to create hierarchical social relations. Hence there is a tension between a representation of communality (el pueblo) and specificity of identity and origin (los pueblos) that resides at the root of the definition of a "popular subject" (Levine 1993a, 1985), and particular attention has to be paid to the language and experiences through, and with which, the tension of a common identity is constructed and diversity approached.

The pueblo that thus emerges has more heterogeneous tendencies than the religious agents which claim authenticity over it can convey. One revealing incident took place in the Anunciación in the summer of 1991, when a conflict broke out between Padre Nemo and two coordinators, Mauricio and Soledad. Mauricio is a construction worker who came from Armería, a village on the Colima coast, in 1988. He was called to Polanco by the priest himself, and they worked in close collaboration, both in constructing the church and promoting the Comunidades group. As his influence over people and his charisma grew, some people became envious, and he had confrontations with some of the coordinators and the nuns. This group put pressure on Padre Nemo, who in a meeting of the coordinators, confronted the situation and blamed Mauricio and Soledad for following their own program and not that of the parish. Since then, Mauricio and Soledad have not been allowed to work in the parish, and have been prevented from participating in other Comunidades activities organized in Guadalajara. This case was distressing for many coordinators because they questioned how the will of a few was used to isolate members of the same Comunidades group. As a consequence of this internal confrontation, some of the coordinators left for a period, and others for good. Other tensions then followed between different lay leaders and activists, leading to a reconfiguration of parish-related activities. "New blood" was involved in the process of decision making, and "old blood" was peripheralized in the process.

When power conflicts arose, Padre Nemo used the notion of a parish program and certain knowledge that Mauricio failed to respect: he could not have his own program, and he could not be a producer of knowledge. Some people complain that the priest and nuns often attend seminars outside the parish, but then do not share that knowledge with group members. Instead, they tend to keep it to themselves, and thus they are the ones "who grow," leaving the others behind. The issue in the confrontation between Padre Nemo and Mauricio was, in fact, not the program itself, but the balance of power between laypersons and clergy, and among laypersons themselves, and tensions arose around issues of authenticity and entitlement of the pueblo.

The two priests make another major distinction between their images of the Church. The Comunidades' attempts to challenge the traditional relationship between Christ, God, and man are based on a strong division between the sacred and profane, between heaven and hell. In the Comunidades' language, Christ is portrayed in his human (rather than super-human) adult dimension,[7] and the exaltation of his humanity increases the spirituality of everyday human interaction. The evangelization of the Comunidades encourages seeing the presence of Christ's spirit in social and interpersonal action, and experiencing sacredness in daily life. In practice, however, social interaction is often seen in terms of the dynamics of power within the social structure, while idiosyncrasies of interpersonal relations are often dismissed. For instance, explanations for why people drop out of Comunidades are often given in terms of individual traits ("por flojera . . . porque le gusta más la tele" [because of laziness . . . because he/she prefers watching television]), but interpersonal problems such as personality clashes are hardly ever mentioned as possible causes.

Many comments (half gossip, half commentaries supposedly made in good faith, which I feel are best not documented here) have circulated in Polanco concerning present and previous coordinators as well as the Jesuits once posted in the colonia and the present and past archbishops. Some rumors concerned the relation between the Diocesan priest, the Carmelite nuns, and the Jesuits. But gossip and rumor are social acts that strategize emotions, the enactment of which can be read as a discursive practice (Abu-Lughod and Lutz 1990: 12). Hence what is said with distraction, or what is understated or revealed only in passing, is a part of a social movement's history and indicates that people may lose interest or fail to mobilize not just because of "false consciousness" or failures (Burdick 1995: 368), but also because of the powerful politics of emotions.

In some cases, issues of authority, legitimization, and interpretation of communality as consensus within the hierarchy are characteristic of the relation between leaders and members of the Comunidades in Polanco, even if many of its organizers would not openly recognize such issues. There are, however, important differences between new and traditional Churches that rest on different boundaries between the sacred and the profane in the interpretation of the Church as a community of people expanding outward, or as a physical, centripetal space, and of the pueblo as subject (agent) or object (a more passive recipient) of evangelization. The narratives of the two priests show that there are differences between these tendencies of the Church, and that the new Church can be a fertile field for empowering its members.

Tensions of Modernity

A number of important themes emerge from the stories of Padre Francisco and Padre Nemo that speak about the character of religious move-

ments, the development of the Mexican Catholic Church, its evangelization, and the nature of modernity. The tension between the new and
traditional Churches as formulated in the language of the Comunidades
expresses the difficulties of combining, in practice, aspects of modernity
with critiques of modernity, both of which form the basis of liberation
theology. The Comunidades embrace a modernity that privileges the
development of the individual/believer partly as an active, freely choosing agent, but they also embrace a critique of modernity, especially in
relation to critiques of capitalism and privatization of faith (Lehmann
1990; Lowy 1990). Thus the new Church's ideal of redemption concerns
participatory democracy and citizen subjectivity, which is itself a project
of modernity.

It has been observed that tensions between the new and the traditional are already part of a bifocal language of modernity. A traditionalist
culture is still part of a modernist (socioeconomic) project (García Canclini 1995) rather than its antithesis. García Canclini argues that these
two dimensions have been conflated into a Mexican cultural hybridity
in such a way that both popular and traditional cultural processes are
not opposed, but are actually part of the reproduction of modernity.[8]
This reproduction of modernity takes place in language and via mediations in language. Language and representations are central to understanding politics of modernity, and the religious field is one means of
its articulation.

The voices of the Comunidades were originally, and still are, medi-
ated by the voices of the Jesuits and diocesans. This very important
mediation has actually given a voice to a political-religious tendency of
social transformation. However, these mediations have also partially ne-
gated real, autonomous representation by laypersons. Hence I want to
draw the reader's attention to the politics of representation, belonging,
and mediations while considering whether a grassroot social movement
reinstates a subordinate position or creates a "politics of the people"
(Guha 1988: 334)—an autonomous domain that escapes, in this case,
the translation of a religious/political elite. I can address this question
by turning, once again, to the emergent and residual formation of new
and traditional evangelization, and to tensions in the language of modernity.

Liberation theology and the Comunidades have not been the exclusive grassroot experience in the whole of the archdioceses of Guadalajara. They have been central to popular mobilization in colonias of the
city where the Movimiento Urbano Popular (MUP) has taken root. I
wish to recall here the connection between urban popular mobilization

for basic services and urban upgrading, and the development of Comunidades evangelization, especially during the period of this research
(late 1970s to late 1990s). There have also been, during and since, other
forms of Catholic and non-Catholic evangelization that have had, and
continue to have, a strong influence on the Guadalajara religious scene.

Fortuny has pointed out that secularization in Guadalajara appears
to be related to an increased religious pluralism (Fortuny Loret de Mola
1999a). New Age religious groups, miscellaneous groups such as the
Mexicanidad (Rostas 1998), Eastern religious practices, and new religions (such as the Luz del Mundo; see De la Torre 1997) are emerging
along with a diversification and pluralization within the Catholic
Church. Charismatic groups such as Renovation of the Holy Spirit are
playing an increasingly important part in Guadalajara Catholic religious
activism (De la Torre 1998). An understanding of this complex religious
field, Fortuny argues, requires a focus on individual identification and
translation of religious beliefs into lifestyles (Fortuny Loret de Mola
1999a: 21).

Religious affiliation can be part of the construction of civil society
not only because of the influence of religious principles. The style in
which religious movements address social goals, and in which their
members embody theological worldviews in everyday practice, also influences society (Foweraker 1995). Studies of the dynamics of Catholic
religious affiliation in the Comunidades have already pointed out a "ro-
manticization" found in previous studies and have unveiled a heterogeneity in members' practices and goals, as well as the maintenance of
an internal hierarchy (Levine 1985; Hewitt 1991; Burdick 1993; Drogus
1995). Thus a positive sense of empowerment and, therefore, of
agency—the capacity to act or have a potential for beneficial action—as
well as a sense of disempowerment can be created through affiliation
with the Comunidades (Hewitt 1991: 86; Levine 1992: 311, 313). The
contentious questions are still "for whom," "in which ways," and "in
what circumstances empowerment or disempowerment takes place."
These questions address two interconnected areas: first, how socioreligious movements articulate boundaries of inclusion and exclusion, and
therefore a micropolitics of identity; second, how specific religious discourses and prisms of belonging grounds the production and appropriation of religious belonging and transfer of knowledge within, as well
as in the questioning of, a creation of a "popular subject" such as "el
pueblo."

Comunidades and Jesuits

The Mexican Church is not a homogenous body (Arias et al. 1981), and translating into action the agenda set by the Puebla, Medellín, and Santo Domingo conventions has been influenced by the structural relation between the Church and the Mexican state. The conferences held by the Congreso Episcopal Latino Americano (CELAM) in Medellín (1968), Puebla (1979), and Santo Domingo (1992) marked a transformation of the Latin American Catholic Church following the Vatican II Concilium (1962–1965). The condemnation of institutional violence, the support of education as a basis for progress among the underprivileged, the centrality of opting for the poor, and the important roles of women, indigenous people, and ethnic minorities are some of the important issues highlighted in those conferences. Needless to say, the conferences also revealed internal divisions between revolutionary, traditionalist, and progressive interpretations of such mandates.

Major divisions between traditional, radical, and progressive tendencies within the Mexican Church, and in its relation with the state,[9] are also reflected in the evangelization efforts in colonias populares, as the stories of Padre Nemo and Padre Francisco illustrate.

Some Catholic parishes limit their action to the pastoral and evangelical spheres, and their orientation toward the poor is organized around concepts of charity and service. Such groups are considered by members of the Comunidades to be part of the traditional Church. The more radical groups of the Mexican Church see the struggle for the poor, leading to social mobilization and structural change of society, and the recognition of human rights as central points of the Catholic message. A good example is the central role of mediation played by Samuel Ruíz and other Comunidades leaders in the negotiation of the Zapatista rebellion in Chiapas (Trejo Delabre 1994). Liberation theology, the basis of Comunidades evangelization, rejects the modern liberal view of separation between the collective and the individual, and between the religious and the political (Lowy 1990). It also rejects the dichotomy between tradition and modernity, attempting instead a synthesis that combines a critique of capitalism with an attempt to restore community as a core value and to defend individual freedom, the right to criticize an authoritarian Church, and play down "unreflective impulses" of popular religiosity (Lehmann 1990: 121). The case of evangelization in Polanco shows how these theological principles, once applied to local practice, can change, and how prisms of belonging within a religious context are produced and appropriated by different lay and clerical agents.

But what has been the discourse on personhood that the Comunidades evangelization has fostered in the urban Mexican, popular sector? Catholic teaching in the Comunidades emphasizes a symbolic interpretation of the biblical message focused on metaphors of renewal and being born again as part of a unified pueblo. The language of the Comunidades stresses self-introspection as a primary component of the identity formation of the subject. A project of modernity emphasizes the "care of the self" and the relation of the self to his/her present (Parameshwar Gaonkar 1999: 11–12) and the Communidades also encourages the rise of meaning through an objectification of reality and a reflection on the relation between the self and his/her present (Chakravorty Spivak 1998: 22). The principles of the Comunidades are expressed in the slogan "veer, pensar, actuar" — to see (in the sense of understanding), to think, and to act. The missionary task of the Comunidades develops at the prophetic, pastoral and sacerdotal levels, in the sense that they promote a vision, a pastoral educational effort, and a particular clergy formation. These are central points of Jesuit teaching about CEBs, and it has been common at meetings in Polanco to hear mention of the notion of "becoming a person," meaning an agent who stands for his/her social and human rights. In the Comunidades, especially under the guidance of the Jesuits, there is a tendency to identify traditional religion with a lack of subjectivity. The Comunidades believe that full personhood is achieved through personal and group consciousness followed by action, while traditional religion is defined as acceptance of reality as it stands and as change of personal aptitudes rather than an impulse toward social action; acceptance calls for identification and lack of separation between the subject and the reality in which he/she lives. In this sense, different movements within the Church have developed distinct processes of identity formation, and offer different sites of subjectivity.

It bears repeating that although Catholic groups are described above as if they are a unitary subject, the Comunidades movement is not homogeneous, and has gone through various transformations over the course of its development.[10] Comunidades have constituted different arenas for interaction: they can be centers for political activism and the challenge of political and religious hierarchies, and they can offer opportunities for reflection and social action, as well as human bonding; but they can also be rather accepting of religious hierarchy and political authority.[11] In some Comunidades gatherings, concepts of change and personal commitment may be discussed but not actively applied in members' daily lives.

Notions and naming of the popular have been points of conflict between different parts of the Church, as reflected by the shifting meaning of the word "Comunidades." In 1987, when José Salazar López was still leading the archdioceses of Guadalajara, the name was identified with groups inspired by liberation theology. However, when Cardinal Posada Ocampo, who had strong ties with the conservative group the Opus Dei, took office in 1987, the scenario changed. With subtle, but highly political implications, the word "Comunidades" began to be applied to other, less radical Catholic groups. It was part of a move to "deradicalize" the CEB movement. Appropriations of politically loaded language have also been used to displace the rhetoric of opposition in contemporary Mexican politics.[12] The use of the terms "Comunidades" or "Grupos" may often indicate a renaming executed by the hierarchy rather than a real transformation of the Mexican Catholic Church. In such cases, "the poor" may be identified as the Church's foundation, but interpreted as including only those who are humble and hold popular religious beliefs rather than the entire class (Levine 1985: 310). By the mid-1990s the Comunidades meeting in the Church of Santa Magdalena were called "Grupos de Barrio," and their agenda was much less radical than that of the Comunidades of the 1970s and 1980s.

At one level, clergy such as Padre Nemo and the Jesuits and some of the lay coordinators involved in the Comunidades have formed an ideal of what the Comunidades should be, based on metaphors of organization, community, consciousness, and awakening to sociopolitical action. Consequently, they tend to view the neighborhood in light of that image. The actual members of the Comunidades, however, often have different ideas about the Comunidades' goals, and different levels of commitment to working toward those goals. Many Comunidades leaders focus on a polarized us and other, with "us" representing the pueblo, the poor, the exploited campesinos, and the "virginal" Mexican soil, and the "other" everything against the pueblo: the Mexican lay and clerical elite; members of the traditional Church; religious sects; and "penetration" by the North American invaders.[13]

However, structural binarisms—such as self opposed to the other, or a center opposed to a periphery—do not account for overlapping categories. This is why the language used by Comunidades leaders about a common identity with its roots in poverty fails to account for the hybridity of urban identities that results from the complex interplay be-

tween communality and difference. García Canclini (1995) has argued
that the hybridization of society requires a renewed understanding of
the relation between social action, symbolic and cultural performance,
and urban space where similarities, metaphorical struggles, and the
"obliquity of symbolic circuits" of culture and power are at play (García
Canclini 1995: 261). In this scenario overlapping categories and struggles
over representations become central.

A struggle of politics of representation in ways of "being the Church"
observable at the micro-level of colonias populares reflects a wider tension. Some of those contrasts are rooted in the long-standing power
struggle between diocesan clergy and the Jesuits within the Roman
Catholic Church. Guadalajara is a stronghold of the Jesuits, and they
are often judged by some diocesan clergy to be politically radical, and
are seen as interfering in parish politics. The Jesuits' evangelization in
Polanco—which began in 1973 and had a twenty-year intervention
plan—targeted social awareness and subsequent popular mobilization
through the training of leaders to carry out the process of evangelization.
For them the continuity between faith and life targeted people's commitment to structural change in society. The colonia thus became a lab-
oratory for the Jesuits' program when it was chosen in the early 1970s
as a place where it would be possible to live with the pueblo and establish
an important center for novices.

Jesuit rhetoric often uses "warrior" metaphors, such as "Life is a
struggle," "We have to fight for justice," and "Faith is a social commitment of the individual" (all mentioned during sermons given as part of
mass). This idea of life as a fight/conquest is embedded in the teaching
of San Ignacio, the founder of the Company of Jesus, the name of the
Jesuits' order. The idea of personal evolution through a development of
the will, the image of leaders as key figures in the process of evangelization, and the priority of personal contact with the inner self through
spiritual exercises are strong characteristics of the Company of Jesus.
Comments about Jesuits from people who are or have been in the Comunidades vary. On one hand, some believe that the Jesuits are the
holders of the real knowledge of the so-called Church of change. On
the other, some see the limitations of Jesuit intervention and see their
interests in power and control as little different from many other Church
groups. One diocesan priest who worked in the colonia feels that the
Jesuits are unable to reach people's hearts: "The Jesuit has the tendency
to lead, but it is necessary to give people what they ask for—not what
one wants to give them."

The Jesuits do not let people grow. This is the problem. They want things done in their way, and if people want it done differently, they tell them that it is not correct, and they say this through reasoning, philosophically . . . so that they convince you. The Jesuits say you are worthy, but that you lack experience and that you need to grow. Therefore people are not appreciated for what they are, and they feel frustrated. The Jesuits already know what they want to do. They do not ask people. (Lalo, who worked with Jesuit youth groups for seven years and considered becoming a Jesuit himself).

Elio, a Comunidades coordinator living in a colonia neighboring Polanco, sees a similar tension:

The Jesuits did not like the fact that the *periferia* was working better than Polanco.[14] They ignored us, they wanted Polanco to be outstanding. The Jesuit priests said what needed to be done and who would be in charge of it. Polanco wanted to use our work, but I did not want to be messed around, it is important that you and your work are taken into consideration.

What emerges through the Jesuits' evangelization is a particular subject position, and an attitude that makes religious lay subjects feel they lack knowledge that the Jesuits have. A condition of ignorance is also associated with the devil, and in the new Church, knowledge becomes the means of salvation. To construct the realm of God is, for the Jesuits, to know the social, political, and economical reality. This challenges the position of the traditional Church, which—Jesuits argue—emphasizes a division between faith and life, and between individual conversion and social transformation. These ontological claims and the objectification of reality carried out by Jesuit evangelization rests on a dividing practice that distinguishes between those who are on the path and those who are not, between those who are with the pueblo and those who are not. This practice, because it tends to conceal its arbitrariness by apparently empowering leaders and followers in the same way, legitimizes the leading position of those who utter it (Gledhill 1994: 141), and to a certain extent it takes away, by a strategy of mediation, the power of "speaking back."[15] Hence it is important to focus on the articulatory nature of micro-differentiations that creates a form of mastery and leadership for some while denying it to others.

To summarize, social movements such as the Comunidades are multifaceted and are related to the subject positions of those who become involved in the process of knowledge production and transfer. It contributes to empowerment, but also to disempowerment, of social subjects. In the following chapters I focus on the empowering effects of Comunidades evangelization activities on women in the field of health care. However, it is also important to understand this process within the history of Guadalajara's social and urban mobilization. As previously discussed, since the beginning of the 1990s and the consolidation of Polanco as a center of the periphery, there has been a contraction in urban mobilization. Social mobilization as social practice has multiple effects on constituting gender subjectivity and strengthening group identity, but in particular forms it may also support hierarchy and subordination. This latter condition is more visible when social mobilization is in decline, and a language of external differentiation between groups renews internal, hierarchical differentiation between clergy and lay members. While forging a popular subject, Jesuit leaders may implicitly, and to a certain extent unwittingly, reinforce the very subordination that grassroot movements such as the Comunidades originally set out to address.

The Traditional Church

The term "traditional" is used by members of the Comunidades to define a certain type of religiosity. The people who participate in groups other than the Comunidades do not call themselves traditionalist, but see themselves as followers of religious traditions. The stress on personal salvation and the transcendental parallels worship that is oriented toward everyday personal and family concerns. People pray for their own well-being while asking God for personal favors. It is within this framework that people make *mandas*—their vows to saints.

The traditional view cannot be attributed exclusively to the elderly or any other specific age group. The cases illustrated below show how traditional religion is a question of degree, and that the division between traditional and new church can be ambiguous. In fact, the word "incompatibility" is often used by laypersons and clerical leaders who have lost control over the parish following a change of priest, so religious affiliation can also be seen as a form of appropriation and maintenance of symbolic capital in the sense of access to resources and attainment of prestige and legitimization within the parish community.

The case of the followers of El Movimiento Familiar Cristiano (MFC) illustrates some discursive similarities and differences between more-traditional movements and the Comunidades. Created in the early 1960s after the dissolution of the ACM (Acción Católica Mexicana),[16] in principle it is a lay movement relatively independent of the religious hierarchy (Concha Malo 1986). The MFC in Mexico has a middle-class base, but has extended its influence into the lower classes. MFC's training plan is a three-year program organized by laypersons together with the clergy and concentrates on the upbringing of children and on family relations. The training course covers various subjects, including the development of a person from childhood to adulthood, relations between couples and children, and the objectives of the Catholic family within the post-Vatican II Church.

For couples in Polanco, belonging to the MFC has given them a chance to get to know many people of different backgrounds and to learn about improving communication within the family. Many say the experience has helped them develop solidarity within the family and to learn to listen to others. There are six basic focuses in the MFC: team life, hospitality, a life of prayer, commitment to service, good use of material goods, and study of family-related topics. Some of these goals are similar to those of the Comunidades, but they can also have different meanings. The idea of service is one such example. The MFC sees service as a form of sanctification, and even marriage itself is considered a responsibility of mutual sanctification between husband and wife. In contrast, for the Comunidades, service is perceived as part of a human bond of social solidarity and communal identity—a redemption of social, rather than personal, sin.

The Holy Spirit is a central theme in MFC prayer, as it is in the charismatic movement. MFC members also believe strongly in miracles and in the power of the Holy Virgin and the Sagrado Corazón (Sacred Heart of Christ). Like members of the Comunidades, they talk about seeking change, but the aim is to change individual attitudes about God and family relationships, not power relations in society. The MFC does, however, hold a modernist attitude typical of a certain type of Catholicism in which pre-Catholic/indigenous beliefs and culture are associated with ignorance rather than seen as a heritage of cultural pluralism. In contrast, the Comunidades seek to integrate that pluralism within the new Church.

The traditional beliefs of the MFC can also be a source of inspiration, as demonstrated by the case of Doña Estrella. For many years, Doña Estrella and her husband, Luis, have been the coordinators of the MFC group in Polanco. She has a negative view of the Comunidades, and is aligned politically with the Catholic-oriented Partido de Acción Nacional (PAN). She has been working in the MFC since the early 1970s, and she was at one time president of the Acción Católica and the Caritas (an international confederation of Catholic organizations) in the parish of the Santa Magdalena. She is resentful of Padre Nemo, who supports the Grupos de Barrio, because he does not pay attention to her and the work of the groups with which she is involved. Estrella does not like the work of the Comunidades because the people who are involved in them call for social change but, she says, do not improve their own behavior: "What can they do to decrease drug addiction? It is not a question of getting rid of the social dirt, but my own dirt, and as a neighbor I ask myself, 'What am I not doing?' . . . They say they do, but they do not do anything."

Estrella thinks we can change our destiny, and that heaven is the reward for our suffering on earth if that suffering is dedicated to the glory of God instead of being used to deny it. For her, the motivation to exalt God is central to the meaning of human action. If people misbehave, their lives will reveal the consequences, and it is the individual who is to blame. Thus drug addiction and poverty are explained in terms of an individual's inabilities, or shortcomings in his or her family's religious education. Although the imagery used by the Comunidades may suggest a "second" birth—and perhaps a break with the past—the MFC is perceived by its members as an extension or continuation of previous forms of Catholic worship. However, the MFC also offers opportunities for self-reflection more characteristic of the Comunidades' work. In the words of Gerónimo—an active member of the Anunciación Comunidades, but who at one time also belonged to the MFC—there is an awareness of the limits of maintaining the other as separate:

In the Comunidades they want to talk about liberation, change of structure, but they do not pay attention to the family and the person. Some people come to the meetings and they leave everything else aside, but this is a mistake. The problem is that in the Comunidades they talk very little about the family, and many people in the Comunidades have pressing family problems. Padre Nemo believes that the MFC has arisen from the right wing of the Church and that it is in opposition to the work of the Comunidades, but many in the parish do not think so.

However, as among the Comunidades, the MFC leaders' visions are often different from those of members. While a leader such as Estrella tends to focus on difference and opposition, members often interpret differences as complementarities; they see people as able to be more flexible in integrating different religious messages into their everyday lives if they are not involved in power struggles within the parish. Thus,

as this case suggests, the analysis of social movements should pay particular attention not only to the language of a group's leaders, but also
to that of its members. The impact and image of a religious social movement result from an internally negotiated process on the meanings and
values given to particular social actions by its members and leaders.

While the MFC can be seen as complementary to the Comunidades,
the Adoración Nocturna, a more traditionalist group, seems to share
little with the Comunidades, who have a very different concept of the
relation between human and divine agents. But again, the differences
are given stronger emphasis in the words of the group's leader (who has
been close to Padre Francisco) than in those of other members of the
Adoración Nocturna and its counterpart group for women, Vela del
Santísimo.

Founded in Mexico in 1900, the Adoración Nocturna is a small but
cohesive group of men who meet the last Saturday evening of each
month in the Church of the Anunciación. As a sacrifice to Christ in
recognition of the suffering he undertook for humanity's salvation, they
pray throughout the night in groups of four, a practice that recalls
Christ's meditation on the Mount of Olives. The women who belong
to the Vela del Santísimo meet to pray to the Most Holy through can-
ticles and rosaries.

As its name suggests, the primary goal of the group is to adore and
guard the reliquary of the Santísimo (Most Holy), where the Eucharist
is stored. Their members (a group of ten to fifteen in the parish of the
Anunciación) stress the idea of mortal sin and the need for divine forgiveness, and members pursue an intimate dialogue with God away
from the distractions of society. In this dialogue, believers confess their
miseries and problems to Jesus, and ask him for the necessary strength
for the final judgment. Members of the Adoración believe that other
people's redemption can be achieved through one's own sacrifice.

The Adoración worship represents a moment of meditation which
implies "amor verdadero" (real love), sacrifice, and expiation.[17] The goal
of prayer is to go beyond the illusory body and get in touch with one's
soul. Matter is conceived as inferior to the soul: "The body is a cover,
we have a heart, a heart which is not the one that the worms eat, it is
the soul; all this [indicating the body] is impregnated with the soul"
(Don Manuel, a member of the Adoración and the Refugianos). So the
soul is a bridge to God and to the knowledge of his will, and a denial
of the body is essential to understand the true nature of the sacred. This
central characteristic of the Adoración Nocturna is opposed to the way

in which Elio of the Comunidades talks about God (see above). God, in the Adoración Nocturna, is the investigator of the human soul, able to see what we attempt to hide: he is a divine Father of his human children. The God/human dialogue is a dual rather than a three-dimensional relation. This duality is also present in the experience of the women who belong to the Vela del Santísimo. In their accounts the figure of Christ is depicted as a physical entity, as a presence, who has come and visited them in their houses in moments of particular suffering or blessing, and who helps to sort out painful situations. If the traditional Church is depicted by the Comunidades as interested in the mystical, but not in everyday reality, paradoxically the language of its members is very physical and oriented toward sensory perception of the divine. Many actually expressed this perception in sensory terms, such as being "touched" on the shoulder by Christ, or "feeling" the presence of the Virgin in one's bedroom. Their own amazement at such experiences — because they were felt in person, and frequently at particularly critical moments of a person's life — was translated into an impulse for faith renewal. So despite the body-matter subordination to the soul, the sensory dimension is actually an important depository of the religious experience.

The leader of Adoración Nocturna group in Polanco is Don Luís. He identifies with the Partido Revolucionário Institucional (PRI) and has become general secretary of the Adoración Nocturna at the regional level, even learning to read and write for the post. Don Luís is close to Padre Francisco and became his so-called right arm while he held the same position. Since Padre Nemo arrived, Don Luís's activity within the Church has been limited to the Adoración Nocturna, and he and others who remain loyal to Padre Francisco attend other churches for Sunday mass. Don Luís had a severe conflict with Padre Nemo, reported concerning money that he and others of Padre Francisco's "old group" were holding in trust for the church construction. At the end of 1988, the situation had become so tense that Don Luís's group asked the archiepiscopacy to remove Padre Nemo. When that request proved unsuccessful, he and those close to Padre Francisco pulled out of the parish. Don Luís assumes that behind the religious activities of laypeople there is always the clergy, and that it is the clergy who mislead the believers: "The priests of the Comunidades send people to the front to get burned." His main criticism of the Comunidades is that members profess love and brotherhood but fail to demonstrate these qualities in their interactions with the wider Catholic community.

The dispute between members of the Adoración Nocturna and the Comunidades shows how affiliation to religious groups within the Catholic Church is not just a question of moral and spiritual convictions, but also of control of symbolic capital (Bourdieu 1987: 4). Status, prestige, and power can be acquired by being in the group supported by the present priest in charge of the parish, but can be lost if the group falls out of grace. It is important, then, to analyze the political dimension of Catholic membership not only in terms of the presence and absence of political and social mobilization, but also in terms of people's self-worth, desire for recognition, and the representation of the body and sensory perceptions.

Membership in Comunidades and traditional religious groups is not mutually exclusive, as counter cases show.[18] Those who are active in both often are seeking a balance between mystical belief and enactment of those beliefs, since the Comunidades' message can be experienced as lacking certain devotional aspects (Drogus 1995: 472). Cases of double membership are therefore not experienced as contradictory, but complementary, even if the clergy emphasize the differences between groups. Membership in different Catholic religious groups emerges out of an interplay between human and divine agents as well as the nature, and the legitimization of, knowledge and power within clerical and lay relationships.

Prisms of Belonging and Religious Discourses

In conclusion, I want to weave together the different strands involved in production and appropriation of prisms of belonging in this particular religious field. I have tried to foreground some of the interpolations between being the Church, ideas of personhood encouraged by different religious affiliations, and the politics of belonging to the Catholic Church in a colonia popular. The prisms of belonging that emerge among different lay and religious agents take place via an appropriation, claiming, and withholding of knowledge that shape boundaries of inclusion and exclusion. Because of their prismatic nature, different angles are refracted and reflected through prisms of belonging. Knowledge-in-the-making is filtered in different ways that may or may not have any resemblance to an original agent's intentionality and intended meaning. In other words, one's sense of belonging and knowledge represent different facets, with each experience refracted in a particular way depending on other individual and group dynamics of belonging and knowledge.

Religious and modern discourses often rely on categorical oppositions and unfold through emergent and residual formations. Traditional approaches tend to focus on maintenance of hierarchical power between clergy and laypersons, change in personal attitudes within the family, an acceptance of rather than an action upon social reality, and an intimate dialogue with God as well as sensory perception and experience of the divine. But the sensory perceptions and the embodied dialogue with the divine are not expression of a residual religious-cultural formation. As evidenced by the growing presence in the archdioceses of Guadalajara of the charismatic movement (which encourages, as does the traditional Church, a similar style of contact with the divine), we cannot assume that traditional religious forms are necessarily extensions of residual formations. Part of their style of practice is a form of emergent spiritual and religious experience. As Raymond Williams (1977) suggests, emergent formations do not appear in opposition to dominant formations, but are somehow part of them.

The Comunidades, on the other hand, emphasize a challenge to the sacred/secular dichotomy and to the hierarchical division of power between clergy and laypersons, but it may leave unaddressed the issues related to everyday politics of affects and sentiments that arise, for instance, in interpersonal clashes (for example, the dispute between Mauricio and Padre Nemo) and in the struggle over the claim of authorship of representations. Therefore, the progressive Church of the Comunidades "presents domestic problems as secondary to the 'really important' issues of the world beyond the household" (Burdick 1992: 176). The heterogeneous practices and their interpretations both within traditional and new Catholic groups address issues not only of race and gender (Burdick 1992; Caldeira 1987; Drogus 1990, 1992), but also of selfhood and human nature, and fields of analysis include, among others, the embodiment of religious practice, boundaries of the body (or, better, bodies), and the social construction of knowledge. Hence the analysis of social movements needs to take into account the negotiation of processes of identity and the production and circulation of knowledge (Escobar and Alvarez 1992), as well as the embodiment of experience.

The activities of the Comunidades may follow a process of construction of knowledge similar to that of the traditional hierarchical Church, where the figure of intermediation, the clergy, is central. The political dimension of the Comunidades has often been linked to the symbolic

FIGURE 5. This sculpture at the Parish of the Anunciación named "El Señor de las Tenteadas" represents an indigenous Christ, and on the board to the right are ex-votos representing various parts of the body. I commissioned a local artist, Alfredo Lopéz Casanova, to create the sculpture in 1992 in memory of my time with the parishioners. As indicated in this photo taken in 2001, it has been transformed into a Christ of *milagritos* (small miracles), another name for the ex-votos left behind by people who come to him and ask for healing. This is another interesting modern twist of faith, curing, agency, and intentionality embraced by an art object, myself, and the people in the neighborhood.

and ritual domains, and as with other social movements, their political role is constrained by the necessity of mediating between popular demands and state institutions, as in the case of mobilization for services discussed in Chapter 1. Once the mediation with institutions ceases, members scatter (De la Peña and De la Torre 1990: 597; Foweraker 1995: 105); however, we are left with the question of what remains after mobilization, and how it gets retranslated into other forms of social action or personal biographies. In Chapters 5 and 6 I explore further how Catholic religious evangelization and the effects of socio-religious mobilization articulate with gender, ritual practices, and the construction of gender subjectivity.

New and traditional Church tendencies may be represented as discordant by some of the diocesan and Jesuit clergy, and by group organizers, but they are experienced as complementary by some of the parishioners. This tension points to a struggle for symbolic capital between some Jesuits and diocesan priests, and the believers closely associated with them, and also indicates a gray area of anxiety (part of a process of modernity) and one in which a certain degree of subordination between leaders and grassroot members takes place.

I have only scratched the surface of this gray area, which, by resisting full categorization and by having overlapping progressive and traditionalist tendencies, indicates that religious affiliation is a process of formation (of the subject) and transformation and revelation (of the self) that can never be completed, but is open-ended. In this respect, these open-ended negotiations and tensions point to an area where lay and clerical subjects of a particular urban history flow into, negate, and reinterpret binarism and tensions of modernity. And prisms of belonging relate to both politics of sentiments and to modernity insofar as they link embodied experiences, particular religious affiliations, and representations of personhood. Group boundaries, theological statements, and religious practices allow specific micro-differentiations that constitute particular socio-religious affiliations. If we want to better understand religious affiliation for configuration of self, subject, and group identity, we need to understand how prisms of belonging reveal aspects of the embodiment of experiences and are also operative and contested categories about the interpretations of these experiences.

When clerical agents and lay leaders use language that essentializes religious tendencies, fixing them in categories that become subtly unchallengeable, they re-create a form of subalternity among believers. When the meaning of "el pueblo" is essentialized in the language of the

Comunidades, it reveals a twofold nature: active and passive. Hence, I invite the reader to think about the pueblo in urban Mexico as an active popular subject, whose image is not essentialized by its leaders—and as an object, the depository of an ascribed, essentialized, and homogeneous representation. However, I have explained in this chapter that idiosyncratic processes of differentation within the pueblo work against an impulse to describe it as a homogeneous entity. These internal differentiations, as well as impulses to homogenization, play an important role in the formation and reproduction of socioreligious movements. Moreover, in this case they become part of a narrative of knowledge production and appropriation that emerges through the prisms of belonging.

CHAPTER 4

Medical Pluralism

Medicina Popular and Medicina Alternativa

Religion, science, and the medicalization of illness always interweave in a dialectical and processual way. The imagery used by those who have been dispossessed as well as empowered through migration reveals how illnesses are treated. People's experiences and the conflicts in the colonia regarding medicine invite us to revisit the meaning of both medicine and religious activism in light of a national health care system that is struggling to deliver services, and a religious movement that promotes a vision of social healing.

In colonias populares, activism is an important part of the way medical options and healing processes are understood and acted upon as part of a social reality. Activism runs through a health movement fostering internally contested agendas. Nonetheless, people make "alternative" and complementary choices about available (or sometimes unreachable) medical health care that are neither default options nor part of an organized movement. Rather, those choices offer open-ended possibilities for redefining religious, social, and personal well-being that mark a path for a vernacular modernity.

The focus of this chapter is on a plurality of specific nontraditional medical practices and raises issues parallel to those explored in the previous chapter regarding the relation between, and different etiologies held by conventional doctors, alternative practitioners, and patients. It also explores how different medical practices coexist.[1] In the process, I examine how those practices are interwoven, as well as how they can clash in people's experience of illness and in formulating strategies to restore health. These practices point to specific notions of agency, the body, as well as social and individual responsibilities.[2] Moreover, I examine this plurality in the context of a (relative) failure of a modern national project of health care coverage for the urban population, and the increasing popularity of alternative medicines as a revealing manifestation of both a challenge as well as a re-invention of modernity.

The first part of the chapter explores different etiologies and the related allocation of responsibility and blame to diverse agents in different contexts, including a group of people who support medicina popular (developed in the work of the Comunidades Eclesiales de Base in the Parish of the Anunciación), others who belong to the traditional Church, and a local *curandero* (native healer).[3] The second part of the chapter explores how homeopathy is practiced in an allopathic, or biomedical, way,[4] and how homeopaths stress the scientific insights of homeopathy, while patients tend to focus on faith/trust in the remedy itself and the healer who provides it. I will then explore what these phenomena reveal about alternative modernity.

Differences between etiologies are emphasized by those who possess a special knowledge of curing or healing, such as the *promotores* (community health organizers) of the medicina popular group, the curandero, and most of the homeopaths who practice in Polanco. The organizers of the *medicina popular* group emphasize the social nature of diseases, arguing that they are caused by the structure of society and the exploitation of the poor by the rich. The curandero emphasizes that disease is caused by personal sin committed either by the sufferer or by those who may have cast a spell upon him/her. The homeopaths argue that their cure is scientific and therefore does not entail religious belief.

These various agents become representatives and mediators of knowledge for group members and/or patients. Nevertheless, coexistence of different non-biomedical and biomedical systems shows that people perceive differences in terms of the methods and styles of curing rather than in terms of etiological systems. Patients are active agents in a "quest for therapy" (Janzen and Arkinstall 1978), choosing between different practitioners and/or therapies rather than between traditional and modern medical systems, which often are not conceptualized as opposed, but combined in the curing process (Stoner 1986).

It has been argued that in urban Mexico the style of curing often consists of an incorporation of new allopathic and homeopathic elements into traditional household remedies (Logan 1988), and a distinction between their etiologies occurs, if at all, only at the time of treatment, and then regardless of the practitioner's view (Mahar Higgins

1975). Homeopaths and supporters of medicina popular see themselves as practicing alternative medicine, a term that embraces diverse etiological views. In this way, alternative medicines develop within a "meta-medical" framework of thought (Worsley 1982) and practices of a religious and social character. Different etiologies refer to distinct attitudes toward the interaction of human and nonhuman agencies, such as health institutions, and government, as well as God and evil. The meanings attached to the term "alternative" vary according to the various interpreting agents: group organizers, group members, homeopaths, and patients.

But what do these medical and healing practices say in their articulation about a state of modernity? To what extent are they a response to a State increasingly perceived as a failing technocracy? Do they offer ways to reinvent or challenge modernity in a postmodern condition? To explore these questions, I first outline the development of the national health care system and the alternative medicine movements to understand the emergence of health care activism and alternative medicine in Polanco. In short, I want to invite the reader into the debate about modernity that hinges on the link between the role of faith in the Mexican healthcare system and the alternative forms of medicine practiced in the colonia popular.

Institutional and Alternative Health Care

There used to be a split in the Mexican health care system between a "well-funded social security sector for the formal labour force, and a poorly funded public health sector for the poor and those in the informal labour force" (Brachet-Marquez and Sherrard Sherraden 1994).[5] The social security agencies have primarily been concerned with curing rather than preventing illness, and their focus has been on work-related accidents, maternity care, family planning, and caring for invalids, especially among the poorest people. IMSS and SSA policies are based on a concern with social issues. The Plan Nacional de Desarollo (1974), in particular, included the Programa de Fomento a la Salud (Program for the Promotion of Health), which focused on prevention of illness and attention to family and community care and targeted social health (for example, epidemiology, health education, improved sanitation and hygiene) as a determining component of both personal health and socioeconomic development.[6] This pathology of poverty revealed a modernist view of society in which technological and economic growth is believed to be a precondition for improving social health (an idea that still influences current devolution reforms that shift primary responsibility to local government agencies).[7] In practice, the national health plan did not succeed because it lacked the resources to turn the government's populist proposal into applicable strategies (Ward 1986). During the 1980s, major cuts were made in the national health care budget, with obvious consequences for the quality of service, and with increased privatization of the social security sector, the funding of health projects actually decreased (Stern 1990).[8]

In the early 1990s spending by the national health care system increased, eventually accounting for 6.1 percent of the gross domestic product, but spending decreased after the 1994 economic crisis and devaluation of the peso. In late 1995, the Mexican government began promoting a national development plan for 1995–2000, with the aim of extending social security coverage to more people by shifting more state resources to regional and federal programs. During the 1990s spending on primary health care was increased considerably through "priorities programs" targeting both rural and urban areas (Nigenda 1997). Nevertheless, long-standing problems with under-servicing and duplication of services in specific areas remained.

In 1998, only slightly more than 50 percent of the population was covered by health insurance, and the new coverage programs focused primarily on the rural and indigenous population, offering primary care, preventive medicine, and birth control. The plan to decentralize health services in major urban areas has led to promotion of new, expanded IMSS coverage, and families without formal labor contracts eventually will be covered by the IMSS, although the program is still being developed. Most people who are uninsured but covered by SSA have to come to terms with lower-quality services than those provided by the IMSS (LACHSR 1998). And despite attempted reforms, deficient social services and misallocation of public health funds continue to be problems.

Along with a decreasing quality of public health services there has been a devaluation of the figure of the participating doctors. Although working for a public agency used to be regarded as superior to working within the private health care system, that is no longer true. Medical training is now oriented toward North American models of efficiency, high technology, and objectification of the patient—elements believed by some to indicate that medical practice is developing in a social vacuum and shaping it into an "international" medical language (Loyoza

Legorreta 1991). Yet the social and structural conditions in which doctors operate create a reality that is often quite different from these models. For example, in the main IMSS hospital units in Guadalajara that serve low-income areas, patients have to wait months to see a specialist, and there are usually long lines for walk-in clinics. Also, doctors have limited access to medications and often prescribe the same remedies for different diseases, knowing that the prescription will not effectively treat all of a patient's symptoms.

People's desire for national health coverage is strong, among both employed and unemployed. In most low-income neighborhoods in Guadalajara, those who are entitled to social security (mainly factory workers) register under the IMSS. Those who work for the state (mainly those employed in schools or police departments) are covered by the Instituto de Seguridad y Servicios Sociales de los Trabajadores del Estado (ISSSTE) and the rest have limited coverage provided by the SSA. The IMSS and ISSSTE give people at least some confidence in their ability to face the insecurities of daily life, but only the person working under a contract and a limited number of his/her nuclear family are covered. Even if a family has IMSS coverage, they may not use it if alternatives are available, because the care is not of good quality. People primarily use IMSS coverage for maternity care, surgery, work-related accidents, and appointments with specialists, and their opinions of IMSS services often depend on whether or not they have been assigned a good doctor.[9]

The general perception that the services provided by the IMSS and the SSA are decreasing in quality can be attributed to two causes. First, many people describe their relationships with doctors as lacking in humanity. Patients feel they often are treated as if they are ignorant and unable to understand what is happening to them, and as if ignorance and poverty were the causes of their health problems. Patients also are increasingly aware that they are treated not for their specific symptoms, but are instead prescribed general remedies used to treat a wide range of ailments.[10] Second, patients are noticing that after being treated for something specific, they frequently develop other symptoms. For this reason, allopathic doctors are often called *matasanos* (a term that translates literally as "killers of the healthy"). As a result, criticisms of social security coverage often are related to an increasing lack of trust in conventional medicine.

Many people in urban neighborhoods are not covered by the IMSS, including construction workers and women employed as private maids.

Nevertheless, they have a number of different options. Those who can afford it consult private doctors, especially in emergencies. Despite the negative opinions often voiced about them, these doctors appear to be kinder in their treatment than those practicing within the IMSS. However, private doctors sometimes appear to be more concerned with making money than helping their patients, and in such cases patients' experiences can be negative and traumatic. As mentioned in Chapter 2, Don Domingo is a longterm diabetic patient without social security coverage who was treated by a doctor in Polanco for severe leg pain. Although he received several expensive injections that he was told would cure him, his condition worsened. Through the help of his godfather, Domingo was able to receive coverage through the IMSS, and I subsequently took him to the hospital. He was diagnosed as having gangrene, and seriously risked having his leg amputated. As it turns out, the costly injections administered by the private doctor were only morphine to ease the pain, not a cure for his condition.

Because many people cannot afford to see a private doctor, self-diagnosis and use of over-the-counter remedies are common. Over-the-counter drugs are also integrated with *remedios caseros* (homemade remedies usually based on herbs and balms), and people often use different remedies at different stages of disease.[11] The advice of a pharmacist or a sales clerk in a drugstore is not only cheaper than a visit to the doctor but is also similar to "a traditional system of self-treatment, that once included only household remedies" (Logan 1988). Many of those who sell drugs, however, lack training, and people often use the same remedies for similar symptoms with adverse consequences.

A third option for those seeking medical treatment includes homeopathy, *hierberos* (herbalists), *sobadores* (body manipulators) and, in cases of chronic illnesses, curanderos. These treatments cost less than a series of visits to conventional doctors (with the exception of some homeopaths, although their fees also include the cost of remedies). Providers of alternative treatments often have different notions about what causes illness, and their analyses reveal an understanding of different types of treatments and the healing powers that people attribute to themselves and to different agencies. In the next section, I examine the development of medicina popular, and its role in primary health care for Mexico's low-income population.

Medicina Popular as Medicina Alternativa

Since the early 1970s there has been a considerable increase in Mexico of the use of alternative therapies, and two distinct trends are apparent. The first is a growing interest in natural diets and holistic medicines, particularly among the well-educated, who comprise a relatively small but increasing segment of the population (Loyoza Legorreta 1990). The second trend involves the large underprivileged segment of the population who, for different reasons, cannot or prefer not to rely on conventional cures. This second trend has been interpreted as a counter-hegemonic discourse, and hence a form of class resistance to the allopathic system of health care (Menéndez 1983). This use of nontraditional treatments rather than biomedicine has been associated with periods of greater "ontological insecurity" and a lack of trust in the capacity to maintain continuity in the narrative of self and group identity (Giddens 1991b). The development of complementary medicines has been specifically associated with postmodernism (Easthope 1993) because this type of medicine challenges a unified, self-contained idea of the body, and a scientifically unitary medical knowledge. However, the fact that complementary medicines focus on notions of responsibility and the self-healing potential of the body raises questions about the construction of notions of holism, the body, and the self in particular cultural contexts by agents who are positioned in particular power relations. Because the relation between a complementary therapist and a patient requires a dialogue in order to form of diagnosis, this dialogue can also be analyzed as a form of narrative of the self, and as a particular literary narrative in itself (Mattingly 1998).[12]

Models used to study complementary medicines in developed countries such as the United Kingdom and the United States (Sharma 1992) are only partially applicable to developing countries like Mexico (Nigenda et al. 2001) because professional requirements and licensing of alternative medicine practitioners are stricter. In Mexico, alternative medicine is often a less regulated and less legally binding relation between patients and multiple providers (who may be competitors, or who may provide complementary types of care). It is thus important to examine the specific actors and agencies involved in the practice of alternative medicine among a low-income population.

Medicina popular has some characteristics in common with alternative medicine,[13] but it is also a combination of different paradigms. It is an umbrella term used for various kinds of alternative medicine (including acupuncture, digitopuncture [using pressure points], reflexology, herbal remedies, and massage) that aim to increase people's awareness and enable them to practice a form of self-help.[14] Medicina popular in Mexico has developed through two channels. During the mid-1970s, the World Health Organization established a program to develop traditional medicine in Mexico by encouraging practical methods of self-help based on the model of the "barefoot doctors" in China.[15] The program incorporated research from the Instituto Mexicano para el Estudio de Plantas Medicinales (IMEPLAM) and later by the Unidad de Investigación en Medicina Tradicional y Herbolaria del Instituto Mexicano del Seguro Social (MTH) (Loyoza Legorreta 1991). Illich's work on iatrogenic diseases (those produced inadvertently as a result of treatment) was also an important stimulus to the promotion in Mexico of traditional medicine at the grassroot level as an alternative to allopathic remedies (Beltrán 1986).

Medicina popular was also spread through networks that overlapped with the Comunidades Eclesiales de Base.[16] The influence of Freire's work on education and consciousness-raising among the poor, and of different works on Marxist medical sociology have become the ideological basis on which medicina popular has developed as a grassroot movement.[17] For Freire, education as a process of raising consciousness should develop critical thinking (Schutte 1993). In the case of medicina popular, critical thinking would help to break ties of domination between doctors and patients through what Freire sees as a communion of organizers' and group members' interests. In practice this is not always the case because of differences between group leaders and local systems of knowledge.

The principles on which medicina popular is based can be traced to a wider conflict and to dependency theory paradigms, in which illness is related to the failure of society to allocate adequate resources for tackling disease, an idea derived from an ideological inter-class conflict. The cause of illness is located in ideological conflicts, which themselves derive from capitalist relations of production. According to this argument, illnesses manifested in the biological body are triggered by the stress and conflict in the social body, and not only ideological class conflict, but also lifestyles and the practice of medical knowledge—which define the sick person—contribute to the genesis of the ill body (Gerhardt 1989).

Having provided some background on health care in Mexico, I now turn to the Vidasana group, which promotes medicina popular among members of the Parish of the Anunciación. This group emerged in late

1990 from the CEBs experience, and some members continue to participate in CEB meetings. Others, however, are not involved in the Comunidades or other parish activities, and with time the group diversified
and moved away from an original plan of CEBs evangelization. Group
members define medicina popular as "medicina alternativa," a term also
used by homeopaths, though often in the sense of being alternative to
allopathy. Thus the ethnography presented below reveals that the semantic field of alternative medicine changes in different contexts.

In the Vidasana group, leaders' and members' notions about causality
and responsibility in the illness process are often quite different. Group
leaders stress the social causes of diseases: they see the *causae efficiens* and
finalis of medicina popular as located in the structure of relations between social classes;[18] consequently, they attribute illness to the sinful
actions of the wealthy and powerful people who exploit the so-called
poor.[19] Different members of the Vidasana group emphasized different
aspects of the process of illness and healing, and stressed the value of
increased self-worth in dealing with everyday health care issues.

The Vidasana Group

The Vidasana group was formed by members of the Anunciación Comunidades in January 1990. Until summer 1991, the group was led by
Mauricio, who was assisted by Soledad. Sister Carlota, and later Sisters
Mónica and Elda, helped Mauricio and Soledad to organize and promote the group. In early 1991, the group split into two factions because
of accusations against the treasurer about mismanagement of the common fund to which the women gave a small contribution each week.[20]

By 1997, and as late as 1999, the original Vidasana group had dispersed into smaller groups that met in different houses, and no longer
in a unified way under the church's umbrella. At its peak, as many as
sixty women participated in the group, but only a few men joined, and
they eventually dropped out. Although some men have good knowledge
of home remedies, they often either did not have the time to attend
meetings or did not feel comfortable being "among many women."
They may have feared becoming the source of gossip, or generating
mistrust among the women's husbands (which is, indeed, what happened to Mauricio, the only man in the group). Apart from activities
related to the church, there are few occasions in which married women
can socialize openly with men. The husbands of the group's members

are often skeptical about what can be achieved by the group, but once they start to receive treatment from their wives (they are often used as guinea pigs!), they become more supportive and less fussy about their wives' participation.[21]

The Vidasana group is part of a wider urban network in the process of development made up of similar groups in five colonias in Guadalajara: Atemajac, Santa Cecilia, La Peñita, Rancho Nuevo, and Polanco. All of them were born out of the experience of the CEBs or were developed by organizers who were inclined to this type of evangelization. Sooner or later, all of these groups achieved a greater independence from direct parish influence. As in the other colonias, the Vidasana group set up a consultation service available to parish members for a small fee, but some of the women did not want the responsibility of prescribing remedies for people outside their family and circle of friends, so only a few were willing to offer consultations.

Vidasana was born, in the eyes of the lay and religious organizers, with the long-term aim of increasing people's consciousness of their situation and of creating forms of medical self-help to counteract economic pressures in poor households. One goal was to retrieve people's knowledge, rooted in their rural past, and combine it with a knowledge of alternative medicines. Another was to make the members proud of their roots, transforming them into axes of belonging rather than seeing them as an element of backwardness in an urban environment. In this case, the prisms of belonging constitute a realm of experiential knowledge that values tradition in modernity and they foster self and community empowerment. If, as discussed below, complementary medicines are part of a postmodern condition, their lay practice combined with traditional self-help medicine indicates an emergent phenomenon that re-inscribes tradition into modernity.

On the first anniversary of the Vidasana group's formation, Mauricio, along with the women, composed a *corrido,* ballad) that summarizes in a playful way some of the characteristics of the group:

> I have very clearly in mind the twenty-fourth of January when,
> on a Wednesday, a group of female companions met.
> They became very aware of problems related to health,
> and studied with complete and total care.
> Seeing all the sicknesses [around them] they searched for solutions.
> Using medical plants, they found the cure.
> They analyzed the problems within the community,
> and together fought to change the reality.

The pueblo needs to rejoice in health
so that united together people work well.
"Fly, fly, little dove to reach the rose bush": awakening to life, the dove
    wants to thank it.
With this I make a greeting, singing this song.
We are at your service at the temple of the Anunciación.

The ballad clearly emphasizes health as a rejoicement of the whole community, and community problem solving as an awakening to life.

To a certain extent the Vidasana group has responded to unsatisfactory power relations between patients and doctors by deprofessionalizing and demedicalizing health care. One of the group's policies is that only symbolic honoraria can be asked for a given remedy, and women who have taken personal (that is, economic) advantage of the knowledge shared within the group are criticized. Power relations between the members pivot around access to the sharing of knowledge about the uses of plants and other self-help methods. Some of the women show veiled resistance to sharing what they know; those closer to whoever is in charge have easier access to information as well as more opportunities to attend provincial or regional meetings. Women in the group defined themselves as *viejas* (old) and *nuevas* (new) in relation to the length of their membership, their degree of knowledge, and their capacity to assimilate knowledge shared in the group.

In the Vidasana group's early days, Mauricio and Soledad stressed self-teaching. They were resistant to inviting so-called experts to come and give talks, preferring instead to encourage the women to share what they knew already, supplemented by photocopies of written sources circulated between medicina popular groups around the country. The basic teaching revolved around the use of herbs in *tintura* (tincture), *microdosis,*[22] *placas* (metallic bars) used to balance energy, as well as massage techniques. Women learned how to use herbs such as *ruda* (rue), arnica, *estafiate* (larkspur), and *sangre de grado* (dragon's blood) in making potions for the cure of menstrual pain, emotional trauma, stomach pain, and infections. Basic nutrition was also discussed, especially in relation to vitamin properties, and inexpensive but nutritious foods such as soy and gluten.

The way in which the group was coordinated by Sisters Mónica, Elda, and later Mercedes differed from Mauricio's policy. A nurse came regularly to teach first aid, and different experts presented workshops about auricopuncture, acupuncture, and relaxation techniques. The most knowledgeable women were invited to participate in a series of homeopathic workshops in the north of the city; that material, however, was not shared by the organizers with the rest of the group. When Mercedes was in charge of the group, some of the women felt they were not given enough support, and that organizers "se tienen el conocimento para ellas" (kept the knowledge to themselves). Their complaints addressed organizers' preferential treatment of the other group that had been meeting parallel to Vidasana since Mauricio ceased to be in charge. The original group now spent entire weeks without touching the subject of homemade herbal remedies, and some women were upset by this shift. Deprofessionalization of conventional medical practice was high on the agenda during both Mauricio's and Mercedes's periods as promotores, but with different emphases on demedicalization. During Mauricio's time the group was oriented toward knowledge grounded in women's everyday practices, whereas the nuns' emphasis was on presenting the knowledge of experts for the women to assimilate.

The resulting struggle for authenticity about different forms of medical experiential knowledge parallels similar politics of authenticity within and between the new and the traditional Churches, discussed above.

Medicina Popular and the Social Nature of Illness

One level of the process of medicina popular lies in the analysis of social reality.[23] The idea that health is the product of social reality as well as being generated by psychological displacement is central. This presupposition is embedded in a cartoon slide show that was shown during a regional meeting in Sayula (Colima) in May 1991 and later used as a teaching tool in Polanco, as well as in an exercise called the "tree of life and death," led by Sister Mónica in the Vidasana group (see Appendix B).

The protagonists of the cartoons are cats and tigers; the world they occupy is a metaphor for society. It is set in a mythical time when all cats lived together in cooperation, equality, and good health, and nature satisfied all their needs. At that time health was in the hands of the people (cats in the story), but with the rise of private property, some cats were transformed into tigers and started to take control of society. When the newly formed state openly took the side of the tigers, people/cats became subjects of exploitation, beginning with their physical bodies. Imperialism resulted in longer work hours for lower wages, economic pressure, and different forms of disease. Some of the cats turned into tigers as they became false prophets. Most of them, however, were able to reestablish harmony, health, and well-being through unity and solidarity. Mauricio and Sister Mónica often referred to this allegory of the cats and tigers. Mauricio would talk about the connection between good health and human rights which should be enjoyed by the pueblo, and how the abuse of human rights was the cause of a sick society—yet another claim to a representation of the pueblo as a subject.

While human rights are explicitly connected to the state of people's health, the *causa materialis* of illness is in conditions in the social environment where poor people live and work; the *causa efficiens* rests on the nature of the social relations between classes and nations. Thus bodily symptoms are interpreted as the outcome of social conditions, and illness is generated by modifications of social habits and deterioration in general living conditions. On one occasion, the group discussed a leaflet on treating chest diseases with *digitopuntura* (hand pressure points), titled "Useful [Pressure] Points for Chest Disease (Due to Poor Living Conditions and Shortage of Clothing)." The discussion had turned to the topic of alleviating respiratory problems with such remedies as eucalyptus and cinnamon. However, women repeatedly stated that the humidity of houses in the rainy season, the air contamination in the nearby old industrial area of the city, and a diet lacking in fresh fruit and greens were the real causes of lung and throat infections. Several women observed how other colonias lacked these conditions and were better-off. The discussion group was then led by the organizers to examine the *causa materialis* of illness in living conditions, and the *causa efficiens* in their inability to maintain basic conditions of living.

A similar approach to the social root of illness was explored by Sister Mónica through the image of the trees of life and death (see Appendix B), reminiscent of Freire's model of alphabetization and the raising of consciousness. Two drawings of trees were shown to the women as models for the types of diseases common in the colonia. The first, called the tree of life, shows how the integration of the tree is the basis of health. Wholeness is located in a sense of community, in class solidarity. The tree needs strong roots in order to develop healthy leaves. The healing process depends upon a balanced relation between the different parts of society, which is metaphorically represented as a living body. The second model, the tree of death, indicates that illness is generated by the distortion of the structure of society that occurs when an elite group of people exploits the majority.

In this exercise, Sister Mónica asked the women to fill in the roots and the trunk with economic and political factors that generate both disease and health. She suggested that illness was a limitation of personal and collective abilities, and that "hay gente muerta que puede dar vida, y gente viva que puede dar muerte" (there are dead people who can generate life, and living people who can generate death). So those who took advantage of the conditions of the poor were committing a sin, not only toward people, but toward life itself. At the time, the women in the group found it difficult to fill in the tree on their own, especially the part representing the roots, so Sister Mónica helped them make the structural connection between their everyday lives and the wider structures of society. Women's opinions had to fit this overall explanation. Mónica then collected the sheets and prepared a polished up version that she distributed as a handout a couple of weeks later. Women in the discussion had identified the seed of death with drug manufacturers who become rich at the expense of the underprivileged. They identified illness as rooted in the selfish acquisition of superfluous goods, and in the envy that this process generates. But there was also resistance to such explanation masked under umbrella phrases — "no alcanzo a comprender," and "es muy dificil para mí" (I am not good enough to understand; it is very difficult for me), which both *nuevas* and *viejas* expressed.

Teresa, a vieja, mentioned the case of a very poor family on her street that had no proper toilet but used a hole in the courtyard. Teresa mentioned that the children of that family were often ill, and that the neighbors in the street had offered to help the family. She blamed the parents for being lazy, for not looking hard enough for work, and for wasting the money donated by the neighbors. She attributed the children's illnesses to their parents, who were *tercos* (stubborn) and *flojos* (lazy).

Teresa viewed them as such because they did not work regularly but seemed to prefer living on charity donations from the parish. Teresa also mentioned to me, outside the group, that she did not understand where in the tree to place *empacho* (an inability to digest food, and a form of food poisoning that can result in diarrhea, fever, and vomiting), but had been too shy to bring up the issue in the group. Discrepancies of this type between the rationales of the promotores and the local people can be interpreted as a form of friction between external and localized knowledge.

A stratification of Polanco has been taking place, and one effect of the centralization of the suburb is that there are people in the colonia who are relatively affluent in comparison to other families, whose combined income barely covers the minimal expenses of growing families. An example of economic stratification is that some impoverished families try to save money by cutting their food expenses.[24]

In Sister Mónica's opinion illnesses such as those experienced by the poor family Teresa had mentioned are due not to the parents' lack of personal responsibility but to their economic conditions. This was an interesting incidence of contradictory and clashing illness etiologies: the etiologies related in a hierarchical way by Sister Mónica were recognized as more valid in the public space of the group, but outside the group, and for the members who did not fully identify with the message of the organizers, gossip continued about neighbors' inability to ensure their own well-being, which was viewed as a consequence of ignorance and weakness. Older women referred to the economic hardship that they had also been enduring, and how they had struggled to maintain their families' well-being.

Of all the examples, group members could most easily see a correlation between their living conditions and the development of *enfermedades de los nervios* (nervous ailments). "Nerves" have been observed as a polysemic phenomenon (individual, social, and political) used in different class spectrums to express powerlessness in gender and marital conflicts, and in conditions of status deprivation—a phenomenon shaped by the medicalization and "rationalization" of the body, which becomes a battleground itself (Scheper-Hughes 1992). People in the neighborhood refer to being sick because of nervios in different contexts. The term is used to cover many physical symptoms, including migraine headaches, gastritis, and ulcers. The causes of nervios were discussed by the group in terms of unhealthy diets, which resulted from pressure on the household economy. Some explained that "el dinero nunca alcanza para la quincena" (money doesn't last the fortnight [wages are often paid every two weeks]). In more private contexts, women mentioned interpersonal conflicts with regard to the control of shared resources, status and gender control, and a sense of loss and lack of support in a migrant's condition. However, rising inflation and increasing economic hardship for the low-income population in Mexico during the mid-1980s, especially, and again after the peso devaluation in 1994 have been taking a toll on people's health, discussed further in relation to women's subjectivity in the last chapter.

Biblical passages were also used in the group to discuss themes related to the trees of life and death. Sister Mónica brought an elaboration of the letter of Paul to the Philippians (4:15–24) to a group meeting. She developed the theme of the difference between "el hombre viejo y el nuevo" (the old and the new man). The old man "takes too many medicines or poisons himself with tranquilizers and sleeping pills. He only hears what concerns himself, thinking about what he is deciding next. He is focused on his unfulfilled ego ('what I said to him, what he said to me')." The new man, by contrast, "seeks help in overcoming his nervous tensions from his mental and spiritual energy. . . . He is interested in himself in a different way. He does not relate the outside to his own 'I.' He listens carefully and understands the feelings/reasons of others." Again, as discussed in the previous chapter, traditional and new become metaphors for notions of a past and a present/future that takes place as an opposition between the individual/selfish and the collective/social. Disease, in this reading of medicina popular, arises when the collective is subordinated to the will or desires of individuals.

The women of the group related the theme of the old and new type of man to their personal lives. Some of them recognized how easily they had slipped into drugs in the past, and how often they had felt caught in a downward spiral. Most felt that the group helped them to see that many other women in the colonia were dealing with the same problems, and that some illnesses are generated from a state of mind that can be changed by different behavior. Sister Mónica feels that this type of reflection helped the group to connect this structural analysis to their personal experiences. In Sister Mónica's reading, the relationship between human guilt, sin, poor health, and the prevention of illness is a form of respect for God's laws. Mauricio also used biblical references to argue that homemade remedies were used in ancient times, and that critical judgments of doctors and the medical profession were being made even during biblical times (Mark 5:26). The idea that illness can be caused by not adhering to God's plan leads to perceiving the act of curing as a social act.[25]

Three interconnected points can be drawn from the analysis of the causes of illness embedded in the thinking of the Vidasana group in Polanco. First, healing is ultimately linked to the reorganization of society and to human solidarity. It occurs through an increase of collective consciousness, the *causa finalis* thus being structural change in society. Second, the defense of life requires active engagement in fighting the causes of death. Preventive medicine can thus be seen as a way of promoting social justice as part of God's realm. This engagement involves sharing knowledge, and practicing knowledge after a time of "practical mimicries"—learning through repetition, observation, and tactile contact (Jackson 1998), as well as through reading. However, some women did show a difficulty in touching for healing purposes, often breaking up over jokes about one's own or someone else's inability to apply the remedy correctly or give the "right" bodily touch. Third, the individual is considered to be the holder of individual responsibility in collective communal action that may create sin/disease; sin, which causes illness, arises from the actions of those who exploit others, and from the structure of society which enables them to do this. In this respect, modernity, with its specific agency and contradictions, is an embracing (García Canclini 1995) but also necessary condition of the healing process. So by embracing this necessary condition of modernity, how do people inscribe their interpretations into these tensions and knowledge? And what consequences are revealed in people's mapping of the world?

Healing and Self-Worth

The notions of healing and of consciousness and self-worth that emerge in the narratives of some group members are accented differently from the accounts of the promotores. Some women in the Vidasana group value their experience both because it increases their self-worth and because of its religious content. Women who have been involved actively in the Comunidades Eclesiales de Base see a connection between medicina popular and divine healing, while those who are not involved with the Comunidades stress pragmatic results and the increased sense of self-worth they derive from practicing what they have learned.

In a meeting of five popular medicine groups in Guadalajara that took place in La Peñita, the participants were asked to describe the reasons for their participation in medicina popular, and the effects of their experience. Below are the responses of four of the women of the Vidasana group.

> *Doña Carmen:* It is to be conscious of what we have lost, and do something for others.
>
> *Doña Mago:* To serve others and learn to heal oneself. . . . It is a message given with the best love and faith we can. . . . This knowledge must be available to everybody.
>
> *Mari Chuy:* It is our offering to society like that of God to the world.
>
> *Doña Marisol:* That we all can give comfort and health through nature and the love of God.

[Doña Carmen: *Es tener conciencia de lo que habemos perdido y hacer algo por los demás.*

Doña Mago: *Servir a los demás y aprender a curarse . . . es un mensaje dado con amor y fe lo más que uno pueda . . . hay que tener este conocimiento a el alcance de todos.*

Mari Chuy: *Es nuestra entrega a la sociedad como la de Dios al mundo.*

Doña Marisol: *Que todos nosotros podemos dar consuelo y salud por medio de la naturaleza y el amor de Dios.*]

Two of the women used the word *todos* to suggest that anybody can participate in the process of healing. As the boundary between those who know and those who do not becomes fluid, the patient-doctor relationship is challenged. As the Vidasana group members believe, the power of healing is intrinsic to our state of being human once we accept becoming active agents through the love of God.

Through the practice of medicina popular, women can give *consuelo y salud* (consolation and health). Each remedy offered is a means through which a part of oneself can be communicated to those who are in need. What is shared is a common pathos, and through this sharing, healing takes place. This process is also one of self-healing because the group experience is meant to be a service to society, which is a fundamental component of being Catholic; thus the healing process becomes part of the process of redemption of the soul and implies a wider process at physical, emotional, and spiritual levels.

Doña Mago, a vieja of the group, is a lively married woman in her mid-forties. One of the most knowledgeable women of the group, she described her experiences with medicina popular as follows: "Up to now I have had positive and negative experiences. For instance, I have placed small metal bars [placas], but frequently [the outcome] depends on the mental state of the person. You can place many placas, but they do not have any effect if the person does not have consciousness of herself or if she does not have trust. If, with the faith you have, you are lazy, you should realize your contradictions." In Doña Mago's mind, it is God who heals, and those who learn have a responsibility to apply the teaching without laziness. She also sees a relation between sickness and healing in which healing cannot take place if either the healer or the patient lacks personal consciousness and faith. Doña Mago feels she has a responsibility to use the knowledge that she has learned in the group, but she also believes that a successful cure depends on a patient's trust and faith in the treatment and in the person who gives it. There is definitely an awareness that it is not just the remedy that cures, but also the process involved in the giving and the taking of the treatment, and that these are central characteristics which actually differentiate medicina popular from conventional medicine. While for the promotores the consciousness that develops out of the experience of illness tends to be more about social relations and solidarity, for some women in the group the focus is more on healing and faith.

Some women in the Vidasana group believe in natural remedies but are less sure about their religious aspects. One young woman, Antonia, has a good knowledge of plants and remedies, but in replying to my questions about the healing power of God, she appeared skeptical. She felt good that she was able to prepare remedies and give advice on nutrition to her family and friends, therefore reducing their expenses in relieving common illnesses, but was not bothered as to whether it was God or some other forces beyond the treatment. Some of the remedies she uses are those that her mother recalls from the rancho. Antonia offers her advice to neighbors, but some of them, she says, lack the patience to use natural remedies. If they fail to see positive results, she interprets it as laziness in using the correct dosage and treatment.

Many women who have participated in the Vidasana group say it has increased their sense of self-worth because it has allowed them to act together and to learn and practice such skills as reading and writing. Although these are some of the aims that the group's leaders hope to achieve, it appears that the women only partly assimilate the ideological message of the social nature of illness (or perhaps resist it by stressing their ignorance and inability to learn such concepts). Once on their own, they may become experts who can offer advise about remedies to members of their community, and they also can use that knowledge to increase personal status and wealth. In this sense, to different degrees, they begin to feel useful in dealing with health issues in everyday practice at the same time as they become strategically minded about their own choices. Their capacity to provide services therefore has an effect on their own and their families' well-being.

Disease and Individual Sin

The etiology of illness used by the medicina popular group allocates blame and responsibility to certain classes and to the structure of society which allows selfish actions to take place. But other forms of etiology that revolve similarly around notions of sin also exist. These see endogenous causes in a person's emotional state, or as generated by the so-called evil eye, so that the sins of another may become the cause of one's own disease (Foster 1978). These explanations identify the *causa efficiens* of illness in personal sin and in resistance to God's will, rooted in what people call "temor de Dios" (fear of God). Members of traditional churches might offer similar interpretations, and this etiology combined with the idea of the evil eye appears in the practice of the local curandero.

Urban curanderismo seems to be more diversified and to use more impersonal practices than rural curanderismo (Press 1971). However, there is no agreement as to whether curanderismo is increasing or decreasing among the urban population. Early studies carried out among the Hispanic population in urban settlements in the southern United States variously showed that the importance of curanderos was decreasing (Edgerton et al. 1970), or that curanderos were still widely consulted, especially for more serious and chronic cases (Trotter and Chavira 1980), and that their practice was changing, yet maintaining the holistic (mind/body) approach to treatment (Trotter and Chavira 1980). Press's analysis — influenced by the Redfield's rural/urban model — argues that the "urban curanderismo process" is a sociocultural phenomenon through which differences in consultation styles are adapted to the increasingly diversified needs of urban populations (Press 1971). The work of curandero Don Eduardo in Polanco can be understood within the context of urban conditions of life, where allopathic medicine is often too expensive, ineffective, or limited, and where connections between sin and illness are still widely believed to be the causes of chronic diseases or accidents.

Don Eduardo is not well thought of by most members of the Vidasana group, who look on his work with skepticism. Still, despite the organizers' claims that his healing does not cure, some people still have faith in it.[26] Don Eduardo is a type of spiritualist healer, because he claims to be a channel through which divine messages are manifested (Trotter and Chavira 1980). He lives in Polanco with his large family in a simple, rural type of house where he keeps animals in the courtyard.[27] There is always a long queue of people waiting for his or one of his assistants' *limpias* (ritual cleansings). The patients are seen in a small windowless room behind a worn-out curtain, but there is no privacy during the healing session because there is a continual stream of new patients. A large altar in one corner of the room is covered with lighted candles and photographs, and on the top there is an image of the divine providence (in the form of the third eye), embellished with red and white flowers. On the wall is a long series of woeful pictures of the Passion of Christ.

Before the first limpia, the patient has a short session with Don Eduardo, who talks about the patient's weakened state, pain, and depression.[28] According to the curandero, people are in great pain because they are distant from God and the Virgin, and the patient's state is due to his or her soul's weakness in resisting evil.

The actual limpia begins with the sprinkling of perfumed water on the patient's body, and the tracing of the body's outline with a big knife and a wooden bar. Then the patient drinks from a small pot of water kept near the altar. At the end, the person is advised to bathe for three days at lunch time with cold water, and to wrap up in a dry towel for a couple of minutes. Patients also are told to pray to God and the Virgin because the cause of their illness is their distance from God, and they are warned not to expose themselves to envy.

One idea conveyed by the curandero is that illness is caused by misplacement. People and things must not be in places they do not belong so that disease will not be caught, as can happen when one is outside one's own house and exposed to other people's scrutiny. Women, especially, should stay at home because they catch diseases more easily if they expose themselves to public places. After the session with Don Eduardo and his assistants, people leave a donation according to their means. I had personal experience of Don Eduardo's cleansing after burglars broke into my accommodation in broad daylight, and I began having trouble sleeping. Although my limpias were rather positive experiences, after which I felt greatly relaxed, my disturbed sleep continued long after.

Don Eduardo's clientele is very heterogeneous in social and economic status, but one experience seems common: other remedies have failed to cure them. Many patients come regularly with a wide range of different symptoms that vary from physical problems to the appearance of spirits in the houses of relatives. Those who have been diagnosed as incurable, or who cannot afford an expensive medical cure, often turn to Don Eduardo. Some patients have been told by allopathic doctors that there is nothing wrong with them.[29] Don Eduardo advises his patients first to try all the other medicines, and he says, "Cuando uno no quiere, santo no puede," equivalent to the English saying, "God helps those who help themselves."[30] When people come to see him, they must "submit themselves to God's will, not come here just to see." He affirms that the best medicine is the will of God, and that we are now living in a very difficult period because people go against God's laws. Transgressing these laws causes sickness in two ways. First, a person can become sick if he or she acts wrongly or sinfully. But a person also can become sick if another person has invoked the devil. The idea that disease can be put into the person by an evil agency is central. According to Don Eduardo, "People get ill because of other people's actions and misbehavior. When we dislike somebody, we can get ill. . . . If we have a quarrel with someone, he says that he will not forget it. In this way people invoke the devil." Sick people thus carry the weight of a range of problems, pain, and suffering related to their own or others' sins. The *causa efficiens* of illness is the existence of evil in humans, and the *causa finalis* is reconciliation and rapprochement with God as a form of redemption from sin. Don Eduardo argues that God and the Virgin heal through him, and that he himself is not the source of healing. He sees his life before and after his conversion (after which he became a channel of God) as two distinctly different existences: the first a life of vice and religious skepticism, the second a life of service.

A similar connection between illness and sin is also made by followers of traditional religion, in which illnesses are often interpreted as a punishment from God; however, pain and sickness also offer the possibility of an individual soul's redemption. Curanderos are viewed in traditional religion as *hechiceros* (wizards). According to Don Luís, curanderos "call upon the Virgin and saints, but cast spells with the devil." Don Luís and the other members of the highly traditional and devotional Catholic group La Adoración Nocturna criticize Don Eduardo's practice not so much for the idea of treating evil as a cause of diseases, but for the fact that curanderos are seen as capable of releasing people from sin—just as priests do—and therefore their patients believe they can be released from evil and pain without going through church absolution. The curandero thus undermines the figure of the priest as a mediator between human and divine agency, and reduces the priest to the level of a layperson.

Estrella, whose membership in the Movimiento Familiar Cristiano I have previously discussed, often suggested that illnesses and accidents make us aware of having gone against God's will. She explained to me that once, on a Saturday night, she was supposed to finish off some work for Caritas in the temple, but decided instead to go to a fiesta of some relatives with her husband. On the doorstep, she hurt her ankle badly and could not leave the house. She felt very depressed because the following day was the marriage of one of her beloved nephews. However, when she woke up the next day, her ankle had "miraculously" recovered, and she was able to go to the wedding mass. She interpreted the accident and the pain in her leg as a message from God about her misbehavior. However, God is so just and loving that he has the power to heal overnight, and in this case He did because she planned to attend a church wedding the following day. Thus, for Estrella, illness can be an expression of disharmony between human and divine will. Her perception of the divine is related to the traditional conception of fear of God, and of God as punisher, and she sees illness and recovery as a means for redemption of personal sin and a sense of guilt.

For Doña Marisol and Doña Mago, healing and recovery also are related to "tuning in" to the divine world, but also imply becoming aware of the relation between oneself, nature, and society. Sickness is not a punishment or a recognition of personal sin, but a potential for awareness. For leaders of the health group, such as Mauricio and Mónica, this awareness is particularly related to social relations, and responsibility for illness is blamed on those who create poverty and exploit people. For Don Eduardo and traditional Catholics, illness is seen as generated by one's own misdeeds and/or other people's evil.

Between Science and Faith: The Allopathic Use of Homeopathy

The connections between illness/healing and between social and individual sin/redemption are central to the discourse of the traditional practice of the curandero as well as to the medicina popular group. Another polarization/continuum also present in low-income areas is between ideas of science versus faith within the medical practice of homeopathy. Homeopaths in Polanco conceive of a linear progression from traditional, idiosyncratic cures related to faith, to new scientific methods such as homeopathy—a distinction that legitimizes and institutionalizes their social practices. Homeopaths, in fact, have an allopathic way of exercising homeopathy, while patients' attitudes toward homeopathic treatment stress the aspect of faith/trust in the remedy and in the figure of the homeopath. Patients use different alternative remedies, often together, and they perceive these different remedies in terms of methods rather than principles—the element of faith and belief being fundamental. This reflects in practice what I see as an allopathic use of homeopathy, and relates to the links between allopathic and homeopathic train-ing.[31]

The practice of homeopathy in Mexico has been assimilated to a dom-inant allopathic model whose principal traits are the transformation of health into a commodity, an asymmetric relation between doctor and patient, and the exclusion of the patient from medical knowledge (Me-néndez 1983). Hence, since consumption is social, relational, and active (Appadurai 1995), this form of alternative medicine also provides insight into how private medical choices indicate particular strategies and ex-periences of social relations. Indeed, for most homeopaths in Polanco, the remedy targets symptoms rather than the symptomatology, and there is no sharing of knowledge between homeopath and patient. Pa-tients are often considered ignorant by homeopaths because they do not know the right food to give their children, or they do not wash what they eat properly, or they do not take enough care of personal hygiene; in other words, they are seen to lack responsibility and to ignore the obvious connection between illness and lifestyle. Patients may use home remedies, but many believe that for real, "lasting" cures, they have to consult homeopaths.

Frequently, homeopaths attend to so many patients in a short time that there is no time for individual diagnosis of a new patient—an ele-ment which is extremely important in both *purista* (pure) and *complejista* (complex) approaches (see Appendix A). Only two homeopaths, Dr. Magda and Dr. Diego, tend to ask varied questions about their patients' personal habits. The others justify their lack of in-depth diagnosis by citing high patient turnover: many patients come just once, and others may come back only after weeks or months. What matters to most ho-meopaths is to "cure" as many people as possible, and gaining psycho-logical insight into the patient's situation during the actual consultation is treated, if at all, as peripheral.

Homeopaths treat patients as people seeking relief from pain. An-tonio and Piso, who were both trained as allopathic doctors but also received training as homeopaths, describe pain and discomfort in terms similar to those used in allopathic medicine: as something to be taken away, not as a possible sign of improvement (if contained and tempo-rary),—which is a strong principle in the purista approach. Being alter-nistas, Antonio, Samuel, and Piso give whatever is needed, both ho-meopathic and allopathic remedies, to patients at the same time. For example, an allopathic remedy may be prescribed for acute symptoms, and a homeopathic remedy for chronic manifestations. They do not offer explanations about the principles on which homeopathy is based, nor do they name the remedies they prescribe. Remedies are normally administered at the level of the sixth or thirtieth potencies (the lowest), and none of the homeopaths write the name of the remedy on the bottle.[32]

Another characteristic of homeopathic treatment that mirrors allopathic practice is bodily contact. The homeopath measures blood pressure and pulse rate, and may examine the tongue or the throat. When asked about the validity of this type of physical inspection for homeopathic treatment, homeopaths answered that the procedure is part of making the real diagnosis, or that what makes homeopathy a medicina alternativa is that it can be "alternative" to allopathy, but can still use allopathic methods. Only Dr. Magda, who uses a complejista approach, pointed out that homeopathy, in its original, pure Hahnemann form (see Appendix A), implies a radically different conception of the body and illness.

The issue of whether homeopathy is scientific or not is a point of debate. Practitioners variously affirm that homeopathy is a form of science, or, as in the case of Dr. Magda, that science is not developed enough to understand its scientific validity. Drs. Diego, Piso, and Antonio prefer to view homeopathy as a science because they say it can be tested objectively.[33] However, the claim to homeopathy's scientific validity—avowed by the practitioners in Polanco—reveals not a truth of the homeopathic principle, per se, but the particular position of the homeopath in relation to the patient and other doctors/healers.[34] Homeopaths tend to associate, to a greater or lesser degree, faith and magic—in evolutionist terms—with everything which is backward and which is "inevitably" going to be overtaken by science. According to Dr. Samuel, "Those who have no basic academic knowledge can be good homeopaths, but they do not know the natural evolution of the illness. . . . It is important that homeopathy is regarded as a science rather than faith and magic." In fact, homeopaths in Polanco attack any self-help use of homeopathy, and they question the status of so-called unofficial homeopaths who lack allopathic training. Some homeopaths believe patients' faith is misguided, and they make a distinction between a faith "for faith" and a "knowledgeable" faith (for example, in the workings of the allopathic remedy). As Dr. Samuel noted, "It is important that people have faith, not because of faith, but because it cures. It is like aspirin. They take it and they know that it is good for them. They know where the remedy goes."

Drs. Diego and Antonio agree that a patient's faith helps to ensure that the patient will take the remedy as prescribed, whereas Magda and Consuelo believe faith to be a necessary, but not a principal, element in homeopathic treatment. For most homeopaths, faith is nonetheless misleading because it obscures the real causality between a remedy and its effects. This shows again how homeopathic remedies are treated analogously to allopathic ones: the effects of a remedy are attributed to the object—the remedy itself—and not to the process undertaken by the patient and the homeopath—acknowledgement of which would, on the contrary, attach a healing dimension to the homeopathic relationship. "I always repeat to the patients not to have faith in me, but in the remedy I give to them," said Dr. Diego. "I explain to them that homeopathy has a slower effect than allopathy, and that one needs to wait for a couple of months to cure problems that have been present for years, so they know that I am not wrong but that it is the remedy which is slow." Nonetheless, patients do attribute great importance to the figure of the homeopath/doctor and to his/her capacity to "guess" the causes of their illness. In their perception of homeopathy, the compartmentalization between science and faith is not emphasized.

In conclusion, then, homeopaths perpetuate the unequal power relations of mainstream medicine with their patients, and they tend to reinforce the opposition between modern, scientific knowledge and traditional experience (McClain 1977)—framing health in an objective, non-humanistic language (Taussig 1980). Moreover, the stress on professionalization or institutionalization of the homeopath is a fundamental element in the practices that constitute the doctor and patient as such.

Patients and the Homeopathic Choice

Patients' perceptions of homeopathy vary depending on their personal experiences and their socioeconomic condition. Those who can afford a consultation with a good allopathic doctor, outside the IMSS system, will usually consult that doctor for a diagnosis, but they often turn later to a homeopath for treatment. People also turn to homeopaths for relief from fevers, infections, digestive problems, diabetes, *los nervios* (nerves), and to treat alcoholism and smoking-related ailments. Children's diseases are often related to malnutrition, especially among those who live in the Cerro del Cuatro, a poorer area south of Polanco. Normally patients do not speak of curing themselves with homeopathy, but instead, curing themselves with *chochitos* (granules).[35] The common perception is that homeopathic remedies do no harm, whereas allopathic medicines are often criticized for relieving one symptom but creating another.

Nati, one of the daughters of Don Jesús (see Chapter 2) and Diana finished her course at the University of Guadalajara and is now working as a consultant researcher at home. She has been combining different remedies for rheumatoid arthritis, from which she suffers. (Many others in Polanco also combine homeopathic and allopathic remedies with *remedios caseros* [home remedies].)[36] She often goes to Dr. Consuelo, but still sees her private doctor. Like others who can afford to consult good allopathic practitioners, she is positive about homeopathy:

I have always been with a private doctor, but I have also been with the naturopath, but I could not carry on with him because it felt worse. I suffer from rheumatoid arthritis. My hands and arms are sometimes especially painful. I have also taken *los chochitos* because I have faith/trust in them, and I also use the teas that my mother knows because they use them in her rancho. When I took *the chochitos,* I was also taking vitamins and other things. I go to the homeopath because I believe in her, but in the end I go to my doctor.

Even those who cannot afford to see a private doctor, and who turn to homeopathy as a last resort, often express a positive opinion.[37] Often they have tried allopathy, but their bodies have developed iatrogenic diseases. The cost of a homeopathic consultancy is one of the reasons people choose it, but it is not the only one. The choice also implies a patient's ability to evaluate it in terms of other medical practices, indicating a dimension of trust and belief in homeopathy, and a sense of its comparative value and worthiness.

The consultancies of Dr. Consuelo and Dr. Magda in Santa Magdalena are much less expensive than those of Dr. Samuel and Dr. Diego. Doña Eva brings her mother to Consuelo for diabetes checkups because at the clinic they tell her nothing is wrong, even though she often feels dizzy and weak. She used to go to Dr. Samuel when he consulted in the Parish of the Anunciación, but now he is too expensive for her. Dr. Consuelo's and Dr. Magda's consultancies are unique in Polanco because, having had their practice in the parish for more than six years and charging affordable prices, they have developed long-term relationships with patients. Many patients come to visit Dr. Consuelo not only when they need homeopathic remedies, but also when they need to talk about their personal problems. In contrast, male homeopaths (who, in Polanco, charge more) are visited less often for advice on personal problems. Male homeopaths prefer to be perceived as doctors who will find the right cure rather than as advisers on human concerns, even if this is not what always happens. Obviously, gender shapes the relationship between patient and homeopath.

Personal counseling is one element that distinguishes homeopathic treatment from the allopathic methods used by the IMSS, whose doctors have less and less time to spend with patients. The therapeutic dimension of counseling, which allows the patient to be heard by a homeopath, is one reason why people have turned to this form of alternative medicine. Many have a need to be listened to while expressing tensions, fears, and problems, and the popularity of counseling suggests that there is much to be said for this new forum for seeking advice on one's own or a family member's health. In this respect, alternative practitioners are sought out for reasons similar to those given for consulting curanderos. The resulting dialogue, especially with female homeopaths, can become for some patients an important means of *desahogo* (letting go).

Whenever I asked patients what they thought los chochitos to be, they associated them with natural remedies such as herbs. In fact, they had no general understanding about the way in which homeopathy works, although they knew it was different from conventional prescription medicine. They see it as causing less harm and being more natural, indicating that their perception of differences between medical systems is not at the level of theoretical principle, but at the level of choice and practical use (Mahar Higgins 1975).

Patients believe that having faith in homeopathic remedies is essential for recovery. They say they use homeopathy "because it works," and because they have faith in it. For patients, homeopathic practice merges effects and causes: it functions because people have faith in it, but they have faith in it because it functions. It is a practical faith, and a faithful practice. Nevertheless, not all who seek treatment are healed. Isabel, the mother of Antonia (an active member of the health group) and Alejandro (a young sculptor and a leader in the Organización de Colonos Independientes de Polanco) — has suffered from los nervios for a long time. Her husband has been rather careless in fulfilling his family obligations, and she has had to provide for him and their six children. After developing migraine headaches as well as kidney and back pain, she tried homeopathy for a little while, but without results. "I do not use the chochitos any more," she said. "I do not know, but I do not have faith, and if someone does not have faith in them, they do not work. Probably I did not trust the doctor so much." For many patients, it seems, their attitudes, and not the remedies, are the most important part of the healing process. The science of the doctor is seen as a form of guesswork, and the result of treatment depends not so much on the remedy but on the doctor's ability to diagnose what is wrong *(atinarle)*. The figure of the doctor and his or her "divinatory" guessing are important for the patients who chose homeopathic treatment.

Most homeopaths who are uncertain about a remedy will look it up in a reference manual. However, in Polanco they do not like to do that in front of patients because they feel that it may make the patient think their knowledge is inadequate. To avoid having to consult the manual, Dr. Antonio and Dr. Diego have put a list of the major remedies under the glass covers of their desks. Remedies are listed with the number codes used by the ground-floor pharmacy. In this case an element of the "oracle"—the list of remedies—is disguised to enhance the professional side of homeopathic practice.[38] However, the vital element for patients is not the objective process induced by the remedy at a biological level, but the faith and trust that he/she has in the remedy and in the figure of the homeopath who prescribes it. In this respect, there is an interesting parallel between the figure of the homeopath and the curandero in people's perception, which could be a rich field for further research. Dr. Diego, for instance, reported a case of a middle-aged man in Polanco who asked to see the "ñomeopata" (a mispronunciation). At the end of the consultancy, he revealed his surprise to the homeopath, because he had expected the room to be adorned with the candles, feathers, and amulets typically used by curanderos. The patient was surprised to discover that Dr. Diego practiced in an environment similar to that of a conventional doctor. When Dr. Diego described his patient's puzzlement at his discovery, he was proud to be seen as a doctor.

In conclusion, even if people in Polanco still seek medical treatment from hospitals and private doctors, they are also exploring other possibilities ranging from the self-help methods of medicina popular, to curanderismo and alternative medicines. Different experiences and interpretations of selfhood embrace these different and overlapping medical domains. The ways in which practitioners represent their work and value those of others reveal some of the politics of identity of a modernity project now bordering on a postmodern condition, which some would call a later stage of modernity. Along with a diversification of medical practice, there has been a financially related constriction in patient choices, and an increased commodification of and competition for medical provisions. That bordering, once again, is indicating a way in which a modernity project is vernacularly opened up and transformed at a local level.

The Emergent and the Residual through Medical Domains

In this chapter I have focused on the different forms of health care that offer alternatives to the allopathic medicine provided by institutional bodies, private doctors, and pharmacies. But although allopathic medicine is, quantitatively, the major form of medicine used in Polanco, faith in its result is not increasing for several reasons, notably the poor service given by medical institutions, the patronizing relationship between doctors and patients, and the cost of prescription medicine. Urbanization, in this respect, has resulted in an increasing coexistence and commodification of competing medical practices.

This diversification, and especially the increased use of alternative medicine, can be seen as part of a project of modernity. Some homeopathic practitioners subscribe to a scientific style, while homeopathy is associated by patients with a "traditional" medical practice (like curanderismo) that can be re-inscribed as an emergent form (Williams 1977). Homeopathic practice can be seen as a logical progression from religious healing and certain forms of self-help medicine, but it is also chosen because allopathic treatments are not working or are becoming too expensive. Homeopathy is thus an emergent form because it combines elements of a dominant allopathic model as well as elements of "traditional" medical practice.

People have been turning to different non-allopathic medical practices—defined as alternative medicine by both the members involved in the Vidasana group and by homeopaths—which identify quite different allocations of responsibility in illness. The etiologies held by promotores, women of the Vidasana group, curanderos, homeopaths, and patients reveal similarities and differences. Some members of the Vidasana group, the curandero, and people in the traditional Church see a relationship between sickness and sin. The case of the Vidasana group is an example of one way of dealing with disease. Some of its members stress the power of the divine and the role of personal consciousness in the healing process; others focus on the pragmatic results and sharing the knowledge that helps them cope with everyday health issues. The organizers often emphasize shifts in perception of illness and the body. The body comes to be a sign, an expression of interrelation within a socially constituted body of humans, and pain, illness, and sin are still individually felt but are also viewed as an expression of the body as society. Pain and sickness become a language through which the promotores transmit their view of the world—one that women may assimilate or resist. People's resistance is manifest in their professed "lack of understanding" of the organizers' explanations, and their emphasis on pragmatic results rather than etiological explanations.

Even if some group members tend to make self-deprecating remarks, these women also find in group participation an opportunity for increased self-worth, and also a chance to socialize. But they may also have to face gossip—especially if a group splits up—and they have to struggle with their husbands to carve out time away from their household duties. Those who express traditional religious views tend to believe illness is related to personal misconduct or someone else's evil (for example, Don Eduardo and some of his patients). However, in all cases—the Vidasana members, the curandero, and the traditional Church—illness is a potential source of redemption, even if the practice of the curandero is denigrated by people who belong to both new and traditional Churches.

If sin and redemption are crucial themes of the medical practices enumerated above, science and faith are central to the practice of homeopathy. In Polanco, homeopaths draw upon a tension, or distinction, between science and faith, but their patients do not recognize such polarization. Patients' choice of homeopathic remedies depends on their access to good allopathic doctors, and on their faith in the figure of the homeopath and his/her diagnosis, rather than on distinguishing and making a conscious choice between medical systems (Mahar Higgins 1975; Stoner 1986). Most homeopaths in Polanco practice in an allopathic way, and perceive a continuity between homeopathy and allopathy. Their aim in practicing allopathy is to diversify their skills and acquire more clients. Patients, in contrast, experience a continuity between homeopathy and traditional healing practices based on notions of faith in the remedy and the giver of the remedy. There is also evidence of a parallel between the figure of the homeopath and the curandero—an interesting theme deserving further research.

Thus, traditional explanations of diseases, centered on personal sin and the evil eye, coexist with political explanations that blame disease on selfish rich people and the structure of society. Scientific explanations compete with aspects of faith and trust in homeopathic practice, and with curanderos' practice. But this coexistence is not without tensions. Curanderos and alternative practitioners alike compete for patients, and the competition leads to claims of scientific competence by homeopaths. Commodification of alternative medicine is clearly well on the way.

Tensions between the distinct social constituencies that embrace specific medical and healing etiologies show how the politics of modernity in urban Mexico emerge from intersecting religious and medical fields. Once again the politics of modernity embraces both traditional and modern practices by continuously re-inscribing what is traditional and, in this case, scientific, via situated agency. So a tension between tradition and modernity is not simply part of a a meta-narrative of a linear, social development, as functionalist readings of migration in urban Mexico have suggested. It is a struggle that involves the empowerment of situated subjects, as well as medical institutions in the process of healing and curing. Moreover, a postmodern (or late modern) approach to the practice of alternative medicine suggests that a vernacular modernity incorporates practices that challenge, from within, modernity itself.

Finally, a relationship between the body, urbanization, and society emerges through the creative tensions in a local, urban articulation of modernity. This relationship brings together different aspects of traditional and modern health practices in the process of curing and healing the body: the body of social and spiritual relations and the individual, somatic body.

CHAPTER 5

Becoming a Mujercita

Rituals, Fiestas, and Religious Discourses

Love is a smoke made for the fumes of sighs,
Being purged, a fire sparkling in lovers' eyes,
Being vexed, a sea nourished with lover's tears.
What is it else?

William Shakespeare, *Romeo and Juliet*

The work of imagination and its transformation of everyday cultural practices is an important feature of modernity. Falling in love and courtship can be a great work of imagination and transformation. One day in her small hairdresser's shop a young woman, Elsa, recalled the day she celebrated her fifteenth birthday with a major fiesta in the village where her parents and husband are from: "I felt fulfilled, and it is better than the wedding celebration because you are innocent about many things, and now I see all the good and bad. . . . At the fifteenth birthday celebration, you are more fulfilled because you do not see what awaits you." Elsa had already found that being married was very different from that time, and that she was no longer the same. Memories of the ritual and her later married life evoke an understanding of the loss of a dream, but also a sense of life's completion.

By paying attention to the work of imagination, including fantasies, and its enactment in popular, ritualized experience, I want to draw some connections between personhood, gender identity, and the unfolding of life cycles. In this chapter I focus on young women's fifteenth-birthday celebrations and show why the quinceañera has become such an important ritual in creating female identity in Mexican low-income neighborhoods. Both the fiesta and the preceding mass, which together constitute the ritual, embody a process of female self-becoming in which not only continuity, but also discontinuities take place (Crapanzano 1992: 262)—and also public recognition of a girl's and her family's social empowerment.

I have chosen to analyze this particular ritual in detail since, whether it is celebrated or not, it plays an important role in the construction of gender subjectivity and sexuality and demonstrates the interplay between residual and emergent cultural forms.[1] It is also important in the reproduction and transformation of symbolic capital betyween generations, and it reveals some of the tension between urban life and the culture of the pueblos. These dynamics offer a further understanding of the reproduction of prisms of belonging in terms of a contested arena of experience and appropriation of knowledge representation which needs to be understood within the particular history of the colonia popular Polanco. This ritual reveals a broader tension between modernity and its imaginative reinterpretations. The ritual is about the female body, which on one hand is inscribed as a sign of a reproduction of religious and social integrity, while on the other, its phenomenological and embodied dimensions point to imagination and desire for female individualization and differentiation.

The specific ritual of the quinceañera marks the beginning of a phase in a girl's life that will be completed upon her wedding celebration. This period is identified as a time of *ilusión*, or dream;[2] it is a time when representations of the nature of sexual relations and life differ sharply from the "reality" of life after marriage. The ritual embodies an experience of "suspended disbeliefs" about what life will be like after marriage. The consciousness of this reality is suspended and replaced by a dream about marriage—both the reality and the dream are positions constitutive of a multiplicity of gender representations that coexist rather than being mutually exclusive.[3] It has been observed, in fact, that in Latin America, gender imagery is composed of multivocal, evocative experiences and is a symbolic reproducer of social inequalities (Melhuus and Stølen 1996). However, motivations for celebrating the ritual of the quinceañera, and for *not* celebrating it, are important for an understanding of its contextual meaning. The following case histories show how decisions about whether or not to celebrate a feast for a girl's fifteenth birthday, and on what scale, depends on a family's religious beliefs, its status in the neighborhood, the family's attitudes about girls' education and training, and also the negotiation of female attributes between clerical and lay agents within and between families.

The Catholic discourse of the Comunidades Eclesiales de Base challenges existing values attached to traditional rituals as far as the balance between religious celebration and popular fiestas is concerned. Priests have introduced a collective Mass in place of individual celebrations of girls' birthdays, and they have criticized the spending of money on these fiestas as aspects of consumerism and family "protagonism" (in the sense of wanting to be a protagonist, over and above others and at the center of attention). As discussed further below, however, the CEBs' discourse tends to privilege the message of the ritual over its performance. And as I have already discussed, it privileges objectification of reality over the sensory, personal/subjective, and family experiences emphasized in the traditional Church and in the charismatic movement.

The language used by priests who are inclined toward the CEBs regarding this celebration points to a particular construction of gender subjectivity based on de-gendering the person in order to achieve humanity. This is mirrored in the language of "defense of human rights" used in Guadalajara during the recent development of civic and religious movements. Extreme conservative civil-religious groups such as the Fuerza de Alianza Opinión Pública have been defending human rights of fetuses against abortion, with a clear idea of female subjectivity. Meanwhile, the CEBs, influenced by the Zapatista rebellion in Chiapas, have been advocating defense of indigenous people's rights to be treated as human and legitimate political actors (De la Torre 1998). But they have not particularly engaged on gender-specific issues.

Through case studies, this chapter analyzes the ritual of the quinceañera on three different levels: the form and content it assumes in the discourse of the CEBs; the exegesis of the religious and sexual symbolism connected with the celebration as part of a process of gender and family identity; and finally, through a more detailed contextual analysis of this exegesis through comparative case studies. Such analyses reveal that the ritual's symbolism is not fixed. Rather, different aspects of its symbolic potential are stressed depending on a girl's family relations and status, as well as the negotiation of gender identity. And these in turn shape a gendered subjectivity (Goddard 1996: 18).

The Establishment of the Quinceañera Celebration

The custom of celebrating a girl's fifteenth birthday is widespread in Mexican society. It consists of a mass celebrated in the church in order to give thanks to God, followed by a fiesta. The size of the party varies according to the means of the family and the godparents. This celebration was originally a feast celebrated by upper- and upper-middle-class families, but it is now common among lower sectors of the population, too. In certain contexts in Polanco, deciding not to celebrate the feast even if having the means to do so, or, conversely, being unable to celebrate it for economic reasons, can be read as signs of distinction or difference, indicating high or low family status.

The origins of the quinceañera feast are unknown to people in Polanco. There is no recollection of such a feast in accounts of the past by old women. Middle-aged women remember that daughters of rich families in their villages of origin did celebrate the feast, but it was a custom only of the *gente de dinero* (rich people). Women younger than forty who were brought up in the city may have celebrated their fifteenth birthdays, but it was usually a small family gathering without a real fiesta afterward, and no special dress was bought or made for the occasion.[4] In recent years, the celebration has gone out of fashion among the upper- and upper-middle classes in Guadalajara. Girls prefer to celebrate their birthdays either at a disco or with a trip abroad, as do those living in Mexico City (Lomnitz and Pérez Lizaur 1987: 166, 167). The fifteenth-birthday celebration was originally celebrated as a ball—a girl's presentation to high society. The symbology used in the feast recalls elements of European culture (for example, waltzes, performances of classical music, maids of honor, and pages). The assimilation of fashionable European trends into Mexican society can be traced back to the dictatorship of Porfírio Díaz (1876–1911), a time when Mexico's indigenous heritage was played down in favor of European and North American culture.

The first reports of quinceañeras appeared in the *Sociales* (social events) section of Guadalajara newspapers in the early 1940s. There are no church records since the ritual is not a sacrament. The fiesta was celebrated in the house and was an occasion for making family connections manifest. It reinforced family status and social cohesion among those of a specific class. Nowadays, press reports still present an ideal model of the celebration with profuse commentary on the family's status, the importance of the guests, the beauty of the girl's outfit, and the luxury of the party or of the premises where the event takes place.

This standard is unattainable by families in low-income neighborhoods in Guadalajara, but still constitutes the standard referred to by the girls and their families.

These ideals are also acquired through mass media and soap operas. There is an important area of analysis, which I cannot fully discuss here, focusing on how soap operas are a primary means through which images of lifestyles and consumption patterns become familiar to the low-income population. It has been argued that they can have a creative function since they allow a manipulation of hierarchical gender roles (Vellinga 1986), and can represent a resistance to so-called happy representations of traditional female roles (Ang 1985: 123). In the unfolding of the narrative, those happy states are never easily achieved and are thus continuously deferred. However, it is through soap operas that dominant class values are transformed into hegemonic ones and acquired as desirable styles and patterns of consumption for many in low-income neighborhoods (reflected, for instance, in the choice of the girl's dress or the ritual paraphernalia for the feast celebration). The consumption of soap opera indicates an area of manipulation of a dominant ideology, as well as the formation of a language that shapes the interaction between different cultural groups (Lomnitz-Adler 1992: 27). This media consumption is a hegemonic cultural space, strategic for the "reconciliation of the masses and reabsorption of social differences"(Barbero 1993: 139).

The message that CEB-inclined priests have attached to the catechism of this ritual in the colonia is directed against the ideal form of celebration, which is associated with individualist consumption and protagonism. In the catechism class that takes place in the Parish of the Santa Magdalena a few days before the celebration, some of these issues are discussed and developed. Themes touched upon in the catechism revolve around the physical and psychological changes that girls experience during this period, and the different means at their disposal for becoming active agents in the church community. The girls are taught by Nubia, a female catechist, that a similar feast was celebrated in the time of the Toltecs and Aztecs. Nubia stresses that at that time, girls who undertook the celebration were ready to be chosen by a man of the tribe and taken to the mountain. Soon after, they became pregnant for the sake of community reproduction.

However, the 'ilusión de los quince' (the dream of the fifteen-year-old) is described as beyond these Mexican origins. In the catechism, references are made to similar feasts celebrated at the beginning of the twentieth century in Jewish communities, and to the balls intended to introduce girls into society celebrated by the upper-middle-class Europeans in the nineteenth century. In this allusive way the subject of sexuality is introduced to the catechism class. The element of continuity with the past, through the celebration of the feast, is related to a natural female sexual status. An invention of tradition can be said to be taking place. However, that continuity is not traced via the girl's own mother or grandmother. The catechist, and some of the girls, are aware that older female relatives have not celebrated this feast. Nonetheless, the celebration becomes a connection with the ancestors, a link with the past that is acted out in the present. The prisms of belonging are often embedded in a mythology of the past which, in order to exist, have to be disembodied from direct kinship genealogy. In order to be possibly imagined, a mythology cannot often incorporate the idiosyncrasy that the present holds.

The Celebration: A Wedding without a Husband

The ritual of the quinceañera involves learning about gender identity and the construction of the female body. It does not correspond exactly to Van Gennep's concept of a rite of passage (Gennep [1909] 1977). Nor is it a process whose fluidity is counterposed to a static social structure (Turner 1974). While it is constituted by moments of separation, liminality, and reincorporation in the stages of the mass and the fiesta, the ritual is not obligatorily undertaken by all the girls in Polanco. They acquire the status of being a woman even if they do not celebrate it. The ritual does mark a passage into a socially recognized female status, because girls who have undergone it start to dress and talk in a different way, as well as change their attitudes and their body language toward the opposite sex. The ritual indicates ways in which a girl's image is constructed by the different actors involved; it also shapes the girl's self-perception and creates forms of social control over the female body.

The rite of passage starts with the mass. The girl arrives at the entrance of the church accompanied by her parents. She wears a ball dress, preferably pink or peach. White is not fashionable, probably because it is the color of real weddings, but some girls do wear it. The ideal style of the dress is nineteenth century, with big round skirts, voile, embroidery, and high-heeled shoes. Many families in Polanco cannot afford this type of dress, so girls choose less expensive versions, often homemade by close relatives. Dresses are seldom bought in the specialized shops in the city center. The girl's hair is often carefully coiffed with various trinkets such as small artificial flowers.

The girl, her parents, godparents, and *chambelanos* (male chaperons) wait for the priest to come to the entrance of the church.[5] Then the girl, on her godfather's arm, walks in a procession toward the altar following the priest, while the chambelano walks just behind her. Tradition calls for the girl to be surrounded by seven *damas* (ladies) and seven chambelanos, all dressed in the same way, but this is hardly ever the case in Polanco celebrations. Whenever possible, there is at least one chambelano. There may be a correlation between the ideal number of damas, chambelanos, and the celebrated girl. Fourteen people (seven chambelanos and seven damas) could stand for the fourteen years, while the quinceañera herself represents the fifteenth year. The stress is therefore on singularity: she represents the odd number, the individuality, everything that stands out unmatched.

After the girl is led by her close relatives to the altar, she is left alone to receive the mass. This part of the celebration can be interpreted as a liminal stage in which the girl is recognized as a newly born *mujercita* (little woman) both in the eyes of God and those close to her. When the mass is over, the girl leaves her bouquets of fresh flowers for the Virgin behind the altar. She then leaves the church arm-in-arm with her chambelano. Although a quinceañera may have a secret boyfriend before her fifteenth birthday, the chambelano is usually not the same person. Normally he is a friend of the same age, or preferably a few years older, but never younger than she is.

Being handed over to the chambelano is the first stage of the girl's reincorporation into the community after the ritual. The chambelano behaves very differently from the way he behaves in everyday life. He dresses up in a suit and tie, is very kind to the quinceañera, and often arrives for the mass with flowers for her—acts which in another public context, at that age, might be interpreted as showing a lack of masculinity. The power relation between the quinceañera and her male counterpart in this ritual shows that she has the leading role, especially in the second part of the ritual, the fiesta. Like the separation, the reincorporation takes place via a protecting male, whose role is to defend the girl from mixing with unfamiliar boys.

The quinceañera's movements toward the male parallel the handing over of the bride to her groom during the wedding celebration—which will bring to a close the cycle begun by the quinceañera celebration. This handing over is symbolized by the *muertito,* a little drama that takes

FIGURE 6. A quinceañera in front of the altar of Santa
Magdalena. (Photograph by the author.)

place in some wedding fiestas in low-income areas as well as in villages
of origin. First the groom is taken away by his male friends and stripped
of some of his clothes. He is then given back to the bride, who will have
to help him to dress again. The muertito represents how marriage ends
the time of indulgences — the time of *parrandas* — typical of a bachelor
lifestyle, and reinforces the image that the groom will be subject to the
exclusive care of his bride.

Most of the quinceañera fiestas that I witnessed in Polanco took place
at home, but I was also able to witness a few celebrations in the pueblos
of Totatiche (in Los Altos de Jalisco) and San Cristóbal de Chapala (see
Chapter 3). The phases of the ritual are always similar: food is given to
the guests after the opening dances, with the godparents served first.
Young guests come to the party especially to dance and drink. The quinceañera dances to the opening music, first with her godfather and then

with her father, or her maternal uncle if her father is absent. A typical passage of the ritual is a special dance with the chambelano and, if present, all of the chambelanos and damas together.

The quinceañera often choreographs a waltz routine that includes one or more chambelanos. Some girls rehearse for up to three months to learn the steps and to acquire enough confidence to perform in front of a large number of friends and relatives. In her performance the quinceañera often directs the movement of the chambelano, publically leading her male counterpart. When asked why they dance a waltz, quinceañeras reply that it is somehow elegant, and that a quinceañera without a waltz is not a real quinceañera. If the music was a cumbia rhythm, there would be no difference between a quinceañera celebration and any other fiesta.

Performance of the waltz is a powerful emotional experience. The girl stands out on her own in the eyes of people, and fear of failing and appearing clumsy are recurrent concerns. Nube recalled, "I was very nervous about the waltz coming out fine. I was afraid about forgetting the steps, of getting embarrassed in front of many people, but never in my life will I forget this moment." Although this dance (which I discuss further below) is often interpreted by the clergy in Polanco as a mere act—a form without a content, for the quinceañera it is an experience of a new ability to perform in public. In this case, a gender performance and embodiment of experience is read as a symbolic act, creating a tension between embodiment and representation.

The ritual also allows the expression of emotions connected with a new self-identity. In fact, the girl's tension usually fades as the dance goes on and she beomes more self-confident. As the fiesta continues, her parents, as well as her older brothers, will make sure that guests who are drinking are kept under control so as to avoid unwanted quarrels before the fiesta is over, which is usually around midnight. Throughout the celebration, it is clear that the nervousness, excitement, and sense of fulfillment that the ritual and fiesta can generate are a bodily and emotional experience for the girls involved.

Religious Discourses: The Changing Form and Content of Traditional Rituals

Anthropological readings of rituals as means of maintaining authority, social control, and social cohesion are very similar to CEB attitudes toward traditional rituals. The absence of, or lessened emphasis upon, certain rituals provides revealing evidence of different group identities within a community. In Polanco, for example, Jehovah's Witnesses do not celebrate quinceañeras or rituals associated with the Virgin. This imagery of the virgin is weaker among non-Catholic fundamentalist groups. In Polanco, as in many other colonias in Guadalajara, there is a relatively large community of Jehovah's Witnesses (Fortuny 1991), and young women's attitudes toward childbearing are different from those of non-Jehovah's Witnesses.

Carla, a girl in her early twenties who was born and raised in a pueblo in Hidalgo, is now living with a Jehovah's Witness family in Polanco. Her sense of personal worth clearly arises from her dedication to Jehovah. She does not envisage herself having children because she believes the time of the apocalypse is coming soon, and she feels the need to dedicate herself completely to Jehovah's cause. She is in love with a boy who assists in the temple. She would like to marry him and go to train in the Jehovah's Witness center of El Belén in Mexico City. "The world is changing," she said. "Now is no longer the time to have children. Instead it is necessary to build up something in the name of Jehovah. The love of a child, I know, is a strong spiritual [experience]. It can be there, and it would not do me any harm, but one feels freer to serve Jehovah without children." Her goal is to marry: "To be fulfilled as a woman is to be a wife. The Bible says 'a man will leave his father and mother and he will settle down.' A wife must act both as mother and father towards her husband—not by supporting him materially, but by sharing his problems."

From Carla's perspective, the importance of her life's project outweighs her desire for motherhood. This raises the point, which I can only mention here, of how membership in fundamentalist religious groups generates changes in female self-perception, and how their discourses impinge on the construction of female identity and life cycles. This often occurs partly in opposition to, but also coinciding with, a dominant Catholic discourse.

To a certain extent, the CEBs also have an understanding of religious rituals and popular celebrations which is distinct from more traditional Catholic interpretations. Their goal, according to Padre Nemo, is to use the symbols of popular religion, "and give them a new interpretation of their real meaning." In other words, the parishes' political goal is to infuse traditional and long-established rituals with new and, in their view, truthful content. One celebration that has been thus transformed by the Comunidades is that of the Virgin of Guadalupe, where, in sermons and social drama, the Virgin becomes an Amazon helping to lib-

erate the enslaved, rather than remaining the passive listener and consoler of human sadness portrayed in the images of the traditional
Church. The Virgin is a polysemic symbol in Mexico, and her imagery
can stand both for suffering which gives strength and legitimacy to
women (Melhuus 1992: 159) and for redemption of the community,
since the power of giving birth and caring for the well-being of children
can be seen as balancing out male political self-interest and corruption
(Martin 1990: 486).

The CEBs' new metaphor of the Virgin fighting for social justice
imports a new sense of resistance to a traditional symbol. Moreover, the
fiestas promoted by the Comunidades focus on the communal gathering
rather than on the staged presentations, the food stalls, and the music.
The mass also is used to carry forward some evangelization on social
and political injustice while less money is spent on diversions associated
with those celebrations, such as fireworks and fairs. Some believers,
though, object to these changes, saying that the fiestas lack the ambience
they had back in their pueblo or rancho. Such believers often do not
participate so actively as before, and may stop participating altogether.
Consequently, the dismissal of traditional devices typical of village fiestas, and the introduction of new, socially and politically oriented content in the celebration of the Mass challenge the traditional Catholic
division between the mundane, the political, and the religious, and raise
questions about what a traditional celebration is, and who controls it.

Celebration of the quinceañera in Polanco raises issues about the new
content of traditional rituals. Since the quinceañera is not one of the
seven Catholic sacraments and is a relatively new ritual, its interpretation
is an open field. Catholic teaching stresses girls' "closeness to nature,"
the purity of their bodies at the Mass providing a chance for them to
honor God for their having arrived "intact" at such a point in life; moreover the Mass also stresses the duty to take a right path and become part
of the community by participating in different activities such as children's catechism, youth theater, choirs, and Comunidades.[6] Failure to
participate in such community activities is interpreted as a lack of ma-
turity and an inability to accept the responsibility which is appropriate
to a mature Catholic person. The model of personhood imbued in such
evangelization is that of a preexisting unity that can be reachieved—a
fully conscious human instead of a model focused on specific gender
aspects and specificity.

Since the arrival of Padre Nemo and Padre Rodolfo, the quinceañera
celebration in Polanco has taken place in groups, but this communal
form of celebration has created tensions between personal and family

empowerment, and community identity. Some families in Polanco have decided to celebrate the quinceañera mass in a parish outside Polanco. In Santa Magdalena, all the quinceañeras whose birthdays fall in the same month go to mass on the last Saturday of that month. Padre Rodolfo and Padre Jorge, emphasize in their sermons that the mass reaffirms the principle of the baptism as a renewed initiation into the life of the Catholic Church.[7] A former priest in Santa Magdalena, Padre Hermilio, points out the problem the Church faces in understanding and interpreting a new ritual that acquires importance in people's lives. However he, like the other priests in Polanco, emphasizes a search for meaning, stressing the word above the act: "There is also—and we must not forget it—a mentality which is not easy to change. It looks for the celebration without catechism, the act without words. . . . The majority of the people want the mass as a step in order to celebrate the fiesta, which is sometimes reduced to an expression of consumerism and of a materialist society" (Cárdenas González 1987: 122, my translation).

The polarization between a meaningful act and a fiesta for its own sake is drawn in the catechism used by the Comunidades. In fact, Padres Rodolfo, Nemo, and Hermilio believe that the mass for the fifteenth birthday entails a transformation of girls' consciousness and focus of action from familial and personal to communal levels. Padre Nemo and Padre Rodolfo affirm that people need to overcome the individualistic/egoistic tendencies which create protagonism. This celebration—to them—becomes an opportunity for strengthening a sense of community rather than an occasion for family status differentiation. In the words of the priests, protagonism is associated with individualism, urban atomization, and materialist culture.

The resistance of part of the population to communal celebration suggests that additional issues are at stake. Priests and their associates understate the importance of the mass and the fiesta as experiences in the process of the creation of female self-identity. The fifteenth-birthday celebration is the girl's special day, and as Padre Hermilio said, "If the priests do not call her by name, it is not her mass." Naming is one key practice in the creation of self-identity, especially in the public space outside the field of kinship relations (Cohen 1994). Naming gains even greater significance in a culture where a girl's name is very rarely used when speaking about her. In Polanco, a girl may be referred to as "the daughter of the woman who sells chickens," "the daughter of those who sell tacos," "the daughter of my godfather," and so on, which implies that she is not recognized as a full person in her own right. Her identity is not referred to by first name but in terms of her other attributes, her location in the social space, and the social function of her parents or close senior relatives. This is an important point: a process of individuation and differentiation is taking place. Issues of renewed female responsibilities and accountability, discussed further in the following chapter, emerge out of subtle incidences of individuation.

The celebration of this feast also highlights a tension between a young woman's desire for freedom and her family's control over her. On one hand, the girl is the center of the feast and expects subsequently to receive more freedom and independence. However, this is rarely the case, and often family control actually becomes greater. Hence tensions highlighted in this celebration are not only about religious acts, but also about family identity and communal celebration. As a form of differentiation of family status, the fiestas constitute an important moment for a girl's self-identity and that of her family. Through the CEBs' evangelization, people are taught that fiestas involve "unnecessary" financial commitments, but many families spend considerable amounts on quinceañeras despite such criticism.

Becoming a Mujercita: The Time of *la Ilusión*

I shall now analyze the symbolism of the fifteenth-birthday celebration in light of the heterogeneity of several case histories. Rituals bring about experiences in the world rather than merely representing them. They are performances both at an utterance level—verbal statements themselves constitute action (Austin 1975)—and at a bodily level—as performative imagination, movement, and orientation in an interpersonal space (Parkin 1992: 16). Moreover, symbolic and hermeneutic interpretations of rituals have to be understood in the context of power relations between the agents involved (Foster 1990).

In everyday conversation, the fifteenth year is referred to as the most glorious for a girl. Phrases such as: "parece de quince" ("you look very well"), "te pusieron como una de quince" (literally "they made you up like a fifteen year-old," meaning that the person has recovered completely from a disease) identify this age as a physically powerful stage. In the imagery used by both young and older women, the fifteenth year represents a period of dreamed possibilities, *la ilusión de los quince*. As Nubia said, "You are like blossoming flowers. . . . What will shine is not your dress, but your soul, the purity of your soul. . . . Now you can start really to be somebody." It is a time when girls hope to enjoy themselves before having to assume responsibility for their own family. The expression "la ilusión" is used to refer to this time of life by women of various ages, but it can also be used by fathers in reference to their daughters. This period continues throughout an engagement, so it revolves around a fantasy of what life, and especially love, can be. On the other hand, the reality of life after marriage, as discussed in the next chapter, is often disillusion.

In Chicano communities this condition of liminality is closely identified with the tension embodied in girls who are available for courtship but not yet desirable as an object of sexual passion (Horowitz 1993: 267). The quinceañera celebration coincides with the acknowledgement by the family (especially the father) that a daughter is ready to have a sweetheart (if she does not have one already). The father gives her permission, the *permiso de puerta,* to see her boyfriend on the threshold of the house for a set period of time during the evening. The frequency and length of these visits depend on the strictness of the father, and the willingness of the mother to cover for daughters when they bend or break the rules.

A girl is expected to fulfill family duties well before her fifteenth birthday and already knows house duties. The quinceañera ritual can mark a transformation of appearance (as in the use of makeup and fashionable clothes, for example), but that is part of an ongoing process that started well before the age of fifteen. In this sense, the quinceañera celebration embodies a process of transformation rather than being a clear-cut step from one irreversible stage to another. In fact, during the fiesta the quinceañera may receive presents ranging from perfumes, tights, and makeup to teddy bears or other cuddly toys that mark a coexistence of childhood and adolescent elements in this age of puberty.

Another noticeable change in a mujercita is her use of language. Some expressions associated with the jargon of street play can no longer be used, and becoming a mujercita is related to the mastery of a language that avoids the use of uncontrolled, youthful expressions. But this control is not perceived as a move away from childhood. One quinceañera named Angelica said, "Now it is necessary to know what one does and why one does it and to be able to decide. But I still feel like a child. We carry childhood within us and we never should lose it. For that reason I like to play with my little sisters."

The extent to which some elements of play and childhood are maintained after the age of fifteen depends on the girl's personality, her relation to the other sex, her role within the family, and also on the degree of family control. In this sense the ritual does not point to a linear evolution but to coexisting, multiple, and sometimes antithetical female aspects, and it does not just imprint a social status on the girl in question, but also brings out the social relations of which she, as a person, is composed (Strathern 1993: 48). Therefore, gender attributes are not just added on to the person but are revealed at different points in time.[8] This revelation is part of the process through which active agents engage in the process of formation of subjectivity.

Some mothers remarked to me that at this age daughters start to be more selfish around their brothers and sisters. They become more helpful in the house, but also start to carve out their own private space, both metaphorically and physically, even if their "territory" is just one corner of a room that is often shared with other sisters. The process of becoming a mujercita also takes place through becoming acquainted with specific female knowledge about such things as changes in bodily shape and female cycles which is not to be shared with men, not even brothers or fathers. The religious message of sexual purity connected to the ritual relates to this body of knowledge.

The mass for a quinceañera is to thank God *de no haber fracasado.* "Fracasar" literally means "to break down" and "break apart." Metaphorically it can signify becoming pregnant and therefore losing virginity, as well as the failing of a relationship. In its first sense, this metaphor reveals that the girl's body is interpreted as an unpenetrated whole. Her purity is a natural one that evokes the transparency of nature. When a girl loses her virginity, she is considered broken, but it is a redeemable state because becoming a mother is valued in itself, whether or not a girl is married (Melhuus 1992: 175). The condition of *fracasada* also highlights the gendered bonds of patriarchal control. As Ruth Behar points out, mothers can become active agents in the maintenance of patriarchal laws of sexual control by objectifying their daughters while subjecting them to a forced marriage, a system of exchange, to redeem an out-of-wedlock pregnancy (Behar 1993: 282–283). Use of the term "fracasado" as part of a patriarchal discourse is generated also through women-to-women relations.

In the quinceañera celebration, through the symbolic values of the elements used in the feast, the ritual constructs an image of female gentleness, beauty, and magic outside of everyday reality. The dress, the hairstyle, the cushions and champagne glasses that she may receive from different godmothers—all refer to dimensions of purity in which both class differences and the evilness (in terms of temptation) of the female body are absent. Many of these items were not exchanged fifteen or twenty years ago. But although a relatively recent introduction, there is now a thriving business in this paraphernalia, as well as an increasing level of exchange between blood and fictive kin.[9]

The fifteenth-birthday celebration, as the beginning of the time of la ilusión, suggests a whole female body celebrated in its integrity, unpenetrated by reality, and protected from penetration so as to enhance the status and reputation of the family (Collier 1986: 101). It is also a contemporary, but not new, attempt to take control over the mystical powers of the female body, connected since Mexican and Spanish colonial times to the powers of menstrual blood and female sexual forces (Behar 1987).

The integrity of a young woman is expected to last until her wedding because sexual intercourse and reproduction are part of that reality associated with the end of a dreamed-of female freedom, and with the subordination of a broken body to family control. But that is not always the case, and there are several single mothers in Polanco. Families react in various ways to pregnancies out of wedlock. If the father of the baby does not want to marry the girl, she is forced to turn to her family. Parents, and fathers especially, may react by having her leave the house while she is pregnant, perhaps sending her to a relative's house. After the birth, however, she is accepted back into family life, her new status as a mother granting her forgiveness. The one condition is usually that she accept considerable limitations on her social freedom.

If for a girl the time of la ilusión is related to ideas of enjoyment and male kindness during courtship, the representation of the time of the reality is characterized by female suffering, male jealousy, and lack of care. Girls of fifteen know that the time of reality is associated with aspects of female suffering and male betrayal—even if they insist that they will marry only a man who will not make life miserable. The experience and imagery associated with the time of la ilusión thus seem to suggest a willing suspension of disbelief rather than belief in the existence of a different kind of gender relation, and it highlights the importance of delaying and withholding in the negotiation of gender positions. It is possible that a girl may indulge in behavior and fantasies in accordance with la ilusión de los quince, and in the eyes of older people, she is not opposing reality but simply deferring it. So, paradoxically, the quinceañera celebration is an experience of self-empowerment, beginning the time of la ilusión, associated with wider freedom, more responsibility, and the possibility of courtship, but also a symbol of control over the female body, and the deferral of the breaking of its integrity.

In the interplay between emergent and residual values, the gendered body can be broken by uncontrolled sexuality at the same time as the social body, as discussed in the previous chapter, can be broken by the mischievousness of human intentions and the lack of social solidarity.

The dynamic of family control and status opened by the quinceañera celebration often creates tensions between individual and familial identity. Weighing the choice of whether or not to invest resources in a feast, especially in families with limited means, is just one example of such tensions. In some people's villages of origin, the feast is celebrated by families hoping to reaffirm their status and their sense of being part of the village, even if the celebrated girl would have preferred to use the money for something else, such as a separate room in the house.

Even if the Catholic symbolism of the quinceañera celebration relates to a girl's virginity, the ritual can be experienced apart from such a meaning. Sometimes the reality of a girl's life is discordant with much of the ritual's symbolic meaning. Such was the case of Tania, a pregnant girl who celebrated her fifteenth birthday and married a few months later. Everyone in the family, as well as the priest, knew about Tania's pregancy, but the celebration took place nonetheless. The feast was celebrated in a lower key than Tania would have expected if she had not been pregnant. The chambelano was her fiancé, and she danced the waltz as would any other quinceañera. She had daydreamed for so long about this event that being pregnant was not enough to prevent it from taking place.

The celebration of the ritual of becoming a mujercita cannot be denied to a girl because she is pregnant, even if unmarried pregnant women should not be celebrated in public, and should not take part in other public rituals. But the experience of being celebrated in the ritual, and the enactment of daydreams, can be stronger than the symbolic message of virginal purity that the ritual embodies in the social and religious context. In this case, the reality of a symbolically broken body coexists with the representation of a time of la ilusión in which the female body is on a symbolic level still unbroken. This coexistence indicates that there is room to maneuver around issues of female sexuality and virginity. Protecting or relinquishing female virginity has been described as a tactic where women are not just passive victims of predatory out-of-wedlock sexual advances, or mere symbols of family honor. Women, through control of their virginity, can leave the family household and establish their own, and they may break accepted codes of behavior for their own advantage (Goddard 1996: 158).

Hence, not merely dreamlike but also real time after marriage can be read as an articulation of values that create meanings out of, and inspire, particular tactics within everyday life. Much of this articulation is at the level of social and personal imagery. The latter is difficult to research using anthropological methods because it is often part of that which is left unsaid. Moore (1994) has stressed that the representative aspect of gender—that is, the imaginative and performative—needs to be re-represented and re-signified through social action such as rituals. This is because the experience of the engendered body often resists social discourse, which imposes a regime of intelligibility of the body itself. The ritual of the quinceañera and the time of la ilusión which the ritual initiates can be understood as imaginative experiences in which gender categories are re-represented and sometimes resisted; they embody fantasies of identity that relate to certain forms of power and agency within and between gendered subjects (Moore 1994: 66). They are articulated in a language of evocation that builds upon and reproduces gender inequalities to a certain degree (Melhuus and Stølen 1996: 271). However, this articulation, when shifted from evocation to re-representation and the appropriation of gender imagery in everyday life, can also become empowering for women (Behar 1993).

In conclusion, the quinceañera fiesta is not a gesture without words, a meaningless or consumptive pattern; it is a real experience of a dream-like time. The Comunidades' emphasis on community rather than on the importance of individual performative acts overlooks the relevance of the drama and performance (Turner 1982) as expressions of distinct goals for specific people (Parkin 1992: 17). The performative aspect becomes central when the quinceañera celebration fails to correspond to its social and religious approved meanings (as in Tania's example) and also explains why many girls decide to celebrate their fifteenth birthdays in parishes outside the colonia, thus opting out of the communal celebration. The celebration, through the emotional experience and the symbolism of the fiesta, the waltz, and the dress, formally introduces girls into a new sexual world, and at the same time defends them from it. But the experience of the ritual cannot be read just at the level of symbolic meaning. It has to be understood through the idiosyncratic aspects of particular sets of social relations.

Celebrating or Not Celebrating

As I have mentioned, not every girl in the colonia celebrates her fifteenth birthday. The decision about whether or not to celebrate has to do with both class and gender identity. When the family is eager to celebrate the daughter's fifteenth birthday, the fiesta can take various forms. The most expensive involves the nuclear family, godparents, and other members of the extended family pooling resources to rent a ballroom. Similar expenses are encountered in fiestas held in the village of origin of one or both of the quinceañera's parents. Opting to celebrate life rituals in the village rather than in Polanco not only informs the community of the status and prestige carried by the migrant family, but also reinforces prisms of belonging on the part of the offspring, even if they were, as is often the case, born in the city. A process of imagination of belonging translates into popular cultural practice via the celebration of the ritual. In these circumstances, the parents may express the wish that one day the quinceañera will marry someone from the village. In other cases, the celebration may take place in the open air, on a farm that a relative or a godfather has put at the disposal of the family. However, in most cases the party is held in the family home, and a stereo system and lighting are rented, or a band is paid to play live music. If the family cannot afford the fiesta, or is not keen on the celebration, the birthday may be celebrated with a generous meal at home among close relatives.

The main reason why some girls celebrate their quinceañera and others do not is economic: the cost varies, but if there is live music, a family will spend close to 1.5 million pesos (equal to about $500 before the 1994 peso devaluation).[10] If a girl's parents can't afford the fiesta on their own, resources are pooled within the extended family. Often godparents help to cover costs by buying the dress or the food, or paying for the music. Financial difficulty is not, however, the only factor that can prevent the celebration from taking place.

Some girls who do not celebrate their fifteenth birthday prefer to spend the money in a different way, such as on a trip to the beach. Others might choose to put the money into savings and eventually buy a car. Choosing not to celebrate a girl's fifteenth birthday in well-off families is a sign of distinction of family status both within the colonia and within the villages of origin. Families such as that of Don Jesús Ortega (see Chapter 2), whose members, both female and male, have achieved a high degree of educational and professional status and who are highly respected within the neighborhood, look down on such a feast. The professional status of the Ortega sisters has put their relationships with men in a different perspective. For this family a quinceañera celebration in Polanco would not have been a sign of distinction because public recognition of the daughters' availability for courtship was not a priority for them at the age of fifteen, but only later, after they had finished their education. A fifteenth-birthday feast would not have improved their status within the community, but would have lowered the family to a social level to which it did not want to belong. The Ortega family's decision could be seen as an attempt at both individual and family emancipation from communal identity. For them, the importance of a personal career has replaced the importance of ritual.

Given this context, the celebration of the quinceañera in Polanco can be interpreted in two ways. It is a demonstration of family status and prestige in the eyes of neighbors and of the branches of the extended family. However, it can also be regarded, by the middle classes especially, as a vulgar celebration that enhances certain aspects of female identity, emphasizing particular patterns of development of female life and sexuality. This is often the case, as observed in other parts of urban Mexico, when improved female education is connected to an older age of marriage and improved socioeconomic status (Levine and Sunderland Correa 1993).

Many girls in low-income colonias populares fantasize about their quinceañera celebration, but by no means all of them. Some are particularly interested in the celebration of the mass, and the holding of a family gathering for such an occasion. Other girls privilege the importance of the fiesta over the experience and content of the mass. Girls who have dropped out of school at an early age and those who are still studying tend to emphasize quite different meanings attached to the ritual. Girls in school are more protected by the family than girls who are already working, and they often have to decide between studying or having a boyfriend (courtship on a regular basis occupies part of every evening). In most cases, girls' freedom of movement after she turns fifteen is reduced because she can see her boyfriend only in the presence of a third person (such as a little brother).

Milena, the fifteen-year-old daughter of Cuca and Juan—two active members of the Movimiento Familiar Cristiano, a relatively traditional Catholic group—had been daydreaming about her quinceañera celebration since she was twelve, and her parents had always encouraged the idea. She had dropped out of school because she was bored, but was not working. Six months before her birthday Milena started to think seriously about it. She looked at dresses, saved up a part of her weekly pocket money, and found a part-time job to help pay for some of the expenses.

Milena had been seeing her boyfriend, who lived two blocks away,

since she turned fourteen. Her parents allowed her to see him, but insisted that they meet in front of the house and that she should not go
to any fiesta with him. Since having a boyfriend, she had dropped other
male friendships. Even her female friendships had been reduced; she
and her boyfriend both considered female gathering a source of unpleas-
ant gossip. For Milena, her fifteenth birthday seemed like the moment
to take the right path: "Up to now I have felt confused. I can be led
astray by friends. But after my fifteenth, I will be able to see what is
more appropriate."

Nubia teaches girls that part of becoming a mujercita includes a new
awareness of male intentions, so that the girls do not let themselves be
manipulated, and they learn to choose. Milena did not trust her boyfriend to take her out on her own before her fifteenth birthday. This
echoes the gender consciousness of the offspring of migrants in comparison to the consciousness imputed to women by Maximiliano (see
his account on the urban experience in Chapter 2), who was brought
up in the rancho. Once again, we can see that coming to the city or
having been brought up in the urban space has specific transformative
effects in the representations and perceptions of gender relations and
individual consciousness.

Milena's case highlights areas of change in male/female relationships.
The saying "Se robó la novia" (he snatched away the girlfriend) is still
used to refer to a boyfriend kidnapping his girlfriend to go and live with
her out of wedlock. Thus, this expression, and the performative act
around it, is part of a style of localism that exists in both the urban
situation as well as in the pueblos and ranchos. However, the way young
women in Polanco talk about this localist style is changing. The implication is that it still exists, but that girls are also in charge, rather than
it being a unilateral decision made by boys for girls. The expression "Se
fueron" (they went) is now also used to show that the couple were
together by mutual consent. Localist styles of acting out gender relations
are challenged by moments of reflection like the one inspired by Milena's
perplexities, but they continue to exist in an urban context.

Like many girls in the colonia, Milena was not sure that the family
could actually afford the celebration until a few weeks before the date.
But eventually, with the help of relatives and godparents, her quinceañera was celebrated, and special guests included some couples from the
Movimiento Familiar Cristiano. The attitude of Milena's mother toward
the celebration was a mixture of pride and worry. Cuca feared that Milena would get married too soon after her fifteenth birthday because she

had already been going out with her boyfriend for a while. Her concern was that "she would stick to the first," making the same mistake as her mother, who regretted having stepped into married life so young and inexperienced.

Milena's power and role within family life changed visibly a few months after her quinceañera. She was more often in charge of the housework, and although she used to play and argue with her younger sister, now she calls her "mi hija" (my daughter), a term of affection also used to mark a status difference.[11] Milena also behaves differently toward her father. She used to hug or kiss him before he left for work, but now she is physically distant with him. She often complains that her brothers do not take her out to fiestas because girls might mistake her for one of their girlfriends.

The case of Sabrina is different. The eldest of Alfonso's four children, she did not consider celebrating her fifteenth birthday with a fiesta. Alfonso, a coordinator of the Comunidades as well as the Movimiento Familiar Cristiano, had to leave his job because of health problems. The household economy is tight, but the children's education is a priority. Sabrina and her parents hope that she will be able to attend the university. Sabrina's parents' experience in the Comunidades made them sensitive to the priority of the mass over the fiesta. Her mother, Elsa, said, "There is no need to spend so much on a fiesta. What is more important is the mass in order to give thanks to God, and to have a small family gathering. There are many people who get into debt in order to have a good fiesta, but it is better to spend the money on schooling." This message was assimilated by the daughter, who asked just to celebrate the mass. She was aware that her father works only part-time, but that her parents were doing their best to support her higher education.

Sabrina never had a secret sweetheart, but after her birthday, she asked her father for permission to date a schoolmate who had asked her out. She clearly stated that she was not going to lose her mind over him. Her energy and efforts were fixed on finishing her current classes and possibly going to university. Instead of spending money on celebrating her quinceañera, she preferred to save up for a small car.

A few weeks before her birthday, Sabrina was surprised when her parents (particularly her father) insisted that they celebrate her fifteenth birthday. Alfonso was aware from his experience in the Comunidades that he did not need to spend a great deal of money, and that other people in the parish would understand. However, Sabrina is the first of his four children, and his only daughter. For Alfonso, it was important that his daughter—toward whom, in Sabrina's words, he is extremely protective and jealous—should celebrate her quinceañera. Her father is very strict with her and justified his insistence on the celebration by stating he wanted his daughter to have a nice memory of her quince, and that, after all, Sabrina is his *consentida* (favorite). In the end Sabrina was delighted to celebrate her quinceañera—even if at home and with reduced costs—because she enjoyed being the center of attention.

The cases of Ester and Julia suggest that a relative prominence of the mass or the fiesta in the quinceañera celebration revolves around greater or weaker family control over the girl's sexual body. Ester has been working since she was ten and now cleans a shop. She is not able to read and write properly, but she appears to be very witty and looks older than she is because she uses makeup and wears tight clothes with con-fidence. Ester was born in a *casa chica*.[12] Since she was young, she has had to find ways to earn money and help her mother, brother, and sisters with the precarious economy of the household. She looks somehow more experienced than her years. She has had a boyfriend since she was twelve, and parties with friends until late at night. Neighbors comment that she hangs around with different male friends, and her mother ad-mits she cannot control her very easily: "She is very rebellious. Some-times I cannot bring her inside at ten, but at eleven. . . . She wants to enjoy herself, but needs to realize that if she finds herself with something [that is, pregnant], then I will not be responsible. She will be."

The godfather and sponsor of her quinceañera celebration was sup-posed to be one of her former employers, but at the last minute he withdrew, although he did donate some meat. So Ester borrowed a wedding dress from a friend, bought some shoes, and paid for the music. After the fiesta, the family was completely broke, and was probably skip-ping meals, but they had spent more on the fiesta (they hired a live band) than other better-off families in Polanco. For Ester, the mass was not so important; it was the fiesta that she really cared about. However, she seemed disappointed at the way the fiesta turned out because toward the end there were a few fights, and the music was not as good as she had expected. She also expressed disappointment that almost none of her extended family, who were expected to come, actually attended.

The glamorous component of a quinceañera celebration, one in stark contrast to her everyday life, seemed to be Ester's strongest motivation for celebrating her fifteenth birthday. Ester's case shows an aspect of femaleness that claims freedom and pleasure, and rejects subordination to parental authority. Ester's precocious habits, her relationship with her mother, and the family's careless housekeeping have been criticized by the neighbors. She is not seen as having honor, nor is her family. These are some of the reasons given by neighbors for not attending the feast, implying an isolation of certain types of families from the shared space of other neighboring families. Thus, the celebration of the fiesta is an important moment when familial and individual processes of identity emerge and merge in the space of the colonia. The celebration becomes an articulation of individual and familial identities with urban identities. The space of the colonia is not a neutral space where the celebration happens, but as already mentioned, is created by the lived experience and by the rhythm of social practices.

Juana seems to be Ester's opposite. She lives around the corner from Ester, and her family's control over her is much stronger. She is studying to be an accountant and is not allowed to go out with friends. She spends a lot of time at home and is described as very responsible by the members of her family. She wears fashionable clothes and light makeup, but without being provocative. Juana has two older sisters and an older brother who pooled money to buy her a quinceañera dress and pay for renting a sound system and lighting equipment. Her father, a chief building worker, bought everything else needed for the party. Although it lacked a live band, Juana's fiesta was considered a success by her family and friends. In contrast to Ester's case, the unity of Juana's family and its respectability among neighbors contributed to the positive realization of the feast.

Juana especially enjoyed the mass and having all of her family around her. After the celebration she described the emotional intensity of being near the altar and receiving her mass. Now she wishes to have more responsibility and to commit herself fully to her study and work. Her mother is protective toward her because she feels that now she has to keep an eye on her—not because she worries about Juana herself, but about the boys who could take advantage of her. In her words, "If the girl has more than one boyfriend, people will talk badly about her afterwards. But the boys can have more than one girlfriend at the same time!" In respecting her family's rules, and accepting the need to be protected from the danger of male sexual intentions, Juana—unlike Ester, who seems to encourage dangerous encounters—ideally embodies the symbolic meaning of the celebration of a quinceañera: submission, virginity, and control of the female body, which requires appropriate dress, language, and social relationships with the same and the opposite sex.

The cases of Ester and Juana show that this rite of passage entails tensions between different aspects of male and female sexuality. Female sexuality is seen as something to be controlled, to be kept away from wandering males. But at the same time virility is measured in relation to a man's capacity to attract and dominate the opposite sex (Wade 1994: 129). Of course, female sexuality, when it is actively expressed in circumstances of male wandering, becomes threatening to family order because it is deceitful and uncontrolled (Martin 1990: 478). Nevertheless, some girls may actively look for sexual encounters. The quinceañera celebration, then, becomes a theater for different, and often opposed, female identities, as is the case in other rites of passage related to female puberty (Wilson 1980: 621). It also reveals a socioeconomic stratification within the colonia, where some girls' celebrations translate into a power related to female sexuality, or to female education for the reproduction or amelioration of family status.

The cases of Milena, Sabrina, Juana, and Ester show that the same ritual can enhance different aspects of womanhood in relation to the lifestyles and religious beliefs of girls' families. A celebration held by a family involved in the Comunidades (such as Sabrina's) tends to be less glamorous than one held by those only involved in more traditional religious groups (for instance, Milena's family), because money may be saved instead for a daughter's education or the acquisition of valuable commodities.

Traditional Ritual, Multifaceted Experiences

A traditional ritual—such as the quinceañera celebration and celebrations of the Virgin—can acquire new meanings, as in the language of the CEBs. Those new meanings suggest a priority of communal identity over family and individual protagonism, and represent the Virgin as a fighter for, rather than just a consoler of, the poor. These shifts in language are aimed to help break distinctions between the sacred and profane, and to help people see everyday life as part of the sacred, which manifests in a spirit of being the Church through communal activities (Levine 1992: 146). Nevertheless, some priests and their assistants search for meanings, indicating a tendency to reject an "act without words" (Cárdenas González 1987) and criticizing and confining traditional fiestas to their functional role of emphasizing the family as a competitive unit that wishes to increase its social status.

The quinceañera celebration clearly carries a meaning of social differentiation and transformation of female social status and gender relations; however, the ritual also constitutes an important moment in the
process of female identity and self-perception because it opens up a time
of negotiation within the family concerning control over, and definition
of, the female sexual body. This cycle ends with married life, when the
time of la ilusión—of suspended disbelief—can be extended no longer.
And, even more, the preservation of the integrity of the female body
has often been read as the reproduction of the integrity of a nation.

That is to say, as discussed in the next chapter, government rhetoric
in Mexico commonly addresses women's issues only in terms of
women's roles as mothers and caretakers. Women have been the repro-
ducers of the domestic sphere that the nation has constructed (Craske
1999), as for instance in the rationalization of female domesticity via
legislation over activities in the domestic and educational sphere
(Vaughan 2000). Nonetheless, recent female participation in party and
grassroot politics in Mexico has shown that the style of female political
participation is changing. By challenging traditional community values
and using them strategically for a female-oriented political agenda (Martin 1990), women are slowly becoming more visible political actors. The
recent increase in visibility of women in politics and their participation
in electoral reforms has translated into new public discussions, including
the defense of pregnant women's right to work (Rodríguez 1998: 8). Of
course, Catholic discourses are still a central arena of tension between
women's reproduction (and consumer) roles and women's rights as social actors.

At the micro-level of the barrio, representations of female subjectivity
and body are molded into religious discourses, but not without tensions.
In fact, the discourse of the CEBs—which often de-emphasizes issues
of gender hierarchy in favor of ideals of the commonality of the poor—
fails, to a certain extent, to grasp the importance of the body and the
embodied experience of the ritual in the process of female identity and
the creation of female subjectivity. A tension between religious discursive practice and gender performativity continues to develop.

At the same time, however, Church evangelization emphasizes the
roots of the ritual in a mythical past, rather than stressing the singularity
of specific pueblos or ranchos. A communal memory—one of a past in
action—is enhanced via the performance of a life ritual. The performances of life rituals are thus a very important part of understanding the
prisms of belonging in urban Mexico. Those prisms emerge in specific

negotiations of knowledge, while bringing to the foreground particular cultural meanings, and often localist styles of cultural performance and domains of personhood. Moreover, as already discussed in terms of the migrant experience, they are also about losses, and both the validation and the invalidation of one's own experience.

At a symbolic level the success of a quinceañera celebration depends on how well la ilusión is dramatized in the experience of the ritual. The drama of the ritual constructs the female body through virginal images (of candor and purity) and metaphors of the body as a vessel that should be preserved intact until marriage. Family unity, and the respectability of the family and of the girl's reputation, are also factors that shape the success of the fiesta. The time of la ilusión, which begins with the ritual, indicates the new complexity of female identity. Girls acquire new responsibilities toward their families, while at the same time, their desire to engage in courtship demands a loosening of family control. Although within the ritual girls are symbolically handed over to the male domain, they also experience self-empowerment. After the ritual, however, their freedom is often reduced, as is their autonomy in relation to the male domain, and this tighter control is one of the causes of early marriage. The ritual thus implies discontinuities as well as continuities in the process of becoming a mujercita.

Forms of resistance to family authority reveal tensions between different gendered attributes. Those differences can also be seen when families choose not to celebrate the ritual, as in the case of better-off families in Polanco in which female choice privileges individual, professional training above marrying and forming a family at an early age. The socioeconomic condition of a family influences not only whether the quinceañera is celebrated or not, but how it is interpreted. This is becoming more noticeable as female education is increasingly seen as a gateway for the improvement of women's lives and the household conditions in many working-class families.

The exegesis of the ritual cannot be reduced, as the CEBs discourse implies, to its functionalist elements of family status differentiation and consumption. On the other hand, the ritual cannot be fully understood solely in terms of its symbolic level of marking sexual boundaries and helping to construct the female body as a vessel which needs to be defended from male philandering. The ritual is a performative act, an experience which may or may not be part of the process of the creation of female self-identity, and which reveals — even in its absence — different forms of female subjectivity shaped within particular sets of family and social relations. In fact, the indigenous exegesis of the ritual (and its absence) needs to be understood within the context of particular sets of family relations — which are heterogeneous — and also within differing contexts of religious discourse and perceptions of class and status, given that economic and other considerations affect peoples' decisions about whether or not to celebrate the occasion, and if so, on what scale.

Finally, the quinceañera ritual can be read as an arena of emergent and residual cultural formations where, as previously discussed, "the locally residual can be confused with the generally emergent" (Williams 1977). In a language of Catholic evangelization, and in its concern with the fiesta's potential for consumption and increased atomization of the community, the celebration is read as a residual formation. Popularization of a higher-class form of introduction to society does not challenge dominant ideas of gender relations and subjectivity; they only reappropriate their forms with a "new" local language. However, the celebration can also be read as an emergent form that shows a potential alternative to dominant discourses of female subjectivity, as submitted to family and local control. Emerging through urban prisms of belonging, a stress on female performance and display can embrace a wider complexity of meaning and embodied experiences that do not only celebrate female virginity and subordinated control, but also the potential for female individuation and desire. A pull to modernity is part of the construction and imagining of a tradition. At the intimate level of intersubjective family and community interaction, the simple dynamics of whether and how to celebrate such a ritual offer fascinating insights into the everyday paradoxes of modernity in urban Mexico.

CHAPTER 6

Neither Married, Widowed, Single, or Divorced

Gender Negotiation, Compliance, and Resistance

The dumb silence of apathy, the sober silence of solemnity, the fertile silence of awareness, the active silence of perception, the baffled silence of confusion, the uneasy silence of impasse, the muzzled silence of outrage, the expectant silence of waiting, the reproachful silence of censure, the tacit silence of approval, the vituperative silence of accusation, the eloquent silence of awe, the unnerving silence of menace, the peaceful silence of communion, the irrevocable silence of death illustrate by their unspoken response to speech that experiences exist for which we lack the word.

Leslie Kane, *Language of Silence*

Soledad: *¿Valentina, por qué no has tenido hijos todavía?* (Valentina, why haven't you had children yet?)

Me: *Bueno..mmm..no es el tiempo todavía.* (Well . . . it is not the right time yet.)

Soledad: *¡Es porque eres cobarde!* (It is because you are a coward!)

Mastery of representation can no longer be achieved (Taussig 1993: 237), but I hope I have been engaging the reader in the promised unfolding and interlinking of different levels of ethnographic analysis. This final chapter recalls the tension surrounding the writing of an anthropological urban study on identity focusing on processes of subject formation and knowledge negotiation, but without doing away with the phenome-nological dimension of experience altogether.[1] As I pointed out in the previous chapter, gender processes are a looking glass that highlights tensions of modernity, its local, mundane, everyday openings, and also one way to engage with both levels of analysis. I aim here to focus on female subjectivity as well as the contradictory nature of female experiences. In the process I address issues of suffering, language, and transformation through contradictions between images, meanings, and engendered life experiences. I also analyze gendered demands and desires, as well as positions in the work place and the community. A complementary thread which I also try to explore in this final chapter is the relation between gender identity and the experience of not-knowing, which I see as a condition of being void of knowledge rather than as a condition of ignorance, or a denial of knowledge.

Gender studies on Latin America have shown that female identity and virtue have been acquired through the presence of a male figure and through motherhood (Melhuus 1992: Levine 1993a; Bohman 1984). They are shaped in continuity with traditional gender roles which portray women as subordinate to their husbands and as good caretakers of their children. The Mexican state has rationalized the domestic sphere since the 1930s through a range of female-targeted projects on health, nutrition, and education. This state intervention from 1930 to 1960 viewed women, and especially rural women, as ignorant victims of their living conditions and therefore as objects in need of state policy rather than active subjects able to formulate women-centered projects (Vaughan 2000). In general, motherhood has been the key area through which women's issues have been addressed in Mexican social state policy, but women's presence and participation in urban social movements have begun to challenge this image of female passivity (Massolo 1992). One of the subjects I examine here is how motherhood shapes gender relations in a colonia popular such as Polanco.

Female identity formation in urban Mexico is dominated by motherhood and concerns different degrees of embeddedness and nonseparation—in matters of sin and responsibility—which define gender boundaries and shape of power relations within particular family sets. Morality and change in contemporary Mexico point out the importance of examining the relationship between power and values in gender identity and discourse, and distinguishing a power that is negotiated between gendered subjects from power that permeates gender relations and imagery (Melhuus and Stølen 1996: 231). However, I believe an exclusive focus on meaning and symbolism misses a third but important step in the unfolding of gendering processes: the embodiment of experience. Hence, in this chapter I acknowledge that traditional aspects of gender relations—namely, female suffering and the woman's unconditional dedication to the husband, as well as the man's status as provider and seat of authority—are being challenged by young women who wish to develop their own skills or choose a life of religious conversion, and by young men who want to enjoy themselves. However, I also wish to stress that other forms of resistance as well as compliance—as expressed through gossip, life crises, and sickness (a bodily experience and expression)—can be interpreted, to a certain extent, as creative redefinitions of gender positions and relations.

These different perceptions and strategies are not designed to overturn traditional gender roles. Processes of change are not linear in the way conceived by some authors who see traditional values of self-abnegation and suffering for the family giving way to new priorities of autonomy and self-sufficiency (Levine 1993a). A critique of traditional aspects of womanhood is rarely implied by women as a claim for their rights: womanhood is still seen as something acquired through motherhood and wifehood, but the forms and the boundaries implied are shifting. And this shifting reshapes the relationship between practical and strategic interests. The meaning of practical gender interests is redefined in terms of the experience of strategic gender interests, since women's interests cannot be identified irrespective of their subjective positions as actors,[2] and a process of identity formation (Molyneux 1998: 233).

However, a focus on meaning-making and the shifting of boundaries should not gloss over an existing incapacity and an uneasiness in defining both the boundaries themselves and the ways in which those boundaries are extended to national, regional, and group identities. As already discussed, intimate cultures draw attention not only to the boundaries between the self and the other that emerge in differences between hegemonic or subordinate cultures, but also to the creative process of a mutual referentiality and internal coherence as bonds which make a particular cultural identity shared and understood (Lomnitz-Adler 1992). The question of the creation of bonds of understanding which can or cannot be shared, as well as the definition and shifting of boundaries, are as important in the prisms of belonging as they are in gender identity and discourse. If, in contemporary Mexico, female identity has been defined in opposition to the male one, while male identity is defined as a continuum in a position relative to other men (Melhuus 1996), the redefinition of female identity embraces both the relations of difference and complementarity with men and among women, as well as an understanding of exactly what that redefinition is or can be.

Controlling through Nurturing and Service: A Form of Traditional Compliance and Resistance

Motherhood has long been considered a central focus of Mexican social practice and political discourse, and motherhood, nurturing, and issues of survival have been central concerns in women's political participation (Kaplan 1982; Martin 1990). In the political discourse of the Mexican state, motherhood has been the central focus for government action on women's issues and has been used to incorporate women (via their nurturing role) in existing political structures (Craske 1993: 140). Motherhood had been considered a central feature of the Mexican woman in earlier culture and personality analyses (Díaz 1966; Díaz Guerrero 1975), which highlighted the fact that mothers seemed to receive support, status, and protection in old age from their children rather than from their husbands, and where the mother-son relationship appeared stronger in terms of intimacy and psychological dependence than that of the father-son relationship (Hunt 1971).

Once again, however, we can see that essentialist psychological categories do not further an understanding of specific social change and gender identity.[3] It has been observed, instead, that we should understand how, in lower-income urban areas, mothers—especially in single-parent households[4]—invest symbolic capital in their children (Mahar 1992). By investing resources in their children's education, women improve their reputations within the neighborhood and build up both a network outside the household and strong bonds within it that are crucial for their present and future statuses (Mahar 1992: 288–289). Investing social capital is a strategy of identity.

Traditional womanhood is attributed by women to other women who "endure everything that the husband does to them and live for their children." It implies particular care for the welfare of children, self-denial, and manipulation of the male spouse (Levine and Sunderland Correa 1993a: 204); it also implies a practice of service to (especially male) children, and the role of acting as a link between children and father. Through service, women actively control the feelings and actions of their kin. This element of motherhood becomes a form of controlling through nurturing. The act of giving oneself away through service—

and being represented as such—stresses the element of continuity in the discursive process of identity formation. Controlling through nurturing can be read as a form of compliance to male authority, but it is also part of a negotiation for power. It is important to remember the significant links between feeding, food, home, and female domestication of male sexuality (Behar 1987; Varley 2000).

Female identity is centered on service not only in the context of motherhood and wifehood, but also of other kinship ties. When ties of marriage and filiation are absent, other kinship ties can acquire qualities of dedication and service that contribute to making a woman a "real" woman. In the previous chapter I discussed how the quinceañera ritual fosters a specific fairy-tale representation of gender relations based on ideas of courtship, grace, male respect, and fidelity. However, both young and older women know that this will not be true of married life, which often proves difficult and marked by male betrayals. This awareness is somehow withheld in a form of a suspended disbelief that makes young girls eager to celebrate their quinceañera despite the reality that a life of hardship awaits. Thus, in this state of suspended disbelief, conflicting gender imagery coexists in the same subject.

Motherhood's representation in Mexico has a strong basis in Catholic imagery, and in the Guadalajara and the Jalisco region these images have been very powerful. Religious imagery provides an ideal model of woman and mother (Paz 1959), though this embraces different qualities ranging from abnegation and submission to valor and independence. It has been pointed out how, at a symbolic level, Catholicism carries a modern message of gender complementarity in a society that privileges traditional dominance and hierarchy between sexes. This appears paradoxical in a male-dominated society that nevertheless places its highest value on the feminine (Melhuus 1992: 240). The association of ideal womanliness with the model of the Virgin (as in *marianismo*) focuses traditional female identity on the connection between motherhood and the morality of action (Norget 1991).[5]

The opposite female image exists in such figures as the Chingada, the passive, powerless mother who has been violated, like Malinche, who helped Cortez conquer Mexico and subdue its population (Paz 1959). This alternative view of motherhood is also found in common derogatory expressions—such as "vale madre" (it is worthless), "es un desmadre" (it's a total mess), and "es una madreada" (it's a wicked thing). So the double nature of gender representations is stressed in the marianismo ideal and in images of *el chingón,* the violating macho, and *la chingada,* the violated, passive woman, respectively associated with a state of closure and openness (Paz 1959: 70). When a woman is seen as open, or broken, as in the case of the widely used term "fracasada" (discussed in the previous chapter), she is seen as disempowered.

The meaning and tensions of these gender representations can only be understood within everyday life histories and strategies. The case of Miranda—a fifty-year-old woman living in Polanco since the early 1970s—and her husband, Rodrigo, embody some of these tensions. I describe the case of Miranda and of other women with the awareness that their life narratives and their experience of pain, rage, or other feelings can become a reenactment that has a potential for healing and redemption, and this self-narrative can be constructed through the appropriation of male symbols imbued with female imagery (Behar 1990).

Miranda was born in a village near Ameca and brought up in the Colonia del Sur in Guadalajara. Her father died when she was very young, and after her mother remarried, her relationship with her stepfather was difficult. Miranda's story shows a woman who has perceived in herself a quality of self-endurance that comes from being a mother and a wife, but who is actually redefining this perception. Womanhood for Miranda is synonymous with total dedication to the good of the family, and assuring that family members' actions lead to family harmony.

Miranda is married to Don Rodrigo, and they have three children. She is an extremely hard worker and has a small grocery stall that she runs with the help of her younger daughter in a permanent market on Avenida Patria, south of Polanco. Rodrigo has a small business, but Miranda earns the bulk of the household's income, and Rodrigo does not contribute to the household expenses. He expects her to fulfill the duties of a good wife: preparing food, doing the laundry, keeping the house tidy, and in her case, also paying the bills. Miranda has become the link between Don Rodrigo and their sons in terms of decision making within the family. These responsibilities—on top of her business activities and the lack of her daughter-in-law's help with housekeeping—put great pressure on Miranda. In fact, she describes feeling overwhelmed by a sense of obligation: "When Rodrigo asked for my hand, I did not want to marry. My idea was to take care of my mother. When I got married, it was like going to the slaughterhouse because there was no enjoyment . . . and he is very impulsive, so one has to do it [have sex] out of obligation." She is especially critical of her husband since she discovered that he had another daughter before he married her, and in twenty-five years he never told his family. She, in contrast, says she had told him the truth when she married. Miranda felt worried that his other daughter might claim rights on their property, which she feels belongs to her children rather than to her husband.

Miranda often claims some of the responsibility for the misbehavior of her two adult sons, and this prevents them from opposing her will in matters of family decision making. Conflicts arise between Don Rodrigo and his sons in part because the father wants his sons to earn a living, yet both like to go on *parrandas* (drinking binges and occasional drug use) and are often out of work. Other arguments concern the sloppiness of the two adult sons. To avoid direct physical confrontations between Rodrigo and the children, Miranda tries to control the flow of information. She does that by lying to her husband about their sons' whereabouts and their financial contributions to the household. She is also selective about which of their father's comments she reports. In other words, female protectiveness toward men reinforces a childhood dimension in adult malehood (Levine 1993a). In women's words, men never grow up: they are eternal *niños* (children), even when married. This characteristic is sometimes attributed to the phenomenon called "mamitis," which occurs when toddlers suffer a separation from their mothers, an experience that can bear consequences for their adult life (Gutmann 1998).

The case of Miranda and Rodrigo exemplifies the importance of motherhood for women's self-identity and the peripheral position of the father. Rodrigo would like to impose his will on the sons and be tough with them, but they listen to what he says without following his advice. Rodrigo may be encouraged to exercise his authority in the house, allowing him to show that he is an "hombre de veras" (a real man), but the sons still spend their time with friends instead of bringing in regular earnings.

For Miranda, filial ties have become more important than those of marriage. Miranda is able to imagine her life without Rodrigo, but he cannot see himself apart from her because she keeps the family and household together. She represents a vital part of his primary location of identity (Vélez-Ibáñez 1983: 154). It seems that Rodrigo holds the appearance of power, but it is Miranda who has actual power (Roger 1975). Roger's notion of actual female power and other studies that claim that women have power in Latin American society because they have informal ways of influencing events have been criticized for being limited to the control of household reproduction. In doing so, they have not taken into consideration women's lack of access to extra-domestic resources and opportunities (Bohman 1984; Elhers 1990), and they have underplayed the presence of gender hierarchy (Jaquette 1980; Benería and Roldán 1987; González de la Rocha and Escobar Latapí 1991). Nonetheless, the actual power in Miranda's case indicates that she controls her own income, but not the one generated by her husband. Her power technique rests on diplomatic maneuvers used to influence her husband's will, rather than on direct confrontation, as well as on control of her children.[6] Miranda may be giving herself away, and putting herself at the mercy of other people, but this very service also gives her control over those who are served. This is a form of symbolic and, to an extent, executive power around which certain types of family dynamics pivot.

When the integration of her family is threatened by Rodrigo's extra-marital affairs, her prime concern is for the children, and it is the expected unconditional service to her husband that is put under question. This does not happen through direct, open confrontation, but through appearing submissive and silent in his company, but overtly expressing her discomfort when talking with other women. In this sense, through silence before her husband and gossip with other women, she resists her husband's authority without changing her formal relationship to him (Herzfeld 1991). The expression of Miranda's self-identity is neither in separating herself, nor in stating openly the different intentions from her husband, but in being the channel for family relations and being embedded in them. However, she experiences the discomfort and contradictions somatically and is often sick, suffering from severe migraines, exhaustion, and back pain. For Rodrigo, the question is not only to defend the honor of the family via the defense of the valor of the women in the household. In a colonia popular such as Polanco his struggle is also about keeping control of the young male side of his family. His reputation is just as tied to the honor of his daughter as it is to keeping his boys from dealing and using drugs.

Honor is fundamental to an understanding of gender in Mexican history. An idiom of honor and courage was used to subject and control women in times of pre-and post-revolutionary Mexican crisis. One example comes from the war against the Apaches in the northern frontier of Chihuahua, studied by Alonso, in which a language of female purity and honor was reinforced by an idiom of male valor and bravery in warfare. Masculinity came to be defined by a tension between *vergüenza* (shame) and *respecto* (respect), and emphasis was placed on the mastery of reason over the passions in warfare. For Chihuahuan peasants, norms and values of warfare began to shape gender subjectivity: a language of honor, respect, and purity runs parallel to a language of warfare and the reproduction of the nation. The honor of gendered subjects became essential to the integrity of the nation (Alonso 1995: 81, 101, 102). It is clear, then, that if there is a crisis of male bravery, then there is also a challenge to female honor and virtue, and potentially a challenge to the reproduction of nationhood.

In urbanized Mexico other forms of contemporary violence and shame are taking place and influencing ideas about male bravery and gender relations. The father-son relationship has to come to terms with challenges to masculinity such as drug addiction, an increasingly common problem among young males. Young drug addicts are vulnerable and often dependent on relatives for financial support, and, in severe cases, in need of personal care. One of Don Rodrigo's sons, for instance, became so addicted to drugs that he could not provide for his three young daughters and the pressures of family life. After his young wife left, his parents had to take care of not only their granddaughters, but also him, as he was incapable of working and often extremely sick. Rodrigo's crisis with Miranda also has to do with his struggle to conceptualize and come to terms with his sons' addictions despite his own beliefs about male bravery and identity.

Miranda distrusts her daughter-in-law, Violeta, because she has two small children but does not look after them properly. She has also failed to help consistently with housework duties. Violeta says that she would like to go back to school, because she got pregnant and married when she was just fifteen, but her husband and mother-in-law are against it because they think she should first take good care of the children and the household. Especially during times of increased economic pressure, there is a greater demand on adult female income generated outside the house, and daughters and daughters-in-law are expected to help with more of the household duties (Moser 1987; González de la Rocha 1994). Violeta, however, is a woman of the new generation, who 'no aguanta tanto' (she does not put up with much). She says she is more interested in going to parties, showing off new clothes, and enjoying herself. As discussed in previous chapters, changes in patterns of consumption, the labor market, styles of courtship, the implication of rural-urban and transnational migrations, and the experience in new religious movements are some of the factors contributing to value changes and contradictory images in female self-identity.

For Violeta, the wish to enhance her personal skills can be read as a challenge to traditional ideals of dedication to children and the home, and it has become a source of intergenerational conflict. Since the colonial period, the relation between mothers and daughters-in-law (and the tensions inherent in the latter's apprenticeship) has been central to the definition of female identity (Stern 1995: 92) and still is in low-income areas. This is because it affects mother-son, husband-wife relations, while it informs physical, moral, and legal issues of authority over house space and over who is entitled to the husband's/son's support (Varley 2000).

For women who strongly believe in traditional Catholic values, responsibility for action and, consequently, the state of sin are conditions that can be transferred between mother and children. There are cases, for example, of older women who refused to take Catholic sacraments when their sons were "living in sin" (that is, refusing to marry the mother of their children) and had become sick, who then recovered only when the sons agreed to marry.[7] Such cases suggest that a son's sin can be a mother's sin, and that there is no clear separation between a mother's and son's sense of responsibility and moral state. Thus traditional motherhood rests on permeable boundaries between mother and children, and daughters (or daughters-in-law) who acquire experiences in different fields often challenge their mothers' self-perception as women. In many cases, the ties between a mother and her children are still more important than the husband-wife relationship, which, because it is seen as sacred in the eyes of God, may be maintained principally on account of moral and religious obligations.

Another sphere of female definition is the capacity to endure pain, which can be seen, for instance, in the different attitudes toward childbirth expressed by women who have been brought up in the pueblo or rancho rather than in the city. These often concern ideas about the act of giving birth as being a "second birth" for the mother. Older women report that in the rancho, during the weeks following a birth the mother used to rest from housework activities, a custom not always respected in urban areas. A mother who has recently delivered should look after herself with special care. Some women still believe that new mothers should not watch much television, should not sew in inadequate light, should not expose their shoulders to a draft, and so on, as if a woman's senses at this stage are as weak as those of her child — this is why it is considered as a second birth for a new mother.

Prisms of belonging re-emerge in another embodied experience, that of motherhood, bringing to the forefront qualities of stamina and en-

durance. In this urban setting, there is a particular evaluation of a localist, rural style of dealing with labor and post-delivery care. It is, of
course, the physical experience of labor in which women are seen to
display qualities of endurance and stamina. But this style is valued differently by women; its interpretation is not homogenous. Young mothers now often want to avoid the pain of childbirth, and many women
choose caesarean sections. Many older mothers criticize this choice because they see a positive connection between female endurance and the
experience of coping in labor. To them, opting for a painless delivery
undermines the central rite of womanhood. To a certain extent it is
important to make women's suffering visible and a subject for discussion, for public recognition strengthens their womanhood (Melhuus
1992: 160). Suffering and the visibility of pain can indicate a claim for
belonging to a moral community. But suffering, when inflicted, can also
be a mark of a rejection of an actual belonging (Das 1995: 176–178). Then
the visible suffering of labor is not just a marker of female moral superiority and endurance. Through prisms of belonging it can be seen as
an inter- and intragenerational dialogical field where there is a tension
of modernity between a self-choosing subject versus a reification of suffering and motherhood as a claim for agency.

A related attribute of femininity is a capacity "de no dejarse," (for not
giving in). "Dejarse" means literally "to let go," and in a sense it indicates
an action of surrender or giving in. The term is used, for example, to
describe situations during which a woman undergoes physical or psychological distress but has still been able to provide decent living conditions for her children. It suggests a situation of material or psychological uneasiness (as in cases of domestic violence) and the ability to
face the contingencies of daily life. To say that a woman "no se deja"
suggests that she has the capacity to act even under hostile conditions
and possesses a strength not undermined by obstacles in the social environment.

Women's strength thus relates to the capacity "de aguantar" (to endure). The extent to which women endure can be a source of conflict
between older and younger generations, and between women who
strongly identify with traditional values and those who do not. The fact
that women endure more than men and give in less implies that women
perceive in themselves an intrinsic strength that is of a different quality
from that of men. It is not uncommon to hear women say they have
qualities of endurance, self-sufficiency, and independence which they see
as alien to men.

This focus on gender representation cannot, however, be separated from the critical impact and consequences of economic restructuring in the feminization of poverty. Women in Latin America tend to carry the burden in livelihood changes, and their strategies in everyday life have to be understood not only through national and state politics, but also as a part of local community citizenship participation (Alvarez 1996). With increasing pauperization, women's struggles for new entitlements and greater agency is part of a redefinition of self-identity as well as of citizenship. A redefinition of citizenship asks for the incorporation of multiple and often apparently contradictory gender interests—these can challenge or reinforce traditional gender roles—so that the emergence of new political and social subjects depends on the contradictory and uneven ways in which multiple levels of structure of domination function (Stephen 1997: 275).

Some of these contradictions are seated in the connection between gender identity and positionality, employment, and redistribution of assets within and between households. The economic crisis that has affected Mexican low-income households since the oil crisis in the early 1980s has had an effect on both female and male participation in domestic labor and chores. In Guadalajara there has been a remarkable increase in female wage labor, which has directly subsidized the basic needs of the household and sometimes substituted the husband's wage (González de la Rocha 1994). In Mexico City changes also have been observed in an increase in male participation in domestic activities such as home improvements and parenting, activities that have definitely been underestimated in gender analysis of livelihood in the capital and other regional cities (Gutmann 1996).

These gender positions draw domains of empowerment and self-empowerment. The story of the Mexican peddler Esperanza, which was mentioned earlier (Behar 1993), not only shows possible ways in which forms of domination and hegemonic values related to ethnicity, gender relations, and national symbolic imagery are part of women's everyday life history, but also that the act of recalling, evoking, and self-narrating can be empowering for both the listener and the storyteller. When Esperanza beats her daughter because she wants her to stop pursuing a man out of wedlock—behaving as her own mother did with her in the past—she experiences the contradiction between being empowered as a controlling, traditional mother, and disempowered because she herself re-creates the conditions of gender inequality to which she was once subjected. Empowerment as a form of extending agency, and disempowerment as a contraction of agency, is thus part of a process of gendered subjectivity.[8] So the analysis of aspects of gender relations at different points in the life cycle inscribes gendered subjectivity in the unfolding of gain and loss of agency. To this I turn in the next section.

Female Self-Perception, Sickness, and Creative Voids

The struggle to adjust self-perceptions and life strategies to traditional gender representations in everyday actions is a central theme for low-income women in urban Mexico. A woman can be single, married, unmarried, or abandoned; the vocabulary used to categorize women indicates that they are defined through their formal relations to men (or the absence thereof), but the reverse is not normally true for men. For instance, the attribute *quedada* refers to both a spinster and a married woman who has been left with her husband's family because he has gone to work in the United States. ("Quedada" connotes a state of passivity, of having missed a chance, and having been left behind.) But men are never referred to as quedados. Of a mature unmarried man, people say that "el vive todavía con sus papas" (he still lives with his parents) or "es un solterón" (he is a mature single man/bachelor). The former expression implies a condition that is a result of active choice (and may potentially change).

Some married women do not see their state as one of abnegation. The degree of resistance to a traditional female role varies, as do the tensions arising from loss of identification with the traditional female gender role; these elements can be read in the search for extramarital affairs, in the rejection of traditional duties of wife and mother, or in a bodily sense (ailments or sickness, for example) of self-loss. However, the term "resistance" can be problematic when it reduces women's actions to their role as the oppressed, as reacting against subordination, thus conflating the complexity of their multilayered subjectivity.

Certain diseases and restlessness occur when there is what I call a void of knowledge on how to reinterpret and give meaning to specific engendered experiences, and how to redefine and actively create a balance between caring and self-fulfillment. Before describing the case of Antonia, I want to point out the difficulty that anthropology has, or has had, with the experience of "not-knowing." Anthropologists deal with what is but often gloss over the "protestation of ignorance" (Fardon 1990: 5). Subjectivities are placed in the knower in the anthropological account, but they are also located in the "not-knowing," in the unspeakable and in ignorance. Silence and the space of not-manifested knowledge have been considered sites of power, domination, and discipline that shape the nature of the knowledge itself and render access to knowledge and definition of ignorance a political act (Foucault and Gordon 1980). However, a view of knowledge as a form of domination could undervalue the potential creativity (as well as distress and sometimes pain) of a state of not-knowing. A condition of not-knowing can be a painful subject position, but it also offers an opportunity for transformation and social change.

There is a creative potential located in the cultural process of contested and contradictory meaning-making—in the transmission of knowledge of which ignorance is a form—and that process is also located in the phenomenological experience of the loss of meaning which has not yet been replaced. Not-knowing has then a bearing in defining the known or what will be known, not only in terms of secrecy or understated, implicit knowledge, but also in the embodied experience of lack of knowledge as a potential for knowledge. In other words, the somatic experience of not-knowing or of loss of knowledge is important to our understanding of the gendered search for knowledge and redefinition of identity. The following cases of Antonia and Soledad ethnographically exemplify this dilemma and redefinition, and how the unknown can be an integral part of empirical reality (Jackson 1993).

Antonia is a woman in her mid-thirties who participates in a health group based on learning self-help therapies and remedies. Her childhood was very difficult, marked by poverty and poor health. The family came from Zacatecas, and her mother was in charge of looking out for the family because her husband drank, did not earn much, and mistreated her. Antonia married young to escape what she refers to as "an unbearable situation." Her husband loves her very much, but she did not marry him for love. After marriage, when she was working in a factory, she started to suffer from depression, which continued well after the birth of her two sons:

I was working in the factory and eating badly. I started to have high blood pressure, and marriage was not as I had imagined. I thought marriage was going out a lot, having a good time. There was no pressure. I was the one responsible. I started to behave badly with my husband and to beat my children. . . . It was depression and sadness and anxiety. . . . I felt I was going to die.

At the time Antonia was not doing housework or attending to her children. Some neighbors decided to take her to see a *brujo*, or witch doctor, who started to see her regularly. An extramarital relationship with him developed while she was recovering from her depression, and gossip eventually reached her in-laws and her husband. Her husband wanted to forgive her for what she had done, and Antonia recalled that her wish to come back to him involved a mixture of self-abnegation and a wish to let go of the sexual burden of the relationship. Her self-denial did not last, though, and she became involved in another extramarital relationship, with a doctor who had his consultancy in the neighborhood, but whom she left a few years later after he became involved with another woman.

Antonia now feels inadequate in the role of lover, but she is not comfortable in her wifely responsibilities either: "I do not want to serve just a man. I want something more serious, lasting longer and stronger. For me to marry is not to serve a man." Antonia's mother, on the other hand, is totally dedicated to her family but has developed problems with "los nervios" (nerves) from having to cope with running the household without help from either her husband or adult children. In Antonia's case, the tensions between her expectation of pleasure in marriage and traditional patterns of gender interaction also emerge in the relationship with her mother. In Antonia's words:

For my mother, just the fact of criticizing somebody is a great sin. . . . For her, saying "Ay! that man is very handsome" is a sin or shows a desire for him. I do not agree with her about many things. For her it is necessary to obey a husband, and I do not agree with it. She is exhausting herself, and she supports her husband . . . and the children still living in the house do not help her. They should make their own way in life! But they depend upon her, and she feels an obligation to them, because they are her children, but she should take care of herself more.

Antonia believes that a woman has to take more care of herself, and therefore has to draw different boundaries for her children, husband, and lovers, which also implies a greater involvement of the former two in running the household. She also states the need to express herself in her own way within her family and community.

On one hand, Antonia challenges the assumption that women's identity is related to the protection and presence (or absence) of a man. However, she cannot relate to her husband in a different way, and though she claims to appreciate her husband's love, she also knows that in being with him, she may fall again into depression. So Antonia knows what she cannot be, but is still exploring alternative forms without knowing what she actually can be. One exploration has her involvement with the medicina popular group, and Antonia cherishes learning and using remedies, and recommending remedies for her children, family, and neighbors. The experience has made her more confident and has also helped to cut costs and move toward a more balanced family diet and improved health. In the end, though, her caring for others has not really translated into better ways of helping herself deal with periods of crisis.

Antonia and her mother believe that illness can be generated by domestic difficulties related to economic pressure, excessive labor demands, and tensions in gender relations. Antonia's story suggests that while women identify with female qualities such as controlling through nurturing, total self-abnegation, unwavering support for husband and children, and generalized notions of shared responsibilities between mother and children, such qualities are also a source of questioning. This questioning and experience of a void of knowledge of alternative possibilities may manifest itself through life crises, illnesses, and a sense of loss of self-identity. This is not to say that women who fall sick or become depressed are necessarily resisting traditional gender roles, but that those bodily experiences can indicate the existence of contradictory forms of female identity related to particular times in a woman's life history. Indeed, one reading of this female questioning is that it goes, underexpressed and silenced, into the female body. However, both what can be negotiated or changed in gender relations through becoming aware of that void and the contradictory expressions of female identity suggest different female life strategies, to which I now turn.

Alternatives to Abnegation: Negotiation of Gender Boundaries

Participation in social and religious movements seems to provide useful tools for negotiating gender positions. Female agents may acquire male qualities, and male agents may withdraw from some aspects of maleness related to male/female relations without being open to accusations of homosexuality, as is described by some Jesuit novices in the neighborhood.[9]

Experiences in social movements within particular women's life histories involving high labor mobility and personal enterprise may include a process of awakening and self-empowerment, and an ability to bring about changes in gender positions and, to a certain extent, in the life of the community. For women these experiences renew a sense of independence and of being able to see themselves as separate from husbands, parental families, and the life of the parish. Thus, at another level, this independence can entail more connectedness with people outside one's own family, and a stronger commitment to new forms of social relationships. In other words, increased independence in family household relationships is often reflected by an extension of the boundaries of the self to responsibilities and agency in expanded networks of social relations.

When I met Soledad in the early 1990s, she was in her early thirties and actively involved in the Comunidades Eclesiales de Base. She is married to Leo, a specialized mechanic, and they have two children. She describes her husband as *suave* (soft), but she was not in love with him when they married. Soledad is a vital center of her family, originally from Zacatecas. Everybody, even her mother, asks for her advice or veto in personal and family decisions about the allocation of resources, the organization of family gatherings, medical proceedings, major purchases, and so on. She had several different jobs in medical consultancies before marrying, some of them quite fulfilling. Soledad has successfully been practicing hairdressing from home, selling imported goods (more before the 1994 pesos devaluation), as well as organizing communal saving schemes with neighbors. Soledad pays the bills and saves for home improvements, while Leo gives her a set allowance for food and the children's needs. Her curiosity about life and her independence, combined with the experience of the Comunidades have made it difficult for her to fit into expected married, female self-definitions that rely on the presence or absence of a male figure:

Here the majority of women want to be in love and get married, but for me it was not so. I knew Leo and I trusted him greatly as a friend, but I did not want to marry him. . . . Because of that I did not accept him. After we married I felt very low. It was very difficult for a year. . . . Every time he came close I felt nearly sick, but I did not understand what it was. The problem is that I do not want to see myself as single, widowed, divorced, or married. I overcame this repulsion with the birth of Rosa. Then there was a reason to be together.

For nearly two years Soledad participated intensively in the activities of the parish. She was a coordinator of a group of Comunidades before falling out with Padre Nemo, and she was also one of the leaders in charge of the medicina popular group until the nuns took over and the group split. These activities absorbed so much of her time that her marriage nearly broke up, and her family thought she was going "mad." Such changes in women's perceptions of the world as a consequence of activity in social movements are sometimes explained in terms of bodily "failure," which can manifest in mental or physical illness. In this sense, women's psychological deviancy is translated physical deviancy. Soledad recalled:

For a long time I longed for something more: a person cannot live just for the day. So when the sisters invited me, I joined the Comunidades without knowing what they were, but I started to hold more responsibility, but then I reached a point that I was neglecting family matters and the household because I felt that what we were doing was important, and Leo did not understand what it was about. During that time we fell apart, and he did not understand why I was so involved in this [the Comunidades]. I reached the point of thinking of leaving but then I thought of the children and what would have happened to them, not really to Leo. . . . I have always thought that I would share Leo with other women one day. I do not see him as my property.

The conflict with her mother had a different impact. Her mother complained she did not have time for the family and that she was starting to have "strange ideas" about the government, and about what people should do as Catholics. In contrast, Soledad's husband's resistance to her involvement in the Comunidades came from her failure to fulfill her family obligations, not a dispute over her ideas about social mobilization. But neither her husband or her mother could really share her process of redefinition of some of her life motivations. Leo seemed not to understand her.

Soledad's case reveals how female self-perception and gender identity are affected by changing boundaries of responsibilities and notions of failure. Gendered self-knowledge cannot be separated from the intentionality, commitments, and responsibility of the agents in action. In other words, when we analyze female self-narratives, notions of responsibility and failure unveil struggles for meanings and embodiment of experiences that take place not only between different gendered agents, but also within the agent, since desires and resistance play important roles in the evaluation of achievement and failures. As the case of Soledad shows, the challenge is to find the capacity to convert apparent failures (such as not caring adequately for the family) into strengths, and the capacity to endure "not-knowing" while recognizing the uneasiness such an experience entails.

Resistance to identification with female images can also be among the motivations for religious conversion. The choice of religious life may broaden a woman's self-perception, because, in religious terms, female qualities need not conform exclusively to traditional Marian, submissive qualities, but are also formed through the appropriation of male imagery and qualities.[10] In the words of the religious sister Carlota of the order of Santa Teresa (Carmelites) in Polanco, it is possible to identify the characteristics of a woman who has grown up in a village.[11] Carlota was born in a little village of Michoacán, the oldest of seven brothers and sisters, and her parents separated when the children were young. Early in her life she assumed part of a father's responsibility as the family breadwinner:

> In my family I was like a father. I have a strong, resolute, and valiant character. . . . Men trust me because I don't disclose what they tell me to other people, but I don't like people to know that I am a sister. There are people that don't confide in me because of this. . . . Women are more resistant to pain. They have fewer outlets than men. Men go out with friends. Man is weaker morally and in everything else.

As for the different path of being a woman in a religious order, she says:

> I admire Saint Teresa for her freedom. I liked her maleness. She was not dependent upon men. She owned herself. She took what she liked. She wanted to go back to the poor and give away all her wealth. . . . Through this path I have gained part of my self-realization and the attainment of my objectives of being able to construct a new society without compromises in a more profound way than through marriage. I don't see the choice not to have a family and to be in control of what I earn as lost possibilities, because there are other forms of personal growth, and the money situation is the same here. I used to give everything to my mother and then she gave some to me, and here it is the same. They give me what I need, but I don't have my own money.

The fact that some women take on male characteristics and accept male responsibilities within the family does not make them more masculine, but instead enhances their womanhood, including their ability to cope in difficult situations, their *valentía* (courage), and their resistance to pain. Notions of courage can belong to both female and male identities, and a macho dimension, currently limited to manhood, was in fact attributed to both sexes during the Mexican Revolution (Paredes 1960). Thus the gender narrowing of this attribution to the male sphere and, more specifically, to mestizo can be read as part of the discursive formation of a modern Mexican nation (Gutmann 1996), and machismo can be interpreted as a historical formation rather than a behavioral pattern (Stevens 1973).

It is clear that the machismo phenomenon is much more multifaceted and complex, comprehending both discursive dimensions and psychological aspects of chivalry, solitude, courage, aggressiveness, and self-centeredness (Mirande 1997), as well as reflecting the political economy between sexual and homosexual bodies (Lancaster 1992).

Perceptions of different forms of coexisting female identities provide a language for redefining choices and life strategies as expressions of the negotiation of power, consumption patterns, and allocation of resources and status. Womanhood is thus a quality that can be weakened by certain types of behavior (for instance, talking too much and gossiping). In the eyes of believers, religious sisterhood guarantees exemption from these negative characteristics. Religious sisters are then women, but also different women. For some young religious sisters, women are not "dueñas de su persona" (owners of themselves), and families can limit forms of self-realization. For them sisterhood represents a type of womanhood that transforms biological filiation into social filiation, and family boundaries into religious community boundaries.

However, in the dynamic of the novices' houses, there have been tensions between younger and older sisters. The images invoked by Carlota's superiors involve a different kind of female imagery. Their focus is more upon the aspects of service and compassion of the Virgin and Sister Teresa. The emphasis on courage and fighting for others is stronger among younger sisters than among their superiors. The former identify with fighting for people by dressing like poor laypeople (wearing open sandals [*guaraches*] and carrying a campesinos' type of bag [*morral*]) and being, to a certain extent, critical of Vatican conservatism. The older sisters instead stress women's morality and subordination within the Church structure as a central point in their religious experience. It is clear that experience has to be problematized by looking to the interpretations that differently positioned agents have of an apparently similar religious life. Here I come back to the idea that "experience" in this sense cannot be taken as a force that unifies women's condition as such, but rather as a terrain where different conditions and interpretations of those conditions diverge and confer.

Hence, the area of power of redefinition of boundaries available to religious sisters is different than for lay women, but sisters' lives refract very crucial dimensions of womanhood which are partly appropriated and articulated in the life of laypeople such as Soledad. Therefore, gender imagery as well as female self-realization should be analyzed in terms of the boundaries and bonds of family and religious communities, and in the light of existing or potential conflicts in discursive practices that arise in the definitions, maintenance, and hierarchies of those boundaries and bonds, both among women and between the sexes.

Gender Subjectivity and Uncertainty

It is 1999, and Soledad is unexpectedly pregnant with her third child. I am staying at her house, and we are talking about the wonders of life. She has been taking a two-year group course in human development at the University of the Instituto Tecnológico y de Estudios Superiores de Occidente (ITESO), and her tuition has been paid by a grant for low-income people. She loves it, both for what she has learned and how she has been transformed because of the course and the people she has met. Her husband is also taking an interest in the course, and both consider their relationship more stable. Life's contradictions have not been solved, but life enfoldments have certainly taken place.

Soledad has carried on the practice of medicina popular, and she is now rather well known, with people coming from different parts of the city to see her for healing and massage. She is not involved in the parish anymore, nor formally part of medicina popular group, though her interests and curiosity have led her to further explore those themes. She has been going to *ferias de salud* (health festivals) in different parts of Mexico, and she has been exploring indigenous dancing in a group of La Mexicanidad, which now meets to dance in the neighborhood. The economy of the household is tight, but the children are at school, and between what she and her husband are able to earn, basic costs are covered. The second-hand truck that they were finally able to buy was stolen just a few months earlier, from right in front of their house. The house looks shabbier and in need of work, but there is no money for repairs.

Soledad is amazed by the developments in her life—the things she has come to know and become involved with. She counts her blessings. She has a passion for life, even if many contradictions have still not been resolved. The resentment toward parish politics has waned, and for her there is no longer a clear future—such as the utopian project developed by the Comunidades—but she is fully engaged in the unfolding of everyday life. There is uncertainty, but it is not only a sign of anxiety and suffering. In her words, "I do not know where I am going, but I keep on walking. Life is incredible." What I see is that a desire for a (religious) meta-narrative has been transformed into a search connected to community and belonging in a specific modality: through learning and practicing healing powers, and through understanding human development.

Vernacular modernities are about letting go of the predicament of the future and its goals, and they are challenges to an equation between urbanization and secularization. Soledad's paradoxes can be read within a period of history in Mexican society filled with uncertainty. The Salinas project of modernization and technologization of the nation has partly taken place via neoliberal reforms and the dismantling of an import-subsidized economy. The Zedillo presidency continued to support this economic project; however, when neoliberal reforms take place without real democratization, a few get richer, but benefits are very slow to trickle down to the lower classes. The benefits and the drawbacks of Vicente Fox's new administration are still unclear at this early stage; nonetheless, it seems likely that this phase is coinciding with a possible North American economic recession, which will undoubtedly restrict the growth of the Mexican economy as well.

For people like Socorro, costs of living are rising well beyond salary increases, and the pressure on the household economy is growing with new offspring. But uncertainty when translated into gender subjectivity highlights not only crisis and suffering, but also an area of possibility for transformation. Soledad is growing in her own way and becoming part of a body of people who offer a plurality of medical and healing choices in a specific urban environment. This personal process is taking place in the context of economic hardship, and of a centralization of the suburb that is engendering class stratification. Nevertheless, people still cling to localist ranchero and pueblo styles, combining them with urban styles through prisms of belonging. These are some of the connections between gender paradoxes, female subjectivity, uncertainty, and transformation in a context of urbanizing space and modernity.

I have explored some of the multiplicities of gendered self-perceptions and the contrasts that arise between these perceptions and the fixed stereotypes of gender representations. These gender representations portray women's experience as one of suffering, self-abnegation, and hard work. But gender relations in the cases studied show that female and male attributes can be negotiated because they are not only based on relations of domination, but also in those of resistance, compliance, and the potentially creative, even if sometimes painful, experience of not-knowing alternative possibilities. And, as I have stressed, being void of knowledge is a condition of uncertainty that has potential for both a crippling as well as a transformative effect.

Different and often contrasting and conflictive qualities of femaleness and maleness (for example, Carlota's maleness in wanting to "own" herself versus Miranda's unconditional self-sacrifice for her family) coexist as aspects of female self-identity. And it is through conflicts with the same and the opposite sex that gender positions are attributed (Wade 1994) so that "by focusing specifically on how gender differences are perceived, talked about, categorised and symbolised in a variety of contexts and how they express and are expression of power relations . . . [can] lead to a better general comprehension of systems of inequality" (Melhuus and Stølen 1996: 14). Difference and inequality in gender relations are both on this agenda.

Specific representations of male identity are linked to being a good breadwinner and to the experience of the paradox of male sexuality, which simultaneously demands fidelity of one's own wife (within wedlock), and the infidelity of one's neighbor's wife (as a potential for an extramarital relation)—the paradox between respectability and reputation, respectively. They are also challenged, though, by an urban condition that brings with it drug addiction and consequent challenges into intergenerational translation of maleness. Female identity discursive formation pivots around attributes of endurance, resilience in everyday life, and serving as a link between different members of the family for the allocation of resources as well as for the transmission of knowledge.

However, the differences among these attributes are matters of degree rather than kind. There is a tension between the binarism of the time of la ilusión in life of the quinceañera and the time of reality after marriage. Attempts to escape this dualistic representation take different forms. Differently positioned women use diverse strategies to address this tension. Traditional women may find their strength in patterns of submission to their husband, suffering for their family and kin, and shouldering moral responsibility on behalf of their children. They can also, however, challenge these patterns through compliance and gossip. Younger women still recognize values associated with motherhood, but they wish to experience a continuity between "enjoyments" and "obligations" (Collier 1986), and many hope to enhance their personal skills before having children.

Prisms of belonging are generationally- and gender-bound. Again, that is not to say that they are homogenous, or that they are read in diametrically opposed ways by different generations. Reality is more complex. It is not only younger women who do not identify with female attributes of self-sacrifice and suffering, as the case of Soledad shows, but when they do, older women at times criticize girls for wanting to maintain their single lifestyle and patterns of consumption. What is clear is that different and often contrasting representations, tendencies, and desires can coexist between different subjects, and within the same subject. It is at the level of this subject complexity that I have attempted to read some of the paradoxes of modernity.

This coexistence also highlights an area of uncertainty that can become a space for a challenge (rather than a subversion) of gender positions, but which can also prompt a collapse, as the case of Antonia suggests: a collapse into the body, rather than an articulated language of transformation of gender positions. Forms of challenge to traditional female roles can be manifested in physical illness and psychological crisis, or in a process of self-empowerment through active militancy in social movements. In such cases a woman is not only the link between her family members, but also a linking agent in a wider set of relations within the community. These experiences—together with experiences of a void of knowledge of alternative gender positions—take various forms that impinge at different levels, including those of representations, social actions, psychological states and the body itself.

The discomfort of living with the contradictions of gender relations also opens up uncertainty as a central force in gender subjectivity—a force that connects anxiety, suffering, the spoken, and the yet-to-be-spoken. A gendering process is both cognitive and embodied; it is an act of translation in language as well as an experience of becoming into language. Although female subjectivity in low-income urban Mexico involves processes of self-identity that still rest on values of physical proximity and mutual care rather than primarily on concepts of autonomy and self-sufficiency, the meaning, boundaries, and experiences of these values and their semantic limits, as well as their embodied experiences, indicate changes and unveil contradictions. Those changes are having different effects on the endurance and renewal of life strategies and the acquisitions or loss of individual agency.

Epilogue

Valentina: *Ya agarré la onda, Don Domingo, ya no necesito preguntarle otra vez.* (At last I have caught the wave, Don Domingo, I don't need to ask you again.)

Don Domingo: *¡Carajo, Valentina, (giggling) ya hablas como nosotros! Te has vuelto Mexicana.* (Damn, Valentina, now you talk like us! You've turned into a Mexican.)

When Don Domingo addressed me in this way, I realized that something had shifted in the way he related to me, and the way I related to the culture he spoke from. I suddenly experienced a sense of home in the language, and a joking but warm recognition of similarity between us; we were co-experiencing our convergencies. I felt I could flow and play with it, and let parts of me emerge in the process. It also reminded me of how we inhabit different me(s) when we abide in the spaces of different languages.

Dwelling on a co-experiencing of convergencies brings me back to what I posed at the beginning as an anthropological tension between two conceptual frames. In this book's journey I have tried to capture an ensemble of contradictory forces, facts, or tendencies to move beyond an either/or conundrum between concepts of phenomenological selves and disciplined subjects. This move is constituted by a reading of a political narrative of identity, language, representations and embodied experience. While the concept of prisms of belonging helps to capture the embodiment of representative, operative categories of time and space in everyday living, it also points to the tensions and sites of difference that arise in their production and appropriation. Even more, by dwelling in the articulation of contradictory forces in a field of urban, religious, and medical knowledge, I have tried to understand how a project of Mexican modernity is engendering subjects through a space of self-imagining.

This articulation, which also evokes a tension between fieldwork and anthropological theory, requires a constant act of translation. To me, capturing the shift from an anthropology *of* to an anthropology *through* the barrio is acknowledging this act of translation, and also recognizing an intrinsic partiality of representations. An urban anthropology through an urban space requires letting go of a close equivalence between places and cultures while it engages with interpretative agents as well as with subject formation.

An articulation of anthropology through the barrio is also about understanding processes of socioeconomic and urban diversification that become meaningful not only for studying demographic, household, and labor changes (which other comprehensive works have analyzed in the case of Guadalajara), but in light of a place and a subject that is ritualized, medicalized, and gendered.

A vernacular modernity emerges from the creation and re-creation of knowledge in a web of politics of difference. I have engaged with a micro-level of the politics of Catholic evangelization, and I have pulled to the forefront some of the complexities of residual and emergent religious formations. My interest has been to see how a major impulse and tension of modernity emerges from "being the Church," and from the different ideas of Catholic personhood embodied in the ways that both lay and clerical agents articulate discourses of belonging and group affiliations. I have highlighted a tension between the legacy of the new Church's modern citizenship project and the long-standing anti-state impulse of the traditional Mexican Catholic Church. However, that tension does not amount to a binary opposition. The evangelization of the Comunidades Eclesiales de Base, especially in the 1970s and 1980s, has been an emergent formation that has been counterpoised to a traditional, dominant Catholic evangelization. It is clear that at the turn of the twenty-first century, this type of evangelization has also not been able to fully capture a dimension of spiritual practice oriented more toward phenomenological and bodily experience. Traditional styles of religious practices and the spread of multiple and diversified religious affiliations in Guadalajara make us aware that spiritual experience is not just a legacy of a set of beliefs and a practice of group affiliation, but also a choice of subject and self-identification.

Those who emphasize discontinuities between new and traditional knowledge in narrating their experiences often have to legitimize their professional activities or their particular place within a church-related group. By doing this they validate or invalidate other people's experiences. Notions of progressiveness and backwardness are intentionally deployed by some agents—such as religious and medical elites. Plural medical choices concern issues of responsibility, agency, and community. Knowledge production, transfer, and appropriation define agency and labeling, and call for a close look at who perceives and represents those labels. Claims about the nature of religious and medical knowledge have to be analyzed through agents' positions in the construction of this knowledge, and the power that legitimization therefore confers. Traditional fiestas (as opposed to the new Church celebrations) and faith (as opposed to the science of homeopathy) are labels used by particular actors to define groups other than themselves. Their use, rather than showing particular essential cultural characteristics, indicates social differentiation and hierarchy between people and groups, and clashes, overlaps, and continuities between embodied knowledge(s): difference in the making.

A language of representations and the claim of authenticity over the traditional and the new processes, and the articulation of related processes of residual and emergent sociocultural formations are more complex than many urban anthropological readings of Mexican society and governments' rhetoric of a modernizing image of the Mexican nation have assumed. Hence I have tried to capture, via a focus on prisms of belonging and emergent and residual formations, some of the dissonances between a process of socioeconomic modernization and a process of embodied experiences of cultural modernity.

A focus on emerging and residual cultural forms and the way they are embodied in family and colonia interactions is essential to understanding people's self-representation, mobilization, their associations with space and places, as well as their identification with, and participation in, civil society. Identity is negotiated between multiple actors and within the same subject, and in Guadalajara it emerges in particular urban histories of religious activism, social mobilization, and traditional gender relations. An emergence from local and intimate culture extends to an understanding of some of the complexities at play in Mexican social and citizen subject formation. The expression "agarrando la onda" (catching the wave) is emblematic of some of these processes of tuning and translation.

Tuning into specific layers of coexisting realities and interpretations is a cognitive and embodied process; it also requires the capacity of the agents to tune in to the right wavelength. "Catching the wave" thus implies movement and translation: the process of understanding is a process that can be caught as much as it can be lost. Processes of emergent and residual sociocultural formations mold dominant formations dialectically and, to a certain extent, imperceptibly. By drawing attention to a micro-focus on interconnected emergent and residual phenomena regarding gender and migrant subjectivity, and religious and medical discourses, I have revisited, in a politics of modernity key, some themes of the culture and personality approach. And I hope that this revisitation can be read in parallel, and therefore as a contribution toward a better understanding of the impact that macro-shifts in the political economy, well-documented aspects of the feminization of poverty, and grassroot mobilization can have on low-income urban Mexico.

Vernacular modernity is about the politics of belonging and identification with national and religious discourses, and about suffering and becoming a person. It is also about the suffering of exclusion and the rearticulation of the world's taxonomy in a migratory and urbanization process—a process at the core of the growth of the Mexican national economy from the 1960s through the 1980s. And it is about a lack of language about a female experience of transformation of gender roles: a gap between an everyday gender experience that articulates emergent and residual forms, and the search for a language to actually describe it. An emergent form, for instance, can be read into the celebration of the quinceañera (or the decision not to celebrate), which pulls together a language of a modern impulse to individuation, a complex network of social capital building, an objectification of the female body as a vessel, and the female body's commodification. At the same time, it reiterates a language of the time of la ilusión before marriage, and the reality after it, that are part of a traditional narrative of gender roles.

Suffering, however, is not merely about the gap between the realm of experience and the possibility of its articulation in language. For some people it is also about the loss of belonging to an imagined community, and the need to reintegrate oneself into the rural-urban relationship. Changes in Jalisco's regional economy reflect the increase of remittances of Mexican migrants to the United States, and the infusion of new national and international capital investment. These developments are shaping the economy and the livelihood of pueblos and ranchos as well as colonias populares, and they are introducing some new socioeconomic differences between those who migrated to Guadalajara in the 1960s, 1970s, and 1980s, and those who either stayed behind or traveled instead to the northern U.S. frontier. In the stories and life strategies of those who have settled in Guadalajara, moments of recollection, interpretations of both rural and urban changes, and fixity are sources of empowerment and anxiety for the migrant subject. Being from the pueblo or from a rancho are narratives about the reconstruction of belonging, and they are also spaces of differentiation for the people who articulate them. Moreover, they are about the inscriptions of moral value into space. They entail the affirmation of belonging to a present spatial order, even if at times it is looked down on (as in the case of a bad, violent urban neighborhood), and an association with a rural space where social relations lack reflexivity and self-consciousness. Migration is recollected and narrated in a language of empowerment and/or suffering that emerges from having come to know another (urban) world, and coming to re-know oneself in it. These narratives are about the partial mastery and failures of the overlap between everyday life experiences, the labor market, desire, and imagination.

James Clifford has argued that the informant in anthropological research is now a "historical subject, neither a cultural type nor a unique individual" (Clifford 1997: 23). Capturing that historical transformation in anthropological writing is a challenge. However, my interpretation of this challenge is that we should not be afraid to engage with the phenomenology of ethnographic encounters in the process of migration, cultural and economic flows, and reconfigurations: narratives are performed, and desires, imagination, and suffering are experienced. They emerge out of historical, socially regulated processes; in mediating and flows and disjunctions between media, financial, and ethno scapes (Appadurai 1990); as well as in the constrictions on these flows that transformations of transnational capital generate (Ong 1999). Nonetheless, they are also phenomenological revelations of selves in the making, which carry with them the burden of the problematization of the informant. For me this phenomenological revelation is something that ethnography cannot jettison without running the risk of becoming an anthropology of rumors.

Modernity as it emerges through a colonia popular is open to interpretations which themselves are engines of the inscription of social difference. Processes of a centralization of the suburb have, at heart, microhistories of land legalization, struggles for housing, and more recently campaigns for relative gentrification. When house tenancy is at risk because gentrification is taking place, a process of socioeconomic stratification and differentiation between homeowners and tenants becomes part of a narrative of increased social atomization for some, while for others it signifies increased civilization and a decreasing violence in the urban environment. Leaving Polanco is for some young, newly formed families about finding their niche in newly urbanizing areas of the city and the possibility of living in modern blocks of flats. But for older families who, because of rent increases, are forced to move to an underserviced area of the city, leaving is about their decreasing economic power in the urban economy. The centralization of a suburb thus produces different narratives of social differentiation, not only about a memory of a migrant past, but also about a present of urban mobility.

Aspects of the relation between modernity and urbanization in Guadalajara emerge from focusing anthropological narratives into the micropolitical history of land tenancy, housing struggles, and socio-urban mobilization. The articulation of this focus can be read both as a process of group identity formation within the development and contraction of an urban popular movement, and as a discourse of subject formation. It is important to remember that social mobilization in Guadalajaran low-income neighborhoods such as Polanco initially emerged at the grassroot level to address local concerns about land issues and housing. However, now that some of those concerns have been addressed, they have been translated into an interest in national agendas of electoral and political transparency, and defense of human rights. I would argue that these emerging concerns in Guadalajaran civil society at large, and specifically in some low-income neighborhoods, are also rooted in specific histories of socio-religious mobilizations and in the spillover effect of years of consciousness raising in the Comunidades, and related activities such as those of the grupo de salud. To understand urban identity, we need to look for threads that reemerge but may get concealed in distinct forms at different moments of local, urban, regional, and national history.

In Mexico, modernity has also been a hegemonic national project of normative citizenship. This project has allegedly involved all ethnic groups and classes, but in reality it has peripheralized the poor and certain ethnic groups, who have not experienced the full benefits of national incorporation and economic growth. And to some extent, the success of this modernizing project has been paradoxically based on the failures of this incorporation. I have tried to show how, through low-income urban space, el pueblo becomes a key force in the national project—a socially diversifying process. In some cases, a self-ascribed or a descriptive category of *el pueblo* is more about political rhetoric than a reflection of a unified force on the ground.

The move to commodify medicine, pluralize health choices, and the turn to natural and alternative medicine (which has been increasingly observed within developing countries) translates through this low-income neighborhood as an interpretative struggle between faith and scientific knowledge. But this interpretative struggle needs to be understood in a context of economic hardship where biomedical cures are often unaffordable and perceived as less effective, even if they are promoted via national and regional health care programs. I have read, then, into interpretative struggles how the agency of subjects is located, and the self is revealed.

Domingo has not been well and is becoming weaker. I cannot stop thinking about an old, rusting car with American plates he used to keep in his courtyard. The car had been turned into a giant metal flowerpot, with plants on the roof, and medicinal cooking herbs and weeds growing underneath and on the sides. The inside had been used as a greenhouse during the colder months. In one of my last visits, the car was gone, but its image still flickers in my mind. Domingo and his family knew well that modernity needs a root in the courtyard. And by the time modernity, like a car, has been left behind, if ever, it has become something different.

Homeopathic Principles

The theoretical principles of homeopathy are distinct from allopathy. Homeopathy derives from the Greek words *homoion,* which means "similar," and *pathein,* which means "to suffer." The basic principle is that the cure is similar to the symptoms. While allopathy attacks and fights disease, homeopathy learns from the symptoms in order to give a remedy that does not stop the manifestation, but actually causes those symptoms in a healthy person. The symptoms are thought to be generated by a disharmony of vital energy, but there is no concept of an internal cause of disease. Generally speaking, for allopathy, the body is seen in terms of the metaphor of a hydraulic system — illness is due to an internal structural disorder (reductionism) or to the modification of a dynamic phenomena (functionalism), or in other words, an alteration of the homeostatic mechanisms (Federspil 1990).

For homeopathy, illness is the sum of its symptoms: there are no diseases, only sick people (Nicholls 1988). According to Samuel Hahnemann, the founder of homeopathy, illness is so subtle that it cannot be perceived through human observation.[1] Therefore, homeopathy shifts from trying to learn the organic cause of illness to understanding the body process of illness. Homeopathy treats the symptomatology of the body following Hering's law, which concerns the order and hierarchy in which symptoms appear and disappear: "Symptoms disappear from within outward, from above downward, from more important to less important, and in reverse order of their appearance" (Weiner and Goss 1989: 61).

The disease disappears from within outward, from spiritual/mental dimensions to bodily, physical expressions.[2] In Hahnemann's thought—which the puristas claim to follow closely—illness is generated from disharmony in the spiritual and etheric bodies which then materializes in the physical body. In fact, homoeopathic remedies are created through "spiritualizing matter" (Dethlefsen and Dahlke 1984). The process of dynamization takes place through a series of infinitesimal dilutions of the original substance in an alcohol base. At higher potencies, there is no longer any molecular presence of the original substance. The more dynamized the substance is, the stronger and deeper the effect on the psychological, mental, and spiritual bodies of the patients. Homeopathic remedies are peculiar to a certain individual, rather than to a particular disease, and their method of validation is experimental. All symptoms can be equally valid, and there is no evident priority or chain of consequentiality. Different aspects of the illness are treated in a synchronic manner. Allopathy, on the other hand, tends to atomize illness, looking "objectively" into its evolutionary process.

The first school of homeopathy in Mexico, the Escuela Libre de Homeopatía, was founded in Mexico City during the dictatorship of Porfirio Díaz. By the end of the 1990s, the only nationally recognized school was the Escuela Nacional de Homeopatía del Politécnico Nacional in Mexico City, according to data provided by the director of the Department of Alternative Medicine at the Universidad de Guadalajara. In fact, the Colegio de Homeopatas de Jalisco, which trains only allopathic doctors, and the school of Homoeopatas Puros de Jalisco, which accepts anybody who is interested, regardless of previous medical training, have not yet been officially recognized. The former leans toward an alternista approach that combines allopathy with homeopathy, while the latter closely follows the teachings of Hahnemann and adopts a holistic view of patients. Those who study at the Homeopatas Puros de Jalisco cannot advertise their practice openly, but publicize their work by word of mouth. Some schools, then, are more official than others.

Trees of Life and Death

Biblical Education

ÁRBOL DE LA VIDA

Salud
* Liberación, conciencización * Servicio,
convivir * Aire puro, servicios públicos * Vivienda
adecuada * Agua * Buena higiene * Salud en manos del
pueblo * Medicina Popular y natural: Herbolaria,
Masaje, Fitoterapia, Magnetoterapia,
Reflexología . . . * Fe, confianza,
esperanza *
Vida
* Democracia y
organización popular
* Ayuda mutua
* Cambiar la estructura
* Conciencia
* Solidaridad * Hermandad * Compartir lo que
conocemos * Tierra y medios de produción en mano del pueblo *

TREE OF LIFE

Health
* Liberation, consciousness raising * Service, living together *
Clean air, public services * Adequate housing
* Water * Good hygiene * Health in the hands of people
* Medicina popular and natural medicine: Herbalism, Massage, Aromatherapy,[1]
Magnetotherapy,[2] Reflexology * Faith, Trust,
Hope *
Life
* Democracy and
popular organization
* Mutual help
* Structural change
*Consciousness
* Solidarity * Brotherhood * Sharing what we know
* Land and means of productions in the hands of the people *

ÁRBOL DEL MUERTE

Enfermedades
*Amargura * Propaganda extranjera
* Casas farmacéuticas * IMSS, ISSSTE * Cólera *
Enfermedades de los nervios * Odio * Drogadicción
* Alcoholismo * Alimentos Chatarra * Falta de servicios
sanitarios * Anemia * Bichos * Falta de amor *
Anticonceptivos * Injusticia, desconfianza
* Ignorancia
Muerte
* Gobierno *
* Control de medio
de comunicaciones *
* Capitalismo (Papá
Estados Unidos) *
* Dominación
subalterna *
* Bajos salarios * Acaparadores de riquezas
* Explotación * Falta de servicios básicos

TREE OF DEATH

Illness
* Bitterness * Foreign propaganda
* Chemical industries * IMSS, ISSSTE * Cholera *
Nervous ailments * Hate * Drug addiction
* Alcoholism * Junk food * Lack of health care services
* Anemia * Worms * Lack of love *
Contraceptives * Injustice, mistrust
* Ignorance
Death *
Government *
Control of the media *
Capitalism (Daddy United States)
* Domination/subalternity *
Low salaries * Monopolizers of wealth
* Exploitation * Lack of basic services

Notes

Introduction

1. There are obviously many exceptions, which I will be discussing later. I am thinking here of the work of, among others, Nestor García Canclini, Claudio Lomnitz-Adler, and Guillermo de la Peña.

2. The dialectic between ethnography and anthropological theory is one of the most challenging and interesting aspects of writing anthropology/ethnography. See the challenge, for instance, of feminist thinking (Gordon and Behar 1995; Visweswaran 1994).

3. Despite the danger of gross overgeneralization, modernity has produced two analyses of the self/subject which have different starting points. Dialectical communitarian theories of the self have stressed that selves are constructed in mutual transformation and tension with society. This core idea of the self has drawn anthropological attention to social practices that constitute held values and beliefs and to phenomenological, interpretative processes of self-revelation. To a certain extent this has been a conceptual frame for a humanistic anthropology. On the other hand, postmodernist and poststructuralist theories have attacked the idea of the existence of a core self which existed a priori of social interaction, and looked instead at how the (gendered) subject is shaped by normative projects and regulatory practices. In this view, even projects of self-invention and self-discovery are not part of a liberatory project, but still the effects of a particular discursive power. Subjects are not revealed, but socially created (Coole 1995: 123–125). Particular attention has to be paid to the historicization of experience and to the generative power that produces the subject through processes of difference and historical sedimentations.

4. The Culture and Personality approach coined an idea of a culture of poverty. Broadly speaking, lower-class people were seen as having behavioral attitudes related to fatalism, sexual exploitation, and drinking behavior that recreated their marginal position in society.

5. Some of these studies were aimed at finding out the laws of urban formation through an objectification of space, and a few were embedded in Marxist and positivist approaches; see, for instance, Higgins's (1983) work on urban Oaxaca.

6. Though not the first to use this expression, Gutmann stresses that gender stereotypes have to be understood via the ways gendered subjects identify with different and mutable domains of gender identity.

7. Through exploring innovative and important issues about the acquisition and representations of voices across borders and their transformational power in historically situated personhood, Behar argues that a peasant peddler woman experiences the contradictions of multiple-gendered identity as existing in her life and in the representations of Mexican national history (Behar 1993). On the other hand, the masculine subject emerges in the contradictions and tensions between popular and dominant understandings, and practices of gender identity within a changing national history and urban popular culture (Gutmann 1996). The existence of a "will to identity" in a low-income neighborhood of Mexico City indicates that there is a creative space for changing social relations such as fatherhood and fathering, as well as machismo imagery.

8. First, there is a tradition of interpretative anthropology that has always had a particular eye to questions of memory, self-narrative, and construction of meaning. This has a structuralist legacy that assumes that there is something unknown to people that the anthropologist's narrative is often able to make known and meaningful. Second, there are the analyses of the subject that dislocate that same self-narrative as essential to a particular political-historical discursive configuration. This view is not interested in a phenomenological approach, which in itself is read as a foundationalist discourse. The thesis of this book suggests that we need both of these approaches, as each gives a different insight into urban identities.

9. The implementation of the PRONASOL program drew criticisms about a hidden presidential agenda behind the setting up of the program itself. The aim of targeting the provision or upgrading of infrastructure did not really create employment and subsequent sustainable growth. The grants were allocated to communities throughout the country who already had a certain degree of internal organization and a capacity for negotiation with the ministerial agencies, rather than reaching the poorest of the poor who often lack literacy (for example, indigenous communities) or were not subscribing to already existing systems of political patronage.

10. It was clear however that Salinas's interest in promoting such programs was to gain back the support of constituencies that had supported the opposition, Partido Revolucionario Democrático (PRD), in 1988 presidential and subsequent mid-term elections (Varley 1994). He had used, once again, forms of patronage and clientelistic relations that have ruled Mexican government politics since the revolution.

11. In fact, the dream of stability was completely shattered by the devaluation of the peso in 1994, which Ernesto Zedillo had to declare despite what he had just promised in his electoral campaign. It was also shaken by the Chiapas re-

bellion (launched in January 1994), which, appealing to international media attention, made it impossible for the Mexican government to kill the rebellion with massive coercive and military force, but obliged it to embark on new processes of negotiation with indigenous groups as political counterparts.

12. Before the 1994 presidential elections, internal divisions began to emerge in the PRI following the assassinations of presidential candidate Luis Donaldo Colosio and Judge José Francisco Ruíz Massieu (this also occurred in the PRD after the election of Cuahutemoc Cárdenas as mayor of Mexico City, during the latter part of the 1990s). They indicated a change and a deep crisis in Mexican politics. It was no longer possible to contain and subdue internal divisions in the major political parties (especially the PRI). However, the connivance and the control by emerging economic forces of political figures (such as Mario Villanueva Madrid, the PRI governor of Quintana Roo who fled the country in April 1999 after allegations were made that he was linked to the Cali drug cartel) have suggested obscure and endangering links in these political changes (Gledhill 1999: 29). Nonetheless, the agenda of the newly elected government of Vicente Fox and the PAN includes ensuring transparency and fighting corruption, but without the witch hunting of former PRI representatives who were involved in previous government connivances. It is still too early to say whether these goals will be matched by substantive action and a radical change in the political mentality of the new Mexican government.

13. At the time this book went to press, Fox's government was proposing a fiscal reform program, known as "La Nueva Hacienda Publica," which would create public revenue with the aim of improving education and tackle social exclusion. Originally, Fox proposed a VAT increase of 15 percent on goods such as food, medicine, and books. However, that proposal was withdrawn after public outcry and heated debate.

14. This is the case of the individualist impulses, which are not yet completely articulated, that emerge in the celebration of the *quinceañera* feast, discussed in Chapter 5.

Chapter 1

1. I wish to thank Renée de la Torre for this and other insightful remarks on this chapter.

2. The cultural conservatism of Guadalajara rests on the importance that the Church has had in the history of the town, and its often antagonistic relation with the national state. This was clearly its case of the Cristiada (1926–1929), a popular protest movement that developed in the Jalisco region in opposition to the post-revolutionary state, perceived as socialist and anticlerical. Moreover, many folkloric characters of Guadalajara and Jalisco have been used as national symbols for identification of Mexican culture—including *charros* (horsemen dressed in special clothes), mariachis (male folk singers)—using originally local cultural expressions in stereotyped national and transnational forms.

3. *Mestizaje* is a problematic term whose debate has been central to much

of anthropology of identity in Latin America (Hall 1997). The only point I wish to stress here is that *mestizaje* has been a discourse about homogenization of the political and the biological body (Nelson 1999: 208) and a revolutionary ideology, in the Mexican case, that has had a unified nation at its core (Lomnitz-Adler 1992: 281). In the process of Mexican state formation the definition of *mestizaje* as complementary or in opposition to indigenous cultures has been a central and contested debate in the definition of the Mexican nation, its political culture, and archetypal imagery (Gutiérrez 1998).

4. First, intensified mechanization of agriculture created pressure on food prices because production was directed toward export rather than internal consumption. Pressure on agricultural wages pushed small landowners to increase cash crops at the expense of staple crop production, and this had obvious repercussions upon the self-sufficiency of the *campesinos* (farmers) in periods of bad harvests. This situation, conjoined with increased concentration of land under the hacienda system, created a mass of landless rural people unable to sustain their life from agricultural activities.

5. An *ejido* is a land corporately owned by a community. Its tenure was assigned by presidential command for the agricultural exploitation of a single person or a group of people who had usufruct rights, but not the right to sell, rent, or transfer the property. This character of strict inalienability, specified in Article 27 of the 1917 Constitution, was eliminated by an amendment promoted by President Salinas in 1992.

6. The population estimate at the end of the 1990s is around four and half million, but we will need to wait for the next INEGI census in 2001 to have new official data. When this book went to press the data was not yet available.

7. Greater Guadalajara is constituted by a cluster of municipalities including Guadalajara and parts of Tlaquepaque (in the southeast), Zapopan (in the northwest), and Tonalá (in the northeast), as well as expanding industrial areas such as El Salto in the south and Tlajomulco.

8. Up to 20 percent of the world production of IBM takes place in the region of Jalisco (Medina Ortega 1997: 125).

9. Maquiladoras are small, sometimes home-based, workshops that receive subcontracts from larger companies to do a part of the production process of manufactured goods, assembling already-made parts such as shoes and technological, electronic, and photographic equipment (Escobar Latapí 1988). Originally they developed on the U.S. border, but this system of production has spread through central areas such as Guadalajara, where infrastructure and government policy are facilitating their installation (Duràn and Partida 1990).

10. Migrants arrived from rural areas or small towns, mainly in the states of Zacatecas, Michoacán, Districto Federal, and especially Jalisco. Up to the mid-1970s nearly half of the migrant population came from the region of Jalisco (Winnie and Velázquez 1987). The areas that have had the highest migration rates have not always been the poorest; it is often relative deprivation between the families of those who have migrated and those who have not, increased by migrants remittances (Massey 1994: 716), which triggers additional migration.

11. I refer here to Bourdieu's notion of symbolic capital, which implies that

within particular fields of forces, actors can acquire (or lose) power through resources related to social connections, communication, and group membership (Bourdieu 1987). I am not engaging here with the criticisms that have been directed to Bourdieu's thinking, but simply want to draw attention to immaterial and empowering aspects of capital (as wealth and resources, not as a process of exploitation) within social relations, in a migratory process, and, as I discuss later in the book, in religious and health care group's memberships.

12. The dichotomy of modern/urban versus traditional/rural is studied through analyses of push and pull factors, which should explain what attracts people to the urban life and repels them from their place of origin (e.g., Redfield 1947; Lewis 1961, 1966). Migrants are considered rational actors who tend to maximize outcomes with reference to their goals (Kemper 1977). Through the reification of universal psychological states, their action is decontextualized from its historical-economic setting. While presenting identity modernization theory, the focus is on the description of life conditions in the countryside as backward, and on the description of values, beliefs, and expectations in relation to urban life. The root metaphors of this approach hinge upon notions of progress, development and acculturation, and on backwards versus advanced. This approach's main problem is that it assumes both socioeconomic homogeneity among the migrants and a universal notion of rationality. On the other hand, the historical structuralist approach, which developed in the 1970s and 1980s, focuses on other aspects of migration (Kearney 1986): on migration's macro-economic causes within capitalist industrialization (Muñoz 1977). Then the focus on urban migration studies shifted to issues of labor distribution, class relations, and changes in the agrarian structures to explain the condition of urban migrants as the proletariat in the capitalist development (e.g., Frank 1971; Roberts 1978; Arizpe 1978; Escobar Latapí 1986; Muñoz 1977; Escobar Latapí and De la Rocha 1987). However, structural, class-based approaches to urban migration tend to underestimate the existence of counterhegemonic processes and overlook the diversification and idiosyncrasies of migrants' experiences. Migrants often do not lose their cultural identity, but they create and re-create their local culture through associations or informal gatherings (e.g., Altamirano 1984; Altamirano et al. 1997; Hirabayashi 1983).

13. Those major services were to include systems for potable water with house meters, electricity, drainage, street lighting, street curbs, paved streets, street names, street trees, parks, and recreation areas.

14. The groups are organized at the level of the street and the colonia, and they are aimed to develop a local knowledge based on personal and social interpretations of the Bible, as well as an impulse for community action. I discuss this movement in full in Chapter 3.

15. The 1990s saw a clear process of mercantilization and individualization of popular housing schemes, such as Infonavit (Instituto del Fondo Nacional de la Vivienda para los Trabajadores), which, rather than expanding the provision and building of low-cost housing, has become instead more of a financial system for family housing loans and savings.

16. Intercolonias is a progressive movement founded in 1985 within the Cath-

olic Church that organized a group of colonias in Guadalajara with the aim of promoting local agendas for better social and urban services.

17. CoReTT was initially constituted as an urban agency to promote urban planning and growth, but it turned out to be an agrarian agency limiting its task to land regulation (Varley 1992: 16).

18. Religious organizations have been particularly central in the process of urbanization in Guadalajara because of the lack of alternative associations. Extended migrant families have not settled in the same area, but have been dispersed in the urban area through a high rate of internal urban migration due to the tight control (before the formation of illegal settlements) on land urbanization. Second, ethnicity has not been a catalyst for urban affiliation because of the cultural homogeneity of migrants' origins (De la Peña and De la Torre 1992: 576–577).

19. At the beginning of the 1990s the proportion of houses with valid ownership papers was estimated as 76.1 percent, leaving 23.9 percent with irregular papers; for instance, receipts of payments, land title transfers, and other documents were not considered official proof of ownership (from the Organización de Colonos Indipendientes de Polanco [OCIP] census of 1991).

20. The history of this legal dispute is complex and detailed, and goes beyond the theme of this book. Nevertheless, it is important to point out the connivance between public and private sectors in violating constitutional laws regarding land expropriation.

21. Since 1974 the Jesuits have set up three training houses in Polanco, making the barrio the center of residence for novices in Guadalajara, with the aim of being closer to the everyday life of the poor.

22. During this period, political parties such as the Partido Socialista de los Trabajadores (PST) and the Partido Comunista Mexicano (PCM) unsuccessfully attempted to take advantage of the political mobilization.

23. A similar case of social mobilization occurred in 1980. In that incident, through a network of rapid communication, people were called in to block the activity of bulldozers with their bodies. The workers had been sent at night by the ayuntamiento to evict thirty-eight families with the excuse/reason that the area had to be transformed into a recreation center.

24. The Comité Popular de Sur is an urban popular movement formed in 1980 in the southern part of the city, and it is composed of representatives of several colonias populares: Lomas de Polanco, Lázaro Cárdenas, Lopez Portillo, Vicente Guerrero, Polanco Oriente, Echeverria, and La Longaniza.

25. The stalls, in principle, can be occupied by anyone willing to pay a fee to the organizers based on the size of the stall. However, I was told that to acquire a good location requires a bribe of some sort.

Chapter 2

1. Some interesting analyses have explored the systemic nature of Mexican sociocultural formations and the practice of talking about changes in different

spheres of life in urban contexts (Arizpe 1989). This study of capitalist development in the Mexican medium-size town of Zamora has shown the lack of an adequate cultural response capable of counterbalancing new forms of social, political, and sexual inequality, with the result being that technological modernization has not been met by practices connected to positive values of modernity (Arizpe 1989: 237).

2. Identity is seen as the point of junction (or fracture) between "intimate cultures"—the system of signs and meaning which is part of a cultural understanding—and a "culture of social relation"—the objectification of different forms of intimate cultures (Lomnitz-Adler 1992). What is important in Lomnitz-Adler's systemic approach is the attempt to see how internalization of cultural practices and values is linked to hegemonic processes, and therefore how identification is a process of power that shapes power hierarchies which are created both between and within identity groups (Lomnitz-Adler 1992).

3. The ritual reenactment of the past and the representation of tradition are central focuses for the construction of collective memory (Connerton 1989), both at cognitive and bodily levels. However, the division between reenactment and representation of the past especially tends to blur while dealing with life stories. The work by Ruth Behar, for instance, shows the overlapping of these two dimensions: while she narrates how her informant—Esperanza—represents her life history to the eyes and ears of the ethnographer, she conveys very poignantly how those representations become moments of reenactment and subsequent transformation of both Esperanza's and Ruth's sense of self (Behar 1993). Memories of past and present experiences of rage and anguish can be redeemably transformed through the telling and the writing of life histories (Behar 1990).

4. The "tales of the city"—the narrativation of urban space—can also be powerful tools to understand the relation between conceptualization and phenomenology of urban space (Finnegan 1999).

5. Mental mapping and cognitive representations have to be integrated with analyses of embodied experience (Csordas 1994). A focus on embodied experience, in my view, sheds light on what Stewart calls the *connaissance,* a local, contingent form of knowing related to particular social space (Stewart 1995) where physiological rhythms (of the body) come together with the rhythms of social practice. Thus the urban space is created by lived experience and performed styles.

6. This concept refers to the lived expression of the articulation of different but interconnected domains—such as the financescape, the ethnoscape, and mediascape—which can often be in articulation through disjunction (Appadurai 1995).

7. In this case I was confronted with different ideas of beauty: my personal view of nature as the most refined form of beauty and elegance, versus their ideas of the human elaboration of a natural theme.

8. Rural life is often associated with healthier, more natural food. Leaving the rancho to come to the city has meant dietary shifts, with animal rennet often being replaced by corn oil, and fruit more readily available (though often ex-

pensive for the average household). *Comida chatarra* (junk food) is widely available, especially in the city, and accounts for a considerable share of the money spent daily on food.

9. When something bad happens to a man, the blame is normally placed on the evil vagos, but if it happens to a woman, people tend to blame her instead, saying, for example, that it happened because she should have not been there.

10. *Bandillerismo* is the phenomenon of bands of juveniles, or gangs. For a good study of this in Guadalajara see Reguillo Cruz 1991. Living in Polanco, one learns to defend oneself from from being hassled by the poorly paid municipal police, who often arrest boys harmlessly hanging around in the street and then ask for money or goods to release them.

11. The Comunidades work at the street level. It is interesting to note years later that many neighborhood streets that used to have a strong group of those involved in Bible study have maintained a stronger character of mutual help than on other streets where such groups were either not strong or were absent.

12. As I pointed out in chapter 1, the control of land invasion through establishment of fraccionamientos populares in the urbanization of Guadalajara has made the settling of kin in neighboring areas difficult (De la Peña and De la Torre 1990).

13. Connerton (1989) describes three different types of memory: personal memories (one's own history), cognitive memories (related to knowledge of our past experiences), and habit memories (acting out memory in a particular performance). In this book I explore the relation between these interconnected forms.

14. The relation between revenge, village identity, family ties, and patron-client relations is the subject of Friedrich's (1986) important ethnography on rural Mexico.

15. I refer particularly to the previous description of urban social movements, where I pointed out that those movements arise where the provision of services by the welfare system is contested by different actors, and to the symbolic experiences analyzed in Chapter 5.

16. Chapala is a lake south of Guadalajara that has long been a tourist attraction (especially for North Americans), but its waters have been receding for some time, having a negative impact on tourism.

17. As pointed out in Chapter 1, in the region of western Mexico (and Jalisco in particular) ethnicity has not recently been a category of imposed or self-chosen identity for most people (with the probable exception of the major indigenous group, the Huicholes, who live in the Sierra Madre between the Jalisco and the Nayarit regions). The indigenous population in the Guadalajara region decreased significantly during the sixteenth century but rebounded significantly in the nineteenth century (Van Joung 1981: 39). The increase in population was a result of land pressure in the countryside and also of economic changes that led to Guadalajara's emergence as an important commercial hub. Guadalajara, then ruled by a mulatto/mestizo elite, was surrounded by Indian pueblos that later became part of what is now Greater Guadalajara.

18. In the past, but no longer, cross-cousin marriage was common.

19. It would be interesting to understand how particular regional features (in the case of Jalisco, a strong Catholicism, deep ranchero rather than indigenous roots, and a desire to migrate to the United States, especially California) affect changes in masculinity, and then compare the material to similar thematic studies elsewhere in urban Mexico (e.g., Gutmann 1996).

20. Don Domingo and his family have started to appreciate their indigenous roots, in part because of their experience of the Comunidades in Polanco and their proximity to a freemason cousin who lives in the village and works in Guadalajara as a judge. This cousin teaches them about the danger of U.S. colonization, and the pride of having indigenous Mexican roots, but most people in the village look down on him for his openly anticlerical views.

Chapter 3

1. Levine (1992: 29) uses *popular subject* to stress the transformation of people from backwards/voiceless objects to self-creating subjects—vital actors in the process of religious and cultural change. I use the term to indicate a condition of subalternity that can be potentially reversed by an active subject who attempts to escape imposed attributed categories within a process of construction and transference of knowledge.

2. There is an extensive literature on the subject of the Comunidades de Eclesiales de Base and liberation theology developed since the 1960s from the reflections of theologians such as Gustavo Gutiérrez and Leonardo Boff. I only wish to mention here the main principles of this theology: the rise of social and political awareness is the base of Catholic evangelization; poverty and its eradication are a theological concern; education is a fundamental step of evangelization; and social justice for the poor is required for the spiritual liberation of the whole society.

3. Jesuits are an internally differentiated group, and they have not been the only religious order involved in this evangelical movement within the Catholic Church in Latin America; therefore, the CEBs movement cannot be associated exclusively with their work. The development of liberation theology, the experiences of the CEBs and the activities of the Company of Jesus are interconnected, but they should not be conflated into the same subject.

4. I particularly refer to the charismatic movement, which has outstripped the importance of the CEBs movement in the archdioceses of Guadalajara and has had an important impact on the Jalisco region since the late 1980s and 1990s. But CEBs discourses also have to be understood in counter-opposition to evangelical Protestant movements and new religions such as the Iglesia de la Luz del Mundo, which has its headquarters in Guadalajara, and the Jehovah's Witnesses, who also have a remarkable presence in this same urban region (De la Torre 1997).

5. For example, consider the opposition between the Mexican state and the

Mexican Catholic Church. I stress once again that the formation of the modern twentieth-century Mexican state has been in opposition to the antimodern rhetoric and conservative position of the Mexican Catholic Church.

6. Posada was cardinal until May 25, 1993, when he was killed (by some accounts, accidentally) in a drug cartel shooting. He was recognized as being very hostile to the liberation theology movement. In Guadalajara, he replaced so-called radical priests (those inclined to liberation theology) with clergy sympathetic to the charismatic movement. Posada had been appointed cardinal in Rome by Pope John Paul II in 1991, and along with the Papal Nuncio (or envoy), Girolamo Prigione, was considered one of the pope's important allies in Mexico (Camp 1997: 230–232).

7. This image contrasts with the images of Christ in pain on the cross, and the infant Christ, both associated with traditional religion. Traditional religion is part of popular religion, as the latter has been characterized as an "ethos" of passivity based on the socialization of time and space (the centrality of reproductive cycles and of one's own community/family), worship of the blessed Virgin, God as the eternal Father, and Christ's birth and his passion on the cross (Dussel 1986).

8. However, Beverley (1999) has argued that this reading assimilates the subordinate/hegemonic axes to the popular/cultured, traditional/modern and fails to unveil how the subaltern operates within modernity and hybridization processes (1999: 128). I am only briefly referring here to the contribution that subaltern studies have had to the debate of politics of modernity in Latin America. Since 1992 the Latin American Subaltern Studies group has rightly pointed out the need to escape the binarism intrinsic to subaltern studies and address instead the blurring area where the dominant overlaps with the subaltern, especially when the latter is associated with the heterogeneous category of "people." The tensions between el pueblo and los pueblos that I discuss in this chapter is a revealing example.

9. Briefly, the historical process of opposition and of negotiation of power between the State and the Mexican Church has been important in the shaping of the latter. For example, the denial of juridical person of the Church in 1917 led to the Cristero Rebellion in the mid- to late 1920s, and later to the formation of conservative political groups in the Guadalajara region. Other topics too complicated to explore in depth here include the peculiarities and reasons behind the strong hold of the Catholic Church in western Mexico: the role that the Church has had in mediating between the State and civil society in Jalisco, and in the city of Guadalajara; the Church's conservative, antimodern stance, particularly in the Jalisco region; and the presence of many novices' houses in Guadalajara. Among the extensive bibliography on these subjects, see, e.g., Meyer 1973; Arias et al. 1981; Laueza 1985; Ortoll et al. 1985; Concha Malo 1986; Canto 1991; Muro 1994; De la Torre 1998; Camp 1997; and Fortuny Loret de Mola 1999b.

10. The experience of the CEBs in Mexico can be divided into three main historical periods: (1) the Renovación Pastoral, or el Nacimiento (1968–1975)

(after the 1968 Medellín conference), when the exchange of experiences and the mobilization of people began to take place at the grassroot level; (2) a second period (1975–1979) (connected to the Puebla convention) marked by a confrontation between proponents of different models of the Church: the dominant model, allied with the State against the pueblo, and the alternative model based on increased participation of laypersons and the underprivileged classes in religious life. The new evangelization focused on promotion at the grassroot level, involving groups such as those practicing *medicina popular* (discussed in Chapter 4), and small cooperatives of production and consumption; and (3) the third stage (1980 to the present), considered to be a period of transformation which has led to increased participation in elections monitoring and defense of human rights.

11. See Levine's distinction between CEBs inspired by "radical ideals," "sociocultural transformation," and "conservative ideals" (1993a: 47).

12. For example, the program of Solidaridad implemented by President Salinas during his sexennium, was said to be designed for investment of government resources in selected social welfare projects throughout the Republic. One of the hidden agendas, though, was the displacement of the main party opposition rhetoric (at the time the PRD). The overall slogan of the projects meant to shift the connotations of a central word in popular understanding—"solidariedad"—away from a left-leaning political discourse to make it part of the political rhetoric of the government and the ruling party.

13. Sexual metaphors are often used to describe the body of society and the body of nations, and in the language of the CEBs, sexual imagery of penetration has become a metaphor used to define boundaries of space and power relations.

14. "Periferia" (suburb) refers to a group formed in 1977 by people interested in the CEBs who were living in the colonias of López Portillo, De la Virgen del Carmen, Balcones del Cuatro, Villa Guerreros, and Echeverria. They, too, needed to organize themselves to lobby for installation of basic services, and in this case the word "periferia" was related to the centrality of Polanco's Comunidades.

15. This critical review of the Jesuits' position is not intended to diminish the positive results of their activities in many colonias populares in various parts of the country, and I am personally indebted to those Jesuits who offered companionship and intellectual support while I was conducting fieldwork.

16. The ACM was formed in 1930 with the aim of strengthening Church action in the social sphere. This organization was closely linked to the clergy, and its goals and style of action always reflected the visions and inclination of the Catholic religious hierarchy rather than the grassroots.

17. This recalls the life of Christ, and especially his suffering, as the root of his holiness. In relation to the Comunidades, the joyful element in the sacred is played down.

18. In the words of Don Pancho, who become an Adorador after many years in the Comunidades:

The message of the Adoración Nocturna is very different; the Adoración Nocturna is an action that I have always known. Nevertheless I had never practiced. I tell the priest that I feel ashamed to have discovered the Adoración at the age of sixty, but I am enthusiastic and God appreciates it. The Adoración Nocturna is to be in dialogue with God our Father and to devote some hours [in prayer] to him, while the Comunidades are more action-oriented. In the Adoración Nocturna one is directed in one way, while in the Comunidades in another.

Chapter 4

1. Defining alternative, complementary, and integrated medicines (as in the case of combinations with biomedicine as forms of "medical marriage" [Featherson and Forsyth 1997]) is a matter of debate not addressed here. However, the term "alternative" is used throughout because it is used at the grassroot level, and the term "complementary" is becoming more widely used among medical health professionals, especially in Britain and the United States. Nonetheless, the term "alternative" is used by such major organizations as the Office of Alternative Medicine (OAM), now called the National Center for Complementary and Alternative Medicine (NCCAM), a remarkably expanding American governmental institution initiated through a U.S. congressional mandate under the 1992 National Institutes of Health (NIH) Appropriations Bill, whose budget in 2000 was more than $64 million.

2. An interesting subfield of medical anthropology has explored the connection between the body, illness, and politics from a phenomenological angle (Jackson 1983; Scheper-Hughes 1992; Scheper-Hughes and Lock 1987) and stresses that a reification of culture has confined the study of the body to symbolic and semiotic fields, leaving the embodiment of experience under-explored (Jackson 1983). Hence, an anthropological study of the embodiment of experience requires attention to the "environment of the way of acting" as the condition present to the experience, which means paying attention to and experiencing "practical mimesis" (joining in and inhabiting the world as others do) (Jackson 1998). Related to this important distinction is another which should also be kept in mind: that between somatics and the body. On the one hand there is the perception of the body from the I-perspective—as the human being perceiving her/himself from the inside. On the other hand the body is perceived as a phenomenon—a body of behaviour—from a third-eye (Hanna 1995: 341, 343): both are coexistent but stress different narratives of the self. In this chapter I concentrate on the body as represented socially in terms of illness, but I am aware that somatics—in the sense of body intelligence and the active sensory-motor responsive wisdom to events—is an important and still much understudied area in anthropological studies on identity.

3. The term "curandero" can be translated as "medicine man," "native healer," or "witch doctor" (the last term following Trotter's classification in his study of curanderos in the southwestern United States [Trotter and Chavira 1980]). I prefer to use the term "native healer" rather than "healer" or "spiritual

healer"—acknowledging, however, the changing nature of the "native," especially in an urban context. The contested and transformative nature of what is "native" in urban contexts is one of the tensions that emerge in a vernacular modernity.

4. For a brief introduction to the principles of homeopathy, the difference between homoeopathic and allopathic medicine, and the development of homeopathy in Guadalajara, see appendix A.

5. National health care in Mexico is divided into two areas: social assistance and social security. Social assistance, provided by the Ministry of Health and financed by state and federal institutions, covers approximately 35 percent of the population (Nigenda et al. 2001: 9). The social security organization has two major branches: the Instituto Mexicano del Seguro Social (IMSS), created in 1944 for full-time employees of private enterprises, and the Instituto de Seguridad y Servicios Sociales de los Trabajadores del Estado (ISSSTE), created in 1960 for state employees. Other government-based institutions, such as the Secretaría de Salubridad y Asistencia, or SSA (part of the Ministry of Health) provide health care for those not covered by social assistance or social security. However, this has been described as only a nominal health service, given that its budget is quite low relative to the number of people it has to cover (Ward 1986).

6. "In reality the premise that health is the cause and effect of development (the fair distribution of wealth) becomes an affirmation, because there is no healthy population without development and this does not take place if the distribution of wealth is unfair and there are poor conditions of health" (Soberón Acevedo et al. 1988) (my translation).

7. A modernist and neoliberal view of society lay behind many of the devolution reforms in health care systems that have been supported by the World Bank (Gupta and Gumber 1999). Devolution, which is the shifting of primary responsibility to local government agencies, is also the foundation of health policy reforms in many other developing countries, such as the Philippines, Honduras, and Tanzania. However, the effects of those policies—which often decentralize responsibility, but not resources—on the well-being of the poor is cause for real concern (Kiefer, personal communication, 1999).

8. In the 1980s, the government budgets for the IMSS, ISSSTE, and SSA were reduced by 40 percent, 61 percent, and 50 percent, respectively (Belejack and Barry 1992).

9. Patients' dissatisfaction with doctors is also related to a lack of continuity in the relationship: a patient is not guaranteed consultation with the same doctor on different visits to the same hospital outpatient clinic.

10. Soledad—one of the former organizers of the group (see Chapter 6)—is particularly critical of the medical profession: "The doctors are enabled to take advantage of the people, the poor. . . . They study to become rich through the suffering of people. . . . What we do in the *grupo de salud* is directed toward those who have not studied, those like us, so that they can learn with what they have."

11. *Remedios caseros* are important not only in Mexican settings but also for

Mexicans and Mexican Americans in the United States, and an increasing number of self-help books targeting Latino women offer information and advice on using those remedies (Delgado 1997).

12. Important studies have examined the healing practices of traditional and folk medicines in Mexico, especially among the indigenous population (Fábregas and Silver 1973; Selby 1974; Ingham 1970; Signorini 1982). Nonetheless, how popular (long-standing and continuously transformed) illness etiologies are related to the contemporary development of alternative health care in urban areas is an increasingly important but still understudied phenomenon (Finkler 1994).

13. One of the roots of alternative medicine is in vitalism (Inglis 1979), which attributes illness to an imbalance of energy fields (e.g., at psychological and/or spiritual levels) that manifests itself in physical symptoms. Instead of being conceived as a recipient of external agents (medicines), the body is considered to have self-healing power (Inglis 1979), and one goal of alternative medicine is to release blockages that prevent such healing. However, because alternative medicine includes a great diversity of practices that do not share a theoretical universal paradigm (as is presumed of allopathic technological medicine) (Grossinger 1980), a general definition of its basic principles is rather arbitrary. The positive side of illness is that it can be a means of becoming aware of disharmony and dis-ease in the physical body, and therefore of latent forces within one's self (Dethlefsen and Dahlke 1992). It differs from allopathic medicine in that practitioners of alternative medicine seek to learn about and acknowledge imbalances rather than simply treating the resulting illness. Therefore, the focus is on symptoms as expressions of the person, rather than symptoms in conflict with the person. Healing can imply a sharing between the healer and the healed—a compassion in the sense of shared pathos. Often the process of healing depends on a change of consciousness, both in the healer and the healed (Dethlefsen 1984). Conventional medicine, in contrast, is symptom-focused and relies on the use of drugs, while the relation between the patient and healer is potentially ignored. Here a reference to allopathic systems is made with the realization that theoretical universal assumptions in their applications may also embrace different, and sometimes conflicting, practices (Hahn and Gaines 1985).

14. "The intent [of *salud popular* (the popular medicine movement)] is to form a wide, self-sufficient and independent organization that, besides preventing and curing illness, defends the rights of the marginal classes by mobilizing communities to demand basic services and fight for better living conditions of life" (Palomar Verea 1988: 260, my translation).

15. During the Chinese revolution, knowledgeable and educated people became involved in organizing forms of primary community health care. Called "barefoot doctors," they treated patients with a combination of acupuncture and homemade remedies, and only referred them to Western doctors if their own interventions were unsuccessful (Worsley 1982: 340). The Chinese traditional medical system has been handed down mainly though written texts and has maintained a certain unity, whereas Mexican traditional medicine has been transmitted orally and is more heterogeneous and fragmented (Loyoza Legorreta

1991), which is one of the main reasons why it has been difficult to establish such self-help training groups in Mexico.

16. In Mexico the World Health Organization's program of medicina popular was hampered rather than facilitated by governmental policy. This is the reason why later efforts have been promoted by universities and religious groups (as in the case of Polanco), outside ministerial health planning, and why they are therefore regarded as a form of resistance to the institutionalized order (Loyoza Legorreta 1990; Beltrán 1986).

17. I refer to those sociological studies based on historical materialist analysis, which uses abstract categories located in particular historical processes, instead of traditional empirical epidemiology, to explain the relation between conditions of health and sickness (Rojas Soriano 1982).

18. I use Dethlefsen's analysis of Aristotelian categories of causality. Aristotle distinguishes four types of causes: the *causa efficiens,* the motive power which induces disease; the *causa materialis,* the material and physical cause; the *causa formalis,* which shapes the result; and the *causa finalis,* the end cause, which is related to the perceived aim (Dethlefsen 1984).

19. I refer here to the discussion in Chapter 3 concerning how "the poor" are not a unified category, but a problematic one, since different agents have different ideas about what is defined as being poor.

20. The treasurer and some group members had been meeting in private houses, supervised by Mercedes, a former nun who lived in the parish with Padre Nemo. Conflicts subsequently arose over allocation of parish resources and Padre Nemo's support. As the original group became divided, the women became critical of each other and often gossiped. Two women who participated in both groups were not fully trusted by other members of the Vidasana group. After Mauricio and Soledad were excluded from parish activities, Mercedes also took on the coordination of the group that meets in the parish, but during her leadership, membership shrank. The history of mismanagement and the conflicts between leaders and participants resonates with the process of appropriation and withholding of knowledge discussed in Chapter 3.

21. The acquisition of knowledge, and its practice, also has an impact on gender relations. In Chapter 6 I discuss how, for some of the women, the experience of learning and practicing self-help remedies and alternative treatments is part of the shaping of their subjectivity.

22. Microdosis is a tincture of a specific herb diluted in an alcoholic solution; normally it is ingested by way of a few drops under the tongue.

23. I do not pretend to give here an exhaustive overview of the politicization of medicine in Mexico. Nonetheless, it is important to stress that the medicina popular movement has also developed in different parts of Latin America, such as among the guerrilla movement in Nicaragua, during and after the Sandinista revolution, and it has been widely implemented in Cuba (C. Kiefer, personal communication, 1999).

24. During particularly difficult periods, a few poorer families would go to the municipal market (Mercado de Abastos) to fetch edible vegetables from piles

of discarded food, and most families had to cut back on consumption of meat and fruit, both more expensive than staple foods.

25. The following quote is from a booklet distributed at the national level within the Comunidades: "Illness is a breaking of God's Law . . . [in the Old Testament] the appearance of poor and marginalized people in society was a clear sign that the alliance was broken and that the law of God was not respected . . . and the bad organization of society was one of the causes that contributed most to people's lack of health" (Mester 1991, my translation).

26. Two women of the Vidasana group were reluctant to give me information about the curandero and his activities. Mari Chuy said, "I do not know what Don Eduardo does, but many people go to him. . . . I have never gone. . . . His house looks very ugly. I believe that he has a lot of money, but he does not want to let it be seen. It is said that he lives in another neighborhood in a very nice house with another woman."

27. The courtyard/waiting room is reminiscent of a rural house in the rancho. Mari Chuy pointed out he kept it as such to make people think that the traditions of the pueblo/rancho were being maintained there. It reminded me of a tendency toward commodification of the "natural."

28. In diagnosing ailments, Don Eduardo often used conversation and the "look" of the patient rather than divination or examination of part of the patient's body (Kroeger 1988).

29. One young woman complained that doctors could not find anything wrong with her, but that she had such severe migraine headaches and anxiety that sometimes she could not leave her bed. As a consequence, she had lost her job and her fiancé, and things were becoming worse and worse in her life. Don Eduardo was the last chance for someone to recognize her pain, and when she came out from the *limpia,* she looked relieved even though Don Eduardo had told her that there was something wrong, and that she would have to come back to see him regularly for a time.

30. Literally it translates as "when one does not want it, the saint can't do it." In this particular context, it also suggests that it is not possible for the curandero to do something for a person who has an agnostic will.

31. Most of the homeopaths in low-income areas had previously trained in allopathy. Doctor Samuel had held a consultancy in Polanco for more than nine years (six years in a consultancy in the Parish of the Anunciación, during the time of Padre Francisco, then in his own consultancy near the market). Dr. Antonio, Dr. Diego, and Dr. Piso consult, or have consulted at different times, in a first-floor studio on the main street (the homoeopathic pharmacy in Polanco is on the ground floor of Dr. Antonio's medical practice). Dr. Consuelo and Dr. Magda consult in the Parish of the Santa Magdalena. Magda is the only homeopath who has not been trained as an allopathic doctor. She had at one time been a lecturer in chemistry at the university, but left her job because it was badly paid. Except for Samuel, who trained at the Colegio de Homeopatas de Jalisco, homeopaths in Polanco are self-taught or have done their training by assisting other homeopaths. All of them are *alternistas* (see Appendix A) except Magda, who is a *complejistas.* However, in cases where biomedical intervention

is needed, she turns for allopathic treatment to Consuelo, who consults in the same room with her in the Santa Magdalena parish four evenings a week.

32. Not writing the name of the remedy on the bottle is intended to prevent patients from reusing it as a form of self-help. Thus whenever a patient needs treatment again, he or she has to pay for another consultation with the homeopath.

33. Emphasis on the inductive side of homeopathy recalls the objective and testable link between the rational thought and empirical method typical of allopathic medicine (Federspil and Scandellari 1985).

34. Homeopathy's scientific validity can, in fact, be demonstrated because it can be empirically tested to provide clinical evidence in humans and animals, especially in low potencies (Ullman 1998). However, this is more difficult for negative testing. The lack of positive results can always be blamed on the incorrect remedy given by the homeopath, rather than on the inefficacy of the right remedy for a specific case (Weiner and Goss 1989). Nonetheless, this inconsistency also can apply to allopathic remedies. The fact that "it is known where the allopathic remedy leads" (see Dr. Samuel's claim in the main text) is an assumption which assumes a concept of a mechanical body. If the body responded just like a hydraulic system, the different efficacies of the same allopathic remedy in different patients would present the same theoretical problem.

35. The word *chochitos* comes from the root verb for "to suck," which refers to the fact that the remedies have to be held under the tongue.

36. The analysis of the use of homeopathy in Campinas, in urban Brazil, shows a similar combination of homeopathy with other alternative remedies. People do not entrust themselves exclusively to any particular form of healing and medicine but use different forms, either simultaneously or in a sequence throughout their history of ill health (Santos 1981).

37. For example, Doña Francisca is a middle-aged woman who earns a little money as a street seller, but she also has to attend to her large family. She suffers constant pain in her lower belly. She was x-rayed in the public hospital and diagnosed as having cysts that had to be removed. Since the diagnosis she has been given antibiotics (for the last two or three years) for her acute syndrome but has never undergone surgery. In her opinion, "In the Social Security, they do not treat you kindly, and they do not change the medicine. [Dr. Diego] has a kinder and more careful touch. I feel that homeopathy does not harm but cures. The other takes away the pain, but it does not cure."

38. Santos describes how in Campinas, in urban Brazil, homoeopathic reference books such as Kent's *Materia Medica* are used as oracles by healers who also practice homeopathy (Santos 1981).

Chapter 5

1. There have been only a few studies of the celebration of girls' fifteenth birthdays in Mexico, primarily focused on urban, non-indigenous populations (Cárdenas González 1987) or Chicano communities in the United States (Ho-

rowitz 1993). Recent literature on gender in urban Mexico and Latin America has focused more on class and ethnicity (Nash and Safa 1976, 1986; Arizpe 1977; Benería and Roldán 1987; Stephen 1991; Tiano 1994), women's participation in social movements (Massolo 1994; Bennett 1995; Logan 1988a; Radcliffe and Westwood 1993; Stephen 1997) and nation-state building (Martínez 1997; Dore and Molyneux 2000), than on the study of rites of passage (Lomnitz and Pérez Lizaur 1987) and life cycles. As already pointed out in the introduction, these latter themes were once developed in Latin American ethnography by scholars working within the culture and personality approach (e.g., Díaz 1966; Fromm and Maccoby 1970; Romanucci-Ross 1973; Díaz Guerrero 1975; Kemper 1977) through an essentialist view of the self.

2. "Ilusión" in this sense means "dream," or "hope," not "illusion," which connotes hopelessness and ephemerality. The Spanish word instead resonates with a hope or a vision that is worth fighting for.

3. I refer here to foci on the embodiment of gender experience, the multiplicity of gendered subjectivity (Moore 1994), and the negotiation of gender attributes also in specific Mexican and Latin American cases (Gutmann 1996; Wade 1994). These perspectives have acquired particular explanatory powers since studies of women's participation in social movements in Latin America have already questioned an essentialist view of women, deconstructed aspects of motherhood, elaborated on the role of the state in gender discourse, and argued for a continuity between public and private spheres (Radcliffe and Westwood 1993; Craske 1999).

4. Levine has pointed out in a study carried out among women in Cuernavaca that this feast has been celebrated by working-class families since the 1950s (Levine and Sunderland Correa 1993: 60).

5. Good (1991) reports that in the Sakandu—a rite of puberty observed in the Tamil Nadu state in southern India—girls also perform rituals similar to a wedding ceremony but their chaperon is always a female relative who is a few years older. Avoidance of contact with a male in the ritual is to avoid the threat to the purity of female sexuality and the girl's family's caste identity.

6. Padre Rodolfo, in the Parish of Santa Magdalena, has introduced a special moment in the Mass for the fifteenth birthdays of girls at which the girls hold each others' hands and recite a prayer: "Lord, I give you thanks for these fifteen years of my life that you have granted me . . . for my parents, my brothers . . . and for the love with which they have educated me. . . . I love and admire this world, that is the work of your hands, the sun, the flowers, the stars, the water, the wind and what is born and grows on this earth. . . . I recognize that the society I join today, with enhanced consciousness, has many negative aspects. . . . Nevertheless, there are many good people ready to give me a hand to follow the good path." This prayer stresses clearly that the positive elements of nature are reinforced in individual life mainly through conscious and communal human action.

7. The girls are made to reaffirm, as in their confirmation, the baptismal vow of the rejection of Satan.

8. This opens up issues about the reversibility of gender acquisitions and therefore the nonlinearity of life rituals, as well as the awareness that metaphors of status completion—which are often used by anthropologists to analyze initiation rituals—hinge on a particular notion of personhood (Strathern 1993). Hence different notions of personhood expressed in social and family relations are shaped by gender attributions but also by partitions (Strathern 1995); in other words, subjects emerge out of divisions, partitions, and to a certain extent losses, not only linear cumulative attributions. This reminds us that in the migrant experience, too, prisms of belonging are also about losses, and both the validation and invalidation of one's own experience.

9. I can only point out here the need for further study of the role of this ritual paraphernalia as a commodity in gender-identity formation as part of a process of commodification of gender relations in Mexico.

10. The basic costs are for the quinceañera's dress and shoes; food, normally *birria* (barbecued or stewed meat), beans, tortillas, soft drinks, and beer; the fee for the mass, which varies from church to church; and the charge for the rental of music equipment.

11. "Mi hija" is also used between adult women who are not blood relatives, and can be used by husbands speaking to their wives. Although an affectionate term, it evokes a status difference between speaker and addressee.

12. A casa chica is a single female parent household formed by a man in an extramarital relationship, and it has been argued that such arrangements arise because of particular Catholic laws on marriage and as a response to the ban on legal divorce (Gutmann 1996: 141). In this case, Ester's father lives in another state of Mexico and rarely comes to see his six children.

Chapter 6

1. As already stated, to understand gender identity we need to have a theory of the subject, and that subject, as Henrietta Moore has pointed out, is the location of multiple and often conflicting subjectivities (Moore 1994: 54, 55). Intracultural differences are played out and embodied in the experiences between subjects, as well as within the gendered subject.

2. Practical gender interests are directly related to women's position in the division of labor and to basic needs of child and daily household care. The fulfillment of strategic gender interests, instead, through the expression of female specificity and the alleviation and/or redefinitions of sexual division of labor, are targeted to overcome women's subordination and increase female consciousness (Molyneux 1985: 233).

3. Since motherhood is a bond that is variedly constructed in particular socioeconomic and phenomenological settings (Scheper-Hughes 1992), it is necessary to pay attention to the coexistent, and maybe contradictory, discourses on it that exist in everyday gender interaction.

4. Many studies have focused on women's productive or reproductive labor

as well as single-female–headed households (Nash 1980; Jaquette 1989; González de la Rocha 1994; Chant 1991) and considered motherhood and marriage relations as conservative forces militating against women's economic emancipation and their negotiation of gender boundaries (Benería and Roldán 1987: 143).

5. Earlier studies of gender in Latin America explored the stereotypical representation of gender roles, which rests on notions of machismo and marianismo, a notion of innate female spiritual superiority (Steven 1973, 1975). However, these gender stereotypes assume that Latin American women and gender divisions can be taken as homogeneous categories, when instead there is a complex interplay between class, gender ideology, female roles, and women's actions (Scott 1986, 1994; Benería and Roldán 1987). Gender analysis has also shown that there can be a reinforcement between capitalist development and increased machismo (Elhers 1990). Nor can malehood be conceived of as a homogeneous category, but more as a malleable and subtly diverse historical hermeneutic, the imagined homogeneity being directly connected to the definition of past and present discourses on nationhood (Gutmann 1996: 240, 241).

6. Women in other positions can use a representation of suffering strategically. Women landlords, for instance, may use a condition of vulnerability and a representation of victimhood to pursue their own strategic agenda in negotiating with government land agencies (Varley 1995).

7. This is the case of Diana Ortega, the wife of Don Jesús, whom I discuss in chapter 2. Diana is extremely devoted to the Virgin and still takes part in the annual procession in her village of origin in Michoacán. She has dedicated her life to raising her ten children. She married her husband because he "se la robó" (kidnapped her) when she was fourteen, not because she was in love with him. Her husband has had many extramarital affairs, and they have been sleeping in separate rooms for many years. These affairs have cost him a considerable part of the family income, to such an extent that years ago Diana had to take up tailoring at home to pay the bills. In Diana's words, all her children have been very good, and she is extremely proud of them. However, it appears that family relationships have been much more conflictual than she admits to outsiders, including me.

8. Gendered subjectivity is a prerequisite for self-identity but is not equivalent to it (Moore 1994: 147), and it unfolds both through empowerment and disempowerment in gender relations.

9. Male motivations for choosing a religious life are multiple. One motivation, however, seems to be an uneasiness with traditional masculine, breadwinning roles. These aspects reinforce right representations of heterosexual masculinity and power, the failing of which, for a layman, would be addressed by his peers as a potential indication of homosexuality.

10. As for the appropriation of images, we also have to account for the withdrawal from gender images in the configuration of gender subjectivity. The issue, for instance, of "not being a man" in a man-to-man or man-to-woman interaction is brought up in an illuminating recent ethnography on transvestites (Kulick 1998: 231).

11. These religious sisters had a novice house in Polanco until 1997. It was taken over by another religious order and is now a house for older, retired sisters who rarely get involved in the life of the neighborhood.

Appendix A

1. Samuel Hahnemann's (1755–1843) key text on homeopathy is *Organon of Medicine*.

2. Paracelsus's and Swedenborg's ideas about continuity between matter and spirit seem to have influenced Hahnemann (Fuller 1989).

Appendix B

1. Aromatherapy involves the use of plant essences (extracted through an alcoholic process) and oils.

2. Magnetotherapy uses magnetic forces (emitted by particular metals) to balance magnetic fields in the body.

Bibliography

Abu-Lughod, L., and C. Lutz. 1990. Emotion, Discourse, and the Politics of Everyday Life. In *Language and the Politics of Emotion*, ed. C. Lutz and L. Abu-Lughod. Cambridge: Cambridge University Press.

Alarcón, R. 1988. El Proceso de Nortenización: Impacto de la Migración Internacional in Michoacán. In *Movimientos de Población en el Occidente de México*, ed. T. Calvo. México, D.F: Cemca.

Altamirano, T. 1984. *Presencia Andina en Lima Metropolitana: Un Estudio Sobre Migrantes y Clubes de Provincianos*. Lima: Pontificia Universidad Católica del Perú, Fondo Editorial.

Alonso, A. M. 1995. *Thread of Blood: Colonialism, Revolution, and Gender on Mexico's Northern Frontier*. Tucson: University of Arizona Press.

Alvarez, S. Concluding Reflections: "Redrawing" the Parameters of Gender Struggle. In *Emergences: Women's Struggle for Livelihood in Latin America*, ed. J. Friedmann, R. Abers, L. Autler. Los Angeles: UCLA Latin American Center publication.

———. 1990. Women's Participation in Brazilian 'People's Church': A Critical Appraisal. *Feminist Studies* 16 (2): 381–408.

Ang, I. 1985. *Watching Dallas: Soap Opera and the Melodramatic Imagination*. London: Methuen.

Appadurai, A. 1990. Disjuncture and Difference in Global Cultural Economy. *Theory Culture and Society* 7: 295–310.

———. 1995. The Production of Locality. In *Counterwork*, ed. R. Fardon. London: Routledge.

———. 1996. *Modernity at Large: Cultural Dimensions of Globalization*. Minneapolis: University of Minnesota Press.

Arias, P. 1985. La industria in perspectiva. In *Guadalajara: la grande cuidad de la pequeña industria*, ed. P. Arias. Zamora: El Colegio de Michoacán.

Arias, P., A. Castillo, and C. López. 1981. *Radiografía de la Iglesia Católica en México, 1970–1978*. Cuaderno de Investigación Social no. 5. México, D.F.: UNAM.

Arias, P., et al. 1982. Consumo y Cooperación Domestica en Los Sectores Populares de Guadalajara. *Nueva Antropología* 6 (19): 165–187.

Arizpe, L. 1977. Women in the Informal Sector: The Case of Mexico City. In *Women and National Development*, ed. the Wellesley Editorial Committee Chicago: University of Chicago Press.

———. 1978. *Migración Etnicismo y Cambio Económico*. México, D.F.: Colegio de México.

———. 1989. *Cultura y Desarrollo: Una Etnografía de las Creencias de una Comunidad Mexicana*. México, D.F.: UNAM, Colegio de México, M. A. Porrúa.

Arroyo Alejandre, J., and A. De León. 1997. *La Internacionalización de la Economía Jalisciense*. Publication of the Universidad de Guadalajara, UCLA Programa sobre México, ed. Juán Pablos. Guadalajara, México: Universidad de Guadalajara.

Austin, J. L. 1975. *How to Do Things with Words*. Oxford: Clarendon Press.

Barbero, J. M. 1993. *Communication, Culture, and Hegemony, from the Media to Mediation*. London: Sage.

Barragán López, E. 1990. *Más Allá de Los Caminos: Los Rancheros del Potrero de Herrera*. Zamora, México: Colegio de Michoacán.

Behar, R. 1987. Sex and Sin, Witchcraft and the Devil in Late-Colonial Mexico. *American Ethnology* 14 (1): 34–54.

———. 1990. Rage and Redemption: Reading the Life Story of a Mexican Marketing Woman. *Feminist Studies* 16 (2): 223–258.

———. 1993. *Translated Woman*. Boston: Beacon Press.

Behar, R., and D. A. Gordon. 1995. *Women Writing Culture*. Berkeley: University of California Press.

Belejack, B., and T. Barry 1992. *Mexico: A Country Guide*. Albuquerque, N. Mex.: Inter-Hemispheric Education Resource Center.

Beltrán, G. A. 1986. La Asistencia Médica Primaria y el Retorno a la Medicina Popular. In *Antropología Médica*, ed. A. Beltrán. México, D.F.: Casa Chata.

Benería, L., and M. Roldán. 1987. *The Crossroads of Class and Gender: Industrial Homework, Subcontracting, and Household Dynamics in Mexico City*. Chicago: University of Chicago Press.

Bennett, V. 1995. *The Politics of Water: Urban Protest, Gender, and Power in Monterrey, Mexico*. Pittsburgh: University of Pittsburgh Press.

Berthe, J. 1970. Introdución a l'Histoire de Guadalajara et de sa Región. *Recherche Coopérative* 1: 69–75.

Beverley, J. 1999. *Subalternity and Representation: Arguments in Cultural Theory*. Durham, N.C.: Duke University Press.

Bohman, K. 1984. *Women of the Barrio: Class and Gender in a Colombian City*. Stockholm Studies in Social Anthropology no. 13. Stockholm: University of Stockholm.

Bourdieu, P. 1984. *Distinction: A Social Critique of the Judgment of Taste*. London: Routledge & Kegan Paul.

Bourdieu, P. 1987. What Makes a Social Class? On the Theoretical and Practical Existence of Groups. *Berkeley Journal of Sociology* 32: 1–18.

Bourgois, P. 1995. In *Search of Respect: Selling Crack in El Barrio*. Cambridge: Cambridge University Press.

Brachet-Marquez, V., and M. Sherrard Sherraden. 1994. Political Change and the Welfare State: The Case of Health and Food Policies in Mexico (1970–93). *World Development Journal* 22: 1295–1312.

Burdick, J. 1992. Rethinking the Study of Social Movements: The Case of Christian Base Communities in Urban Brazil. In *The Making of Social Movements in Latin America*, ed. A. Escobar and S. Alvarez. Boulder, Colo.: Westview.

————. 1993. *Looking for God in Brazil: The Progressive Catholic Church in Urban Brazil's Religious Arena*. Berkeley: University of California Press.

————. 1994. The Progressive Catholic Church in Latin America: Giving Voice or Listening to Voices? *Latin American Research Review* 29(1): 184–197.

Burdick, J. 1995. Uniting Theory and Practice in the Ethnography of Social Movements: Notes toward a Hopeful Realism. *Dialectic Anthropology* 20: 361–385.

Butler, J. 1992. Contingent Foundations: Feminism and the Question of "Postmodernism." In *Feminists Theorize the Political*, ed. J. Butler and J. W. Scott. New York and London: Routledge.

Caldeira, T. 1987. Mujeres Cotidaniedad y Política. In *Ciudadanía y Identidad: Las Mujeres en los Movimientos Sociales Latino-Americano*, ed. E. Jelin. Geneva: U.N. Research Institute for Social Development (UNRISD).

Camp, R. 1997. *Crossing Swords: Politics and Religion in Mexico*. Oxford: Oxford University Press.

Canto, M. 1991. Los Movimientos Sociales y Los Cristianos en México. In *El Estudio de Los Movimientos Sociales: Teoría y Método*, coord.V. G. Muro and M. Canto. México, D.F.: Universidad Autónoma Metropolitana, Colegio de Michoacán.

Cárdenas González, H. 1987. Los Quince Años: Ritos y Rectos para la Confirmación? *Teología y Catequesis* 21: 115–122.

Chakravorty Spivak, G. 1998. Subaltern Studies: Deconstructing Historiography. In *Selected Subaltern Studies*, ed. R. Guha and G. Chakravorty Spivak. Oxford: Oxford University Press.

Chant, S. 1991. *Women and Survival in Mexican Cities: Perspectives on Gender, Labour Markets, and Low-Income Households*. Manchester, England: Manchester University Press.

————. 1992. Women's Work and Household Change in Mexico in the 1980s. In *Mexico: The Dilemma of Transition*, ed. N. Harvey. London: Institute of Latin American Studies and British Academy Press.

Chase, M., and C. Shaw. 1989. The Dimension of Nostalgia. In *The Imagined Past*, ed. M. Chase. Manchester, England: Manchester University Press.

Clifford, J. 1997. *Routes: Travel and Translation in the Late Twentieth Century*. Cambridge, Mass.: Harvard University Press.

Cohen, A. P. 1985. *The Symbolic Construction of Community*. London: Tavistock Publications.

———. 1993a. Introduction to *Humanizing the City? Social Contexts of Urban Life At the Turn of the Millennium*, ed. A. Cohen and K. Fukui. Edinburgh, Scotland: Edinburgh University Press.

———. 1993b. The Future of the Self: Anthropology and the City. In *Humanizing the City? Social Contexts of Urban Life at the Turn of the Millennium*, ed. A. P. Cohen and K. Fukui. Edinburgh, Scotland: Edinburgh University Press.

———. 1994. *Self Consciousness: An Alternative Anthropology of Identity*. London: Routledge.

Collier, J. 1986. From Mari to Modern Woman: The Material Basis of Marianismo and Its Transformation in a Spanish Village. *American Ethnologist* 13(1): 100–107.

Concha Malo, M. 1986. *La Participación de los Cristianos en el Proceso Popular de Liberación en México (1968–1983)*. México, D.F.: Siglo Veintiuno.

Conciencia Pública (Guadalajara). 1975.

———. 1987.

Connerton, P. 1989. *How Societies Remember*. Cambridge: Cambridge University Press.

Coole, D. 1995. The Gendered Self. In *The Social Self*, ed. D. Bakhurst and C. Sypnowich. London: Sage.

Cornelius, W. A. 1975. *Politics and the Migrant Poor in Mexico City*. Palo Alto, Calif.: Stanford University Press.

Coronil, F. 1997. *The Magical State: Nature, Money, and Modernity in Venezuela*. Chicago: University of Chicago Press.

Crapanzano, V. 1992. *Hermes' Dilemma and Hamlet's Desire: On the Epistemology of Interpretation*. Cambridge, Mass.: Harvard University Press.

Craske, N. 1993. Women's Political Participation in *Colonias Populares* in Guadalajara, Mexico. In *Viva: Women and Popular Protest in Latin America*, ed. S. Westwood and S. Radcliffe. London: Routledge.

Craske, N. 1999. *Women and Politics in Latin America*. Oxford: Polity Press.

Csordas, T. J. 1994. *Embodiment and Experience: The Existential Ground of Culture and Self*. Cambridge: Cambridge University Press.

Das, V. 1995. *Critical Events: An Anthropological Perspective on Contemporary India*. Delhi and New York: Oxford University Press.

De la Peña, G. 1981. *A Legacy of Promises: Agriculture, Politics, and Ritual in the Morelos Highlands of Mexico*. Austin: University of Texas Press.

———. 1984. Ideology and Practice in Southern Jalisco: Peasants, Rancheros, and Urban Entrepreneurs. In *Kinship Ideology and Practice in Latin America*, ed. R. Smith. Berkeley: University of California Press.

———. 1986. Mercado de Trabajo y Articulación Regional: Apuntes sobre el Caso de Guadalajara y el Occidente Mexicano. In *Cambio Regional, Mercado de Trabajo y Vida Obrera en Jalisco*, coord. G. De la Peña and A. Escobar Latapí. Guadalajara, México: Colegio de Jalisco.

———. 1989. Poder Local y Intermediación Política: Las Organizaciones Vecinales en Guadalajara. Unpublished paper, presented at Centro de Investigación y Estudios Superiores en Antropología Social (CIESAS) Occidente Seminar Series.

De la Peña, G., and R. De la Torre. 1990. Religión y Política en Los Barrios Populares de Guadalajara. *Estudios Sociológicos* 8: 571–602.

———. 1992. Irregularidad Urbana, Contradicciones Sociales y Negociación Politica en la Zona Metropolitana de Guadalajara. Unpublished paper presented at Centro de Investigación y Estudios Superiores en Antropología Social (CIESAS) Occidente Seminar Series, Guadalajara.

———. 1996. Identidades Urbanas: Guadalajara al Final del Milenio. In *Globalización y Regionalización,* coord. H. González Chavéz and J. Arroyo Alejandre. Guadalajara, México: Universidad de Guadalajara.

De la Peña, G., and A. Escobar Latapí. 1986. *Cambio Regional, Mercado de Trabajo y Vida Obrera en Jalisco.* Guadalajara, México: Colegio de Jalisco.

De la Rosa, M., and C. Reilly. 1985. *Religión y Política en México.* México, D.F.: Siglo XXI.

De la Torre, R. 1997. *Los Hijos de la Luz: Discurso, Identidad y Poder en la Luz del Mundo.* Guadalajara, México: Centro de Investigacion y Estudios Superiores en Antropología Social, Universidad de Guadalajara.

———. 1998. *La Ecclesia Nostra, la Arquidiócesis de Guadalajara desde la Perspectiva de Los Laicos.* Ph.D. thesis, Centro de Investigación y Estudios Superiores en Antropología Social (CIESAS), Universidad Guadalajara, México.

Delgado, J. 1997. *Salud!* New York: Harperlibros.

Dethlefsen, T. 1984. *The Challenge of Fate.* Boston: Coventure.

Dethlefsen, T., and R. Dahlke. 1984. *The Challenge of Faith.* Boston: Coventure.

———. 1992. *The Healing Power of Illness: The Meaning of Symptoms and How to Interpret Them.* Shaftesbury: Element.

Diaz, M. 1966. *Tonalá: Conservatorism, Responsibility, and Authority in a Mexican Town.* Berkeley: University of California Press.

Díaz Guerrero, R. 1975. *Psychology of the Mexican: Culture and Personality.* Austin: University of Texas Press.

Díaz Guerrero, R., and L. B. Szalay. 1991. *Understanding Mexicans and Americans: Cultural Perspectives in Conflict.* New York: Plenum Press.

Donham, D. L. 1999. *Marxist Modern: An Ethnographic History of the Ethiopian Revolution.* Berkeley: University of California Press.

Dore, E., and M. Molyneux, eds. 2000. *Hidden Histories of Gender and the State in Latin America.* Durham, N.C.: Duke University Press.

Dreyfus, H. L. and P. Rabinow. 1986. *Michel Foucault: Beyond Structuralism and Hermeneutics.* Brighton, England: Harvester Press.

Drogus, C. 1990. Reconstructing the Feminine: Women in Sao Paulo's CEBs. *Archives de Sciences Sociales des Religions* 71: 63–74.

———. 1992. Popular Movements and the Limits of Political Mobilisation at the Grassroots in Brazil. In *Conflicts and Competition: The Latin American Church in a Changing Environment,* ed. E. Clearly and H. Steward-Gambino. Boulder, Colo.: Lynne Rienner.

Drogus, C. 1995. The Rise and the Decline of Liberation Theology: Churches,

Faith, and Political Change in Latin America. *Comparative Politics* 27 (4): 465–477.

Durán, J. M., and R. E. Partida. 1990. Industria y Fuerza de Trabajo: El Caso de El Salto, Jalisco. In *Crisis, Conflictos y Sobrevivencia*, ed. G. de la Peña et al. Guadalajara, México: Universidad de Guadalajara and Centro de Investigacion y Estudios Superiores en Antropología Social.

Dussel, E. 1986. Popular Religion as Oppression and Liberation: Hypotheses on Its Past and Present in Latin America. *Concilium* 186: 83–85.

Easthope, G. 1993. The Response of Orthodox Medicine to the Challenge of Alternative Medicine in Australia. *Australian and New Zealand Journal of Sociology* 29: 289–301.

Edel, M. and R. G. Hellman. 1989. *Cities in Crisis: The Urban Challenge in the Americas*. New York: Bildner Center for Western Hemisphere Studies.

Edgerton, R., M. Karno, and I. Fernandez. 1970. Curanderismo in the Metropolis. *American Journal of Psychotherapy* 24: 124–134.

Elhers, T. 1990. Debunking Marianismo: Economic Vulnerability and Survival Strategies among Guatemalan Wives. *Ethnology* 13(1): 1–16.

Escobar, A., and S. Alvarez 1992. Theory and Protest in Latin America Today. In *The Making of Social Movements in Latin America: Identity, Strategy, and Democracy*, ed. A. Escobar and S. E. Alvarez. Boulder, Colo.: Westview.

Escobar Latapí, A. 1986. *Con el Sudor de Tu Frente: Mercado de Trabajo y Clase Obrera en Guadalajara*. México, D.F.: Colegio de Jalisco.

———. 1988. *The Manufacturing Workshops of Guadalajara and Their Labour Force: Crisis and Reorganization (1982–1985)*. Texas Papers on Mexico. Austin: University of Texas Press.

Escobar Latapí, A., and G. de la Peña. 1990. Introduction to *Crisis, Conflicto y Sobrevivencia: Estudios sobre la Sociedad Urbana en México*, coord. G. de la Peña et al. Guadalajara, México: Centro de Investigacion y Estudios Superiores en Antropología Social and Universidad de Guadalajara.

Escobar Latapí, A., M. González de la Rocha, and B. Roberts. 1987. Migration, Labour Markets, and the International Economy: Jalisco, Mexico, and the United States. In *Migrants, Workers, and Social Order*, ed. J. Eades. London: Tavistock.

Fábregas, H., and D. Silver. 1973. *Illness and Shamanic Curing in Zinacantan*. Palo Alto: Stanford University Press.

Fardon, R. 1990. *Between God, the Dead, and the Wild: Chamba Interpretations of Religion and Ritual*. Edinburgh, Scotland: Edinburgh University Press.

Featherson, C., and L. Forsyth. 1997. *Medical Marriage*. Forres, Scotland: Findhorn Press.

Federspil, G. 1990. La Malattia Come Evento Biologico. *Minerva Medica* 81: 845–854.

Federspil, G., and C. Scandellari. 1984. Medicina Scientifica e Medicina Alternativa. *Medicina* 4: 433–442.

———. 1985. Medicina Scientifica e Medicina Alternativa (seconda parte). *Medicina* 5: 89–104.

Ferguson, J. 1999. *Expectations of Modernity: Myths and Meanings of Urban Life on the Zambian Copperbelt.* Berkeley: University of California Press.

Finkler, K. 1994. Sacred Healing and Biomedicine Compared. *Medical Anthropology Quarterly* 8: 178–197.

Finnegan, R. 1999. *Tales of the City.* Cambridge: Cambridge University Press.

Fortuny Loret de Mola, P. 1991. Listening to the Word of God: Impact of Modern Missionaries and Evangelists in Latin America. Paper presented at the American Anthropological Association annual meeting, Chicago.

———. 1999a. Introduction to *Creyentes y Creencias en Guadalajara,* coord. P. Fortuny Loret de Mola. México, D.F.: Centro de Investigacion y Estudios Superiores en Antropología Social, Consejo Nacional para la Cultura y las Artes, Instituto Nacional de Antropología y Historia.

Fortuny Loret de Mola, P., ed. 1999b. *Creyentes y Creencias en Guadalajara.* México, D.F.: Centro de Investigacion y Estudios Superiores en Antropología Social, Consejo Nacional para la Cultura y las Artes, Instituto Nacional de Antropología y Historia.

Foster, G. M. 1978. Introduction. In *Medical anthropology,* ed. G. M. Foster and B. G. Anderson. New York: Wiley.

———. 1979. *Tzintzuntzan: Mexican Peasants in a Changing World.* New York: Elsevier-New York.

Foster, G. M., and B. G. Anderson. 1978. *Medical Anthropology.* New York: Wiley.

Foster, S. W. 1990. Symbolism and the Problematic of Postmodern Representation. In *Victor Turner and the Construction of Criticism,* ed. K. M. Ashley. Bloomington: Indiana University Press.

Foucault, M., and C. Gordon. 1980. *Power/Knowledge: Selected Interviews and Other Writings, 1972–1977.* Brighton, England: Harvester Press.

Foweraker, J. 1995. *Theorizing Social Movements.* Boulder, Colo.: Pluto Press.

Foweraker, J., and A. L. Craig. 1990. *Popular Movements and Political Change in Mexico.* Boulder, Colo.: Lynne Rienner.

Frank, A. G. 1971. *Capitalism and Underdevelopment in Latin America: Historical Studies of Chile and Brazil.* Harmonsworth, England: Penguin.

Friedrich, P. 1986. *The Princes of Naranja: An Essay in Anthrohistorical Method.* Austin: University of Texas Press.

Fromm, E., and M. Maccoby. 1970. *The Social Character of a Mexican Village.* Englewood Cliffs, N.J.: Prentice-Hall.

Fuller, R. C. 1989. *Alternative Medicine and American Religious Life.* New York: Oxford University Press.

Gallegos Ramírez, M. 1990. Migración y Marginalidad en Guadalajara. Master's thesis. Universidad de Guadalajara, División de Estudios Politicos y Sociales.

García Canclini, N. 1995. *Hybrid Cultures: Strategies for Entering and Leaving Modernity.* Minneapolis: University of Minnesota Press.

Gennep, Van A. [1909] 1977. *The Rites of Passage.* London: Routledge and Kegan Paul.

Gerhardt, U. 1989. *Ideas About Illness: An Intellectual and Political History of Medical Sociology*. New York: New York University Press.

Giddens, A. 1991a. *The Consequences of Modernity*. Cambridge: Polity Press.

Giddens, A. 1991b. *Modernity and Self-Identity: Self and Society in the Late Modern Age*. Stanford, Calif.: Stanford University Press.

Gilbert, A., and A. Varley. 1991. Landlord and Tenant, Housing the Poor. In *Urban Mexico*. London and New York: Routledge.

Gledhill, J. 1994. *Power and Its Disguises: Anthropological Perspectives on Politics*. London: Pluto Press.

———. 1998. Neoliberalism and Ungovernability: Caciquismo, Militarisation, and Popular Mobilisation in Zedillo's Mexico. In *Encuentros Antropologicos: Power, Identity, and Mobility in Mexican Society*, ed. V. Napolitano and X. Leyva Solano. London: Institute of Latin American Studies.

———. 1999. Getting New Bearings in the Labyrinth: The Transformation of the Mexican State and the Real Chiapas. Paper presented at the University of Durham, England (n.d., seminar series sponsored by the Department of Anthropology).

Goddard, V. A. 1996. *Gender, Family, and Work in Naples*. Oxford: Berg.

González, L. 1979. *Pueblo en Vilo: Microhistoria de San José de Gracia*. México, D.F.: Colegio de México.

González de la Rocha, M. 1990. La Familia Urbana Mexicana Frente la Crisis. In *Crisis, Conflicto y Sobrevivencia: Estudios Sobre la Sociedad Urbana en México*, coord. G. de la Peña. Guadalajara, México: Centro de Investigacion y Estudios Superiores en Antropología Social, Universidad de Guadalajara.

———. 1994. *The Resources of Poverty*. Oxford: Blackwell.

———. 1999. Impacto de la Exclusión Laboral en los Hogares Urbanos Mexicanos. Paper presented to the annual meeting of the Society of Latin American Studies, Cambridge.

González de la Rocha, M., and A. Escobar Latapí. 1991. *Social Responses to Mexico's Economic Crisis of the 1980s*. San Diego: Center for U.S.–Mexican Studies, University of California, San Diego.

Good, A. 1991. *The Female Bridegroom*. Oxford: Clarendon Press.

Gordon, D., and Behar, R., eds. 1995. *Women Writing Culture*. Berkeley: University of California Press.

Griffin, J. 1986. *Well-Being: Its Meaning, Measurement, and Moral Importance*. Oxford: Clarendon Press.

Grossinger, R. 1980. *Planet Medicine: From Stone Age Shamanism to Post-Industrial Healing*. Garden City, N.Y.: Anchor Press.

Guha, R. 1998. On Some Aspects of the Historiography of Colonial India. In *Selected Subaltern Studies*, ed. R. Guha and G. Chakravorty Spivak. Oxford: Oxford University Press.

Gupta, A. 1998. *Postcolonial Developments: Agriculture in the Making of Modern India*. Durham, N.C.: Duke University Press.

Gupta, A., and J. Ferguson. 1997. *Culture, Power, Place: Explorations in Critical Anthropology*. Durham, N.C.: Duke University Press.

Gupta, D. B., and A. Gumber. 1999. Decentralisation: Some Initiatives in Health Sector. *Economic and Political Weekly* 34: 356–362.

Gutiérrez, N. 1998. What Indians Say About *Mestizo:* A Critical View of a Cultural Archetype of Mexican Nationalism. *Bulletin of Latin American Research* 17: 285–302.

Gutmann, M. C. 1996. *The Meanings of Macho: Being a Man in Mexico City.* Berkeley: University of California Press.

———. 1998. *Mamitis* and the Trauma of Development in a *Colonia Popular* of Mexico City. In *Small War: The Cultural Politics of Childhood*, ed. N. Scheper-Hughes and C. Sargent. Berkeley: University of California Press.

Hahn, R. A., and A. D. Gaines. 1985. Among the Physicians: Encounter, Exchange, and Transformation. In *Physicians of Western Medicine: Anthropological Approaches to Theory and Practice*, ed. R. A. Hahn and A. D. Gaines. Boston: D. Reidel.

Hale, C. R. 1997. Cultural Politics of Identity in Latin America. *Annual Review of Anthropology* 26: 567–590.

Hanna, T. 1995. What is Somatics? In *Bone, Breath, and Gesture: Practices of Embodiment*, ed. D. Johnson. Berkeley: North Atlantic Books and the California Institute of Integral Studies.

Hannerz, U. 1996. *Transnational Connections: Culture, People, Places.* London and New York: Routledge.

Harvey, N. 1993. The Difficult Transition: Neoliberalism and Corporativism in Mexico. In *Mexico: Dilemmas of Transition*, ed. N. Harvey. London: Institute of Latin American Studies and British Academy Press.

Herzfeld, M. 1991. Silence, Submission, and Subversion: Towards a Poetic of Womanhood. In *Contested Identities: Gender and Kinship in Modern Greece*, ed. P. Loizos and E. Papataxiarchis. Princeton, N.J.: Princeton University Press.

Hewitt, W. E. 1991. *Base Christian Communities and Social Change in Brazil.* Lincoln: University of Nebraska Press.

Hewitt de Alcántara, C. 1984. *Anthropological Perspectives on Rural Mexico.* London: Routledge and Kegan Paul.

Higgins, M. J. 1983. *Somos Tocayos: Anthropology of Urbanism and Poverty.* Lanham, Md.: University Press of America.

Hirabayashi, L. R. 1983. On the Formation of Migrant Village Associations in Mexico: Mixtec and Zapotec in Mexico City. *Urban Anthropology* 12: 29–44.

Horowitz, R. 1993. The Power of Ritual in a Chicano Community: A Young Woman's Status and Expanding Family Ties. *Marriage and Family Review* 19(3/4): 257–280.

Hunt, P. 1989. Gender and Construction of Home Life. In *Home and Family*, ed. G. Allan and G. Grow. London: Macmillan.

Hunt, R. 1971. Components of Relationships in the Family: A Mexican Village. In *Kinship and culture*, ed. F. L. K. Hsu. Chicago: Aldine Publishing Co.

Ingham, J. 1970. On Mexican Folk Medicine. *American Anthropologist* 72: 76–87.

Inglis, B. 1979. *Natural Medicine*. Glasgow, Scotland: Fontana/Collins.

Jackson, M. 1983. Knowledge of the Body. *Man* 18(2): 327–345.

———. 1996. *Things As They Are: New Directions in Phenomenological Anthropology*. Bloomington: Indiana University Press.

———. 1998. *Minima Ethnographica: Intersubjectivity and the Anthropological Project*. Chicago: University of Chicago Press.

Janzen, J. M., and W. Arkinstall. 1978. *The Quest for Therapy in Lower Zaire*. Berkeley: University of California Press.

Jaquette, J. 1980. Female Political Participation in Latin America. In *Sex and Class in Latin America*, ed. J. Nash, H. Icken Safa. New York: Bergin.

———, ed. 1989. *The Women's Movement in Latin America: Feminism and the Transition to Democracy*. Boston: Unwin Hyman.

LACHSR (Latin American and Caribbean Regional Health Sector Reform Initiative). 1998. *Mexico, Country Report*. Clearinghouse on Health Sector Reform in Latin America and the Caribbean (www.Americas.Health-Sector-Reform.org).

Kane, L. 1984. *The Language of Silence: On the Unspoken and the Unspeakable in Modern Drama*. Rutherford, N.J.: Fairleigh Dickinson University Press; London: Associated University Press.

Kaplan, T. 1982. Female Consciousness and Collective Action: The Case of Barcelona, 1910–18. *Sign* 7: 546–566.

Kearney, M. 1986. From the Invisible Hand to the Visible Feet: Anthropological Studies of Migration and Development. *Annual Review of Anthropology* 15: 331–361.

Kemper, R. V. 1977. *Migration and Adaptation: Tzintzuntzan Peasants in Mexico City*. Beverly Hills: Sage Publications.

Kroeger, A. 1988. Enfoque Popular de la Enfermedad: Explicaciones, Diagnóstico y Tratamientos Populares. In *Conceptos y Tratamientos Populares de Algunas Enfermedades en Latinoamérica*, coord. A. Kroeger and W. R. Cano. Cuzco, Peru: Centro Medicina Andina.

Kulick, D. 1998. *Travesti: Sex, Gender, and Culture among Brazilian Transgendered Prostitutes*. Chicago: University of Chicago Press.

Lancaster, R. 1992. *Life Is Hard*. Berkeley: University of California Press.

Laueza, S. 1985. Notas para el Estudio de la Iglesia en el México Contemporáneo. In *Religión y Política en México*, coord. M. Y. de la Rosa and C. A. Reilly. México, D.F.: Siglo Veintiuno.

Lehmann, D. 1990. The Church Return in the Centre Stage. In *Democracy and Development in Latin America*. Cambridge: Polity Press.

Levine, D. H. 1985. Continuities in Columbia. *Journal of Latin American Studies* 17: 295–317.

———. 1986. Religion, the Poor, and Politics in Latin America Today. In *Religion and Political Conflicts in Latin America*. ed. D. H. Levine. Chapel Hill: University of North Carolina Press.

———. 1992. *Popular Voices in Latin American Catholicism*. Princeton, N.J.: Princeton University Press.

————. 1993a. Popular Groups, Popular Cult, and Popular Religion. In *Constructing Culture and Power in Latin America*, ed. D. H. Levine. Ann Arbor: University of Michigan Press.

————. 1993b. Constructing Culture and Power. In *Constructing Culture and Power in Latin America*, ed. D. H. Levine. Ann Arbor: University of Michigan Press.

Levine, S., and C. Sunderland Correa. 1993. *Dolor y Alegría: Women and Social Change in Urban Mexico*. Madison: University of Wisconsin Press.

Lewis, O. 1959. *Five Families: Mexican Case Studies in the Culture of Poverty*. New York: Basic Books.

————. 1961. *The Children of Sánchez: Autobiography of a Mexican Family*. New York: Random House.

————. 1966. The Culture of Poverty. *Scientific American* 125: 183–202.

Leyva Solano, X., and V. Napolitano. 1998. Introduction to *Encuentros Antropológicos: Power, Identity, and Mobility in Mexican Society*, ed. V. Napolitano and X. Leyva Solano. London: Institute of Latin American Studies.

Logan, K. 1984. *Haciendo Pueblo: The Development of a Guadalajaran Suburb*.Tuscaloosa: University of Alabama Press.

Logan, K. 1988. "Casí Como Doctor": Pharmacists and Their Clients in a Mexican Urban Context. In *The Context of Medicine in Developing Countries*, ed. S. Van der Geest and S. R. Whyte. Dordrecht, Holland: Kluwer Academic.

Lomnitz, L. 1977. *Networks and Marginality: Life in a Mexican Shantytown*. New York: Academic Press.

Lomnitz, L., and M. Pérez Lizaur. 1987. *A Mexican Elite Family, 1820–1980: Kinship, Class, and Culture*. Princeton, N.J.: Princeton University Press.

Lomnitz-Adler, C. 1982. *Evolución de una Sociedad Rural*. México, D.F.: Fondo de Cultura Económica.

————. 1992. *Exits from the Labyrinth: Culture and Ideology in the Mexican National Space*. Berkeley: University of California Press.

Lovell, N. 1998. Introduction to *Locality and Belonging*, ed. N. Lovell. London: Routledge.

Low, S. 1994. Embodied Metaphors: Nerves As Lived Experience. In *Embodiment and Experience*, ed. T. Csordas. Cambridge: Cambridge University Press.

————. 1996. The Anthropology of Cities: Imagining and Theorizing the City. *Annual Review of Anthropology* 25: 383–409.

Lowy, M. 1990. Modernité et Critique de la Modernité dans la Theologie de la Liberation. *Archives des Sciences Sociales des Religions* 71: 7–23.

Loyoza Legorreta, X. 1990. Medicina Tradicional y Crisis. In *Salud y Crisis en México*, ed. I. A. Bay. México, D.F.: Siglo Veintiuno.

Loyoza Legorreta, X. 1991. La Medicina Tradicional y la Atención a la Salud in América Latina. In *Otra América en Construcción, Medicinas Tradicionales y Religiones Populares*, coord. E. Pinzón and R. Suarez. Bogotá: Instituto Colombiano de Cultura.

Lynch, K. 1960. *The Image of the City*. Cambridge: Technology Press.

Lyon, M., and J. Barbalet. 1994. Society's Body: Emotion and the "Somatization" of Social Theory. In *Embodiment and Experience: The Existential Ground of Culture and Self*, ed. T. Csordas. Cambridge: Cambridge University Press.

Mahar, C. 1992. An Exercise of Practice: Studying Migrants to Latin American Squatter Settlements. *Urban Anthropology* 21: 275–309.

Mahar Higgins, C. 1975. Integrative Aspects of Folk and Western Medicine among the Urban Poor of Oaxaca. *Anthropological Quarterly* 48: 31–37.

Malkki, L. H. 1995. *Purity and Exile: Violence, Memory, and National Cosmology among Hutu Refugees in Tanzania*. Chicago: University of Chicago Press.

Marcus, G. 1989. Imagining the Whole: Ethnography's Contemporary Effort to Situate Itself. *Critique of Anthropology* 9 (3): 7–30.

Márkus, G. 1978. *Marxism and Anthropology: The Concept of "Human Essence" in the Philosophy of Marx*. Assen, Netherlands: Van Gorcum.

Martin, J. 1990. Motherhood and Power: The Production of a Women's Culture of Politics in a Mexican Community. *American Ethnologist* 17(3): 470–490.

Martínez, R. L. 1997. Beyond Mexico's Woman: Negotiating Gender and Race in Dominant Narratives of Nation. *Social Justice* 24: 45–64.

Massey, D. 1987. *Return to Aztlán: The Social Process of International Migration from Western Mexico*. Berkeley: University of California Press.

———. 1994. An Evaluation of International Migration Theory: The North American Case. *Population and Development Review* 20: 699–751.

Massolo, A. 1992. *Por Amor y Coraje: Mujeres en Movimientos urbanos de la Ciudad de México*. México, D.F.: Colegio de México Programa Interdisciplinario de Estudios de la Mujer.

———. 1995. *Mujeres y Ciudades: Participación Social, Vivienda y Vida Cotidiana*. México, D.F.: Colegio de México Programa Interdisciplinario de Estudios de la Mujer.

Massolo, A., coord. 1994. *Los Medios y Los Modos: Participación Política y Acción Colectiva de Las Mujeres*. México, D.F.: Colegio de México.

Mattingly, C. 1998. *Healing Dramas and Clinical Plots: The Narrative Structure of Experience*. Cambridge: Cambridge University Press.

McClain, C. 1977. Adaptation in Health Behaviour: Modern and Traditional Medicine in a West Mexican Community. *Social Science and Medicine* 11: 341–347.

Medina, A. 1996. *Recuentos y Figuraciones: Ensayos de Antropología Mexicana*. México, D.F.: Universidad Nacional Autónoma de México, Instituto de Investigaciones Antropológicas.

Medina Ortega, M. A. 1997. Internacionalización de las Manufacturas Jalisciense y Su Impacto Territorial. In *La Internacionalización de la Economía Jalisciense*, coord. J. Arroyo Alejandre and A. Arias de León. Guadalajara, Los Angeles, Mexico City: Universidad de Guadalajara, UCLA Program on Mexico, Juan Pablos, editor.

Melhuus, M. 1992. Morality, Meaning, and Change in a Mexican Community. Ph.D. thesis, Department of Anthropology, University of Oslo.

————. Power, Value, and the Ambiguous Meanings of Gender. In *Macho, Mistresses, and Madonnas,* ed. M. Melhuus and K. A. Stølen. London: Verso.

Melhuus, M., and K. A. Stølen. 1996. *Machos, Mistresses, Madonnas: Contesting the Power of Latin American Gender Imagery.* London: Verso.

Menéndez, E. 1983. *Hacía una Práctica Médica Alternativa.* Cuadernos de la Casa Chata. México, D.F.: Secretaría de Educación Pública and Centro de Investigación y Estudios Superiores en Antropología Social.

Mester, C. 1991. *Los Profetas y la Salud del Pueblo.* Cuernavaca, México: Biblistas Populares Ediciones.

Meyer, J. 1973. *La Cristiada.* México, D.F.: Siglo Veintiuno.

Miraftab, F. 1994. (Re)Production At Home. *Journal of Family Issues* 15: 467–489.

Mirandé, A. 1997. Hombres y Machos: Masculinity and Latino Culture. Boulder, Colo: Westview Press.

Molyneux, M. 1985. Mobilization Without Emancipation? Women's Interests, the State, and Revolution in Nicaragua. *Feminist Studies* 11(2): 227–254.

————. 1998. Analysing Women's Movements. *Development and Change* 29 (2): 219–245.

Moore, A. 1973. *Life Cycles in Atchalán: The Diverse Careers of Certain Guatemalans.* New York: Teachers College Press.

Moore, H. L. 1994. A *Passion for Difference: Essays in Anthropology and Gender.* Bloomington: Indiana University Press.

Morfín Otero, G. 1979. Análisis de la Legislación Urbana, Su Aplicación y Consecuencia. El Caso de Lomas de Polanco. Master's thesis, Department of Law, Universidad de Guadalajara, México.

Moser, C. 1987. The Experience of Poor Women in Guayaquil. In *Sociology of Developing Societies, Latin America*, ed. E. Archetti, P. Cammack, and B. Roberts. Basingstoke, England: Macmillan Education.

Muñoz, H. A., O. de Oliveira, and C. Stern. 1977. *Migración Desigualdad en la Ciudad de México.* México, D.F.: Instituto de Investigaciones Sociales, UNAM.

Muro, V. G. 1994. *Iglesia y Movimientos Sociales en México: Los Casos de Ciudad Juarez y el Istmo de Tehuantepec.* Red Nacional de Investigación Urbana and Colegio de Michoacán.

Murphy, A. D., and A. Stepick. 1991. *Social Inequality in Oaxaca: A History of Resistance and Change.* Philadelphia: Temple University Press.

Napolitano, V., and X. Leyva Solano, ed. 1998. *Encuentros Antropológicos: Power, Identity, and Mobility in Mexican Society.* London: Institute of Latin American Studies.

Nash, J. C., and H. I. Safa. 1976. *Sex and Class in Latin America.* New York: Praeger.

————. 1980. A Critique of Social Science Roles in Latin America. In *Sex and Class in Latin America*, ed. J. Nash, H. Icken Safa. New York: Bergin.

————. 1986. *Women and Change in Latin America*. South Hadley, Mass.: Bergin and Garvey.

Needham, R. 1981. Inner States As Universal: Sceptical Reflections on Human Nature. In *Indigenous Psychologies: The Anthropology of the Self*, ed. P. Heelas and A. Lock. London: Academic Press.

Nelson, D. 1999. *A Finger in the Wound*. Berkeley: University of California Press.

Nicholls, P. 1988. *Homeopathy and the Medical Profession*. London: Croom Helm.

Nigenda, G. 1997. The Regional Distribution of Doctors in Mexico, 1930–1990: A Policy Assessment. *Health Policy* 39, 107–122.

Nigenda, G., E. Orozco, M. Guzman, G. Mora, L. Lockett, C. Pacheco. 1998. The Role of Priority Programmes in the Provision of Health Services in the State of Oaxaca, Mexico. *Health Policy* 43(2): 125–139.

Nigenda, G., L. Lockett, C. Manca, and G. Mora. 2001. Non-Biomedical Health Care Practices in the State of Morelos, Mexico: Analysis of an Emergent Phenomena. In *Sociology of Health and Illness* 23(1): 3–23.

Norget, K. 1991. La Mujer Abnegada: Notes on Women's Role and Status in Oaxaca, Mexico. *Cambridge Anthropology* 15(2): 1–23.

El Occidental (Guadalajara). 1975.

Ong, A. 1999. *Flexible Citizenship*. Durham, N.C.: Duke University Press.

Ortner, S. 1984. Theories in Anthropology Since the Sixties. *Comparative Studies in Society and History* 26: 126–166.

Ortoll, S., M. De la Rosa, and C. Reilly. 1985. *Religión y Política en México*. México, D.F.: Siglo Veintiuno.

Pader, E. J. 1993. Spaciality and Social Change: Domestic Space Use in Mexico and the United States. *American Ethnologist* 20: 114–137.

Palomar Verea, C. 1988. Una Experiencia de Trabajo en Salud Popular Con Mujeres de la Ciénaga de Chapala. In *Mujer y Sociedad: Salario, Hogar y Acción Social en Occidente de México,* coord. L.Gabayet et al. Guadalajara, México: Colegio de Jalisco.

Parameshwar Gaonkar, D. 1999. On Alternative Modernities. *Public Culture* 11: 1–18.

Paredes, A. 1967. Estado Unidos, México, y el Machismo. *Journal of Inter-American Studies* 9(1): 65–84.

Parkin, D. 1985. *The Anthropology of Evil*. Oxford: Blackwell.

————. 1992. Rituals as Spacial Direction and Bodily Division. In *Understanding Rituals*, ed. D. de Coppet. London: Routledge.

————. 1998. Foreword to *Locality and Belonging*, ed. N. Lowell. London: Routledge.

Paz, O. 1959. *El Labirinto de la Soledad*. México, D.F.: Fondo de Cultura Económica.

Pérez Martínez, H. 1993. El Vocabulo Rancho y Sus Derivados: Génesis, Evolución y Usos. Paper presented at the conference "Rancheros y Sociedad Rancheras," El Colegio de Michoacán, México, Zamora.

Pockock, D. 1985. Unruly Evil. In *The Anthropology of Evil,* ed. D. Parkin. Oxford: Blackwell.

Press, I. 1971. The Urban Curandero. *American Anthropologist* 73: 741–756.

Radcliffe, S. A., and S. Westwood, eds. 1993. *Viva: Women and Popular Protest in Latin America.* London: Routledge.

Ramírez Saíz, J. 1992. Los Comités Municipales de Vecinos en Guadalajara y los Movimientos Urbanos Populares: Un Estudio de Caso. In *Vivir en Guadalajara: La Ciudad y Sus Funciones,* coord. C. Castañeda. Guadalajara: Ediciones Ayuntamiento de Guadalajara.

———. 1996. La Internacionalización y las Identidades del Movimiento Urbano Popular en la Area Metropolitana de Guadalajara. In *Globalización y Regionalización, El Occidente de México,* coord. H. G. Chávez and J. A. Alejandre. Guadalajara, México: Universidad de Guadalajara.

Ramírez Saíz, J. M., and J. R. Santillán. 1995. *¿Olvidar o Recordar el 22 de Abril?* Guadalajara, México: Centro Universitario de Ciencias Sociales y Humanidades, Universidad de Guadalajara.

Redfield, R. 1947. The Folk Society. *American Journal of Sociology* 52: 293–308.

Regalado Santillán, J. 1995. *Lucha por la Vivienda en Guadalajara: Historia, Política y Organización Social, 1980–1992.* Guadalajara, México: Centro Universitario de Ciencias Sociales y Humanidades, Universidad de Guadalajara.

Reguillo Cruz, R. 1991. *En la Calle Otra Vez, Las Bandas: Identidad Urbana y Usos de la Comunicación.* Guadalajara, México: Instituto Tecnológico y de Estudios Superiores de Occidente.

Roberts, B. R. 1978. *Cities of Peasants: The Political Economy of Urbanization in the Third World.* London: Arnold.

———. 1986. Industrialización, Clase Obrera y Mercado de Trabajo. In *Cambio Regional, Mercado de Trabajo y Vida Obrera en Jalisco,* coord. G. De la Peña and A. Escobar Latapí. Guadalajara, México: El Colegio de Jalisco.

———. 1995. *The Making of Citizens: Cities of Peasants Revisited.* London: Arnold.

Rodriguez, V. E. 1997. *Decentralization in Mexico: From Reforma Municipal to Solidaridad, to Nuevo Federalismo.* Boulder, Colo.: Westview.

———. 1998. *Women's Participation in Mexican Political Life.* Boulder, Colo.: Westview.

Rofel, L. 1999. *Other Modernities: Gendered Yearnings in China After Socialism.* Berkeley: University of California Press.

Roger, S. 1975. Female Forms of Power and the Myth of Male Dominance: A Model of Female/Male Interaction in Peasant Society. *American Ethnologist* 2(3): 727–73.

Rojas Soriano, R. 1982. *Capitalismo y Enfermedad.* México, D.F.: Folios Ediciones.

Romanucci-Ross, L. 1973. *Conflict, Violence, and Morality in a Mexican Village.* Palo Alto, Calif.: National Press Books.

Rostas, S. 1998. Performing "Mexicanidad": Popular "Indigenismo" in Mexico City. In *Encuentros Antropológicos: Power, Identity, and Mobility in Mexican So-*

ciety, ed. V. Napolitano and X. Leyva Solano. London: Institute of Latin American Studies.

Rouse, R. 1992. Making Sense of Settlement: Class Transformation, Cultural Struggle, and Transnationalism among Mexican Migrants in the United States. In *Towards a Transnational Perspective on Migration: Race, Class, Ethnicity, and Nationalism Reconsidered,* ed. N. Glick Schiller, L. Basch, and C. Blanc-Szanton, pp. 25–42. Annals of the New York Academy of Sciences no. 645. New York: New York Academy of Sciences.

———. 1995. Questions of Identity, Personhood, and Collectivity in Transnational Migration to the United States. *Critique of Anthropology* 15: 351–380.

Sanchez Van Dyck de Levy, M. 1979. Le Phenomène de Fractionnements Populaires a Guadalajara, Jalisco, Mexique. Ph.D. thesis, Ecole des Hautes Etudes en Sciences Sociales, Department of Sociology.

Santos, J. 1981. Homeopathy in Campinas: A Study of the Socio-Symbolic Field. Ph.D. thesis, University of London, Department of Anthropology.

Scarry, E. 1985. *The Body in Pain: The Making and Unmaking of the World.* New York: Oxford University Press.

Scheper-Hughes, N. 1992. *Death Without Weeping: The Violence of Everyday Life in Brazil.* Berkeley: University of California Press.

Scheper-Hughes, N., and M. Lock. 1987. The Mindful Body—A Prolegomenon to Future Work in Medical Anthropology. *Medical Anthropology Quarterly* 1: 6–41.

Schutte, O. 1993. Consciousness on the Side of the Oppressed: The Theology of Liberation and Christian-Marxist Dialogue. In *Cultural Identity and Social Liberation in Latin American Thought.* Albany: State University of New York Press.

Scott, J. 1992. "Experience." In *Feminists Theorize the Political,* ed. J. Butler and J. W. Scott. London: Routledge.

Scott McEwen, A. 1986. Women in Latin America: Stereotypes and Social Science. *Bulletin of Latin American Research* 6(2): 21–27.

———. 1994. *Divisions and Solidarities: Gender, Class, and Employment in Latin America.* London and New York: Routledge.

Selby, H. A. 1974. *Zapotec Deviance: The Convergence of Folk and Modern Sociology.* Austin: University of Texas Press.

———. 1987. Battling Urban Poverty from Below: A Profile of the Poor in Two Mexican Cities. *American Anthropologist* 89: 419–424.

Selby, H. A., A. D. Murphy, and S. A. Lorenzen. 1990. *The Mexican Urban Household: Organizing for Self-Defense.* Austin: University of Texas Press.

Sharma, U. 1992. *Complementary Medicine Today: Practitioners and Patients.* London: Tavistock/ Routledge.

Signorini, I. 1982. Pattern of Frights. *Ethnology* 22: 313–323.

Smith, C. 1991. *The Emergence of Liberation Theology: Radical Religion and Social Movement Theory.* Chicago: University of Chicago Press.

Soberón Acevedo, G., J. Kumate, and J. Laguna. 1988. *La Salud en México:*

Testimonios, 1988. México, D.F.: Secretaría de Salud, Instituto Nacional de Salud Pública.

El Sol de Guadalajara. 1991.

Soria Romo, R. 1991. Migración, Ingresos y Asentamientos Humanos Irregulares en la Zona Metropolitana de Guadalajara. *Carta Económica Regional* 4: 3–11.

Stephen, L. 1991. *Zapotec Women.* Austin: University of Texas Press.

———. 1997. *Women and Social Movements in Latin America: Power from Below.* Austin: University of Texas Press.

Stern, C. 1990. Cambios en las Condiciones de Sobrevivencia Infantil en México y Estrategia para el Futuro. *Salud Pública de México* 32: 532–542.

Stern, S. J. 1995. *The Secret History of Gender, Women, Men, and Power in Late Colonial Mexico.* Chapel Hill: University of North Carolina Press.

Stevens, E. 1973. Machismo y Marianismo. *Society* 10(6): 57–63.

———. 1975. Marianismo the Other Face of Machismo in Latin America. In *Female and Male in Latin America,* ed. A. Pescatello. Pittsburgh: University of Pittsburgh Press.

Stewart, L. 1995. Bodies, Visions, and Spacial Politics: A Review Essay on Henri Lefebvre's The Production of Space. *Society and Space (Environment and Planning D)* 13(5): 609–618.

Stoner, B. 1986. Understanding Medical Systems: Traditional, Modern, and Syncretic Health Care Alternatives in Medically Pluralistic Societies. *Medical Anthropology Quarterly* 17: 44–48.

Strathern, M. 1993. On Rituals. In *Carved Flesh/Cast Selves,* ed. V. Broche-Due, I. Rudie, and T. Bleie. Oxford: Berg.

———. 1995. Gender: Division or Comparison? In *Practising Feminism,* ed. N. Charles and F. Hughes-Freeland. London: Routledge.

Talpade Mohanty, C. 1992. Feminist Encounters: Locating the Politics of Experience. In *Destabilizing Theory,* ed. M. Barrett and A. Phillips. Stanford, Calif.: Stanford University Press.

Taussig, M. 1980. Reification of the Consciousness of the Patient. *Social Science and Medicine* 14b: 3–13.

———. 1993. *Mimesis and Alterity: A Particular History of the Senses.* New York: Routledge.

Taylor, C. 1989. *The Sources of the Self.* Cambridge, Mass: Harvard University Press.

Tiano, S. 1994. *Patriarchy on the Line: Labour, Gender, and Ideology in the Mexican Maquila Industry.* Philadelphia: Temple University Press.

Tiano, S., and C. Ladino. 1999. Dating, Mating, and Motherhood: Identity Construction among Mexican Maquila Workers. *Society and Space (Environment and Planning A)* 31: 305–325.

Tonkin, E. 1992. *Narrating Our Pasts: The Social Construction of Oral History.* Cambridge: Cambridge University Press.

Torres Montes de Oca, A. 1997. Reinserción de Jalisco a la Economía Internacional: Cambios en Su Sector Externo, 1980–1994. In *La Internacionalización de la Economía Jalisciense,* coord. J. Arroyo Alejandre and A. de León Arias. Guadalajara, México: Universidad de Guadalajara.

Trejo Delabre, R. 1994. *Chiapas: La Guerra de las Ideas.* México, D.F.: Editorial Diana.

Trotter, R., and J. Chavira. 1980. Curanderismo: An Emic Theorethical Perspective of Mexican-American Folk Medicine. *Medical Anthropology* 4: 423–487.

Turner, V. W. 1969. *The Ritual Process: Structure and Anti-Structure.* Chicago: Aldine.

———. 1974. *Dramas, Fields, and Metaphors: Symbolic Action in Human Society.* Ithaca, N.Y.: Cornell University Press.

———. 1982. *From Ritual to Theatre: The Human Seriousness of Play.* New York: Performing Arts Journal Publications.

Ullman, D. 1998. *Homeopathic Medicine for the Twenty-first Century.* Wellingborough: Thorsons.

Van Young, E. 1981. *Hacienda and Market in Eighteenth-century Mexico.* Berkeley: University of California Press.

Varley, A. 1989. Settlement, Illegality, and Illegalization: The Need for Reassessment. In *Corruption, Development and Inequality,* ed. P. Ward. Routledge: London.

———. 1992. *Gender, Household Structure, and Accommodation for Young Adults in Urban Mexico.* Paper presented at the Institute of Latin American Studies seminar series, University of London.

———. 1994. Delivering the Goods: Solidarity, Land Regularisation, and Urban Services. In *Dismantling the Mexican State?* ed. R. Aitken, N. Crasre, D. Stansfield. London: Macmillan.

———. 1995, Neither Victims nor Heroines: Women, Land, and Housing in Mexican Cities. *Third World Planning Review* 17 (2): 169–182.

———. 2000. Women and the Home in Mexican Family Law. In *Hidden Histories of Gender and State in Latin America,* ed. E. Dore and M. Molyneux. Durham, N.C.: Duke University Press.

Vaughan, M. K. 2000. Modernizing Patriarchy. In *Hidden Histories of Gender and the State in Latin America,* ed. E. Dore and M. Molyneux. Durham, N.C.: Duke University Press.

Vázquez, D. 1990. *Guadalajara: Ensayos de Interpretación.* Guadalajara, México: El Colegio de Jalisco.

Velázquez Gutiérrez, L. A., and J. Papail. 1997. *Migrantes y Transformación Económica Sectorial: Cuatro Ciudades del Occidente de México.* Guadalajara, México: Universidad de Guadalajara Centro Universitario de Ciencias Económico Administrativas.

Vélez-Ibañez, C. G. 1983. *Rituals of Marginality: Politics, Process, and Culture Change in Urban Central Mexico, 1969–1974.* Berkeley: University of California Press.

Vellinga, M. 1986. Masculinité et Feminité dans la "Fotonovela" Latino-Americaine. *Cahiers Internationaux de Sociologie* 80: 161–179.

Visweswaran, K. 1994. *Fictions of Feminist Ethnography*. Minneapolis: University of Minnesota Press.

Wade, P. 1994. Man and the Hunter: Gender and Violence in Music and Drinking Contexts in Colombia. In *Sex and Violence*, ed. P. Harvey and P. Gow. London: Routledge.

Walton, J. 1977. Creating the Divided City. In *Cities in Change: Studies on the Urban Condition*, ed. D. E. C. Walton. Boston: Allyn and Bacon.

Ward, P. 1986. *Welfare Politics in Mexico: Papering over the Cracks*. London: Allen and Unwin.

———. 1999. *Colonias and Public Policy in Texas and Mexico: Urbanization by Stealth*. Austin: University of Texas Press.

Ward, P. M. Weiner, M. A., and K. Goss. 1989. *The Complete Book of Homeopathy*. Garden City, N.Y: Avery.

Williams, R. 1973. *The Country and the City*. London: Chatto and Windus.

———. 1977. *Marxism and Literature*. Oxford: Oxford University Press.

Wilson, D. 1980. Rituals of First Menstruation in Sri Lanka. *Man* 15: 603–625.

Winnie, W., and L. Velázquez. 1987. *La Encuesta de Hogares en Guadalajara:* Instituto de Estudios Economicos y Regionales, Universidad de Guadalajara.

Worsley, P. 1982. Non-Western Medical Systems. *Annual Review of Anthropology* 11: 315–348.

Index

Adoración nocturna, 89–91, 205n18
Agency: and healing, 116–18; gendered, 171–72, 178–79; and medical practices, 125–26; and religiosity, 90; and rituals, 144–46
Alonso, Ana María, 163–64
Alternative medicine, 96, 102, 104, 206n1, 208n3; and homeopathy, 118–25
Alternative modernity, 5, 11, 12, 70, 177, 182, 187, 206n1, 208n13; and illness and healing 124–25, 127, 187; and prisms of belonging, 10
Anthropology, of the barrio, 2, 3, 5, 11, 182, 185, 186
Appadurai, Arjun, 12, 14, 41, 119, 185, 201n6
Arizpe, Lourdes, 200n1

Barefoot doctors, 208n15
Behar, Ruth, 7, 142, 143, 145, 160, 161, 167–68, 201n3, 196n7
Barragán Lopez, Esteban, 58
Barrio. See Colonia popular; Neighborhood; Polanco
Beltrán, Aguirre, 103, 209n16
Belonging, 41; anthropology of 5; representations of 42, 57, 67; and time, 57; and urban space, 41. See also Migration; Identity
Beverley, John, 204n8
Bourdieu, Pierre, 91, 198n11

Bourgois, Philippe, 3, 47
Burdick, John, 70, 78, 80, 92
Butler, Judith, 5

Cárdenas, Lázaro, 21
Casa chica, 150
Comunidades Eclesiales de Base, 4, 7, 49, 69–70, 72, 73, 75, 79, 80, 81–86, 92, 204n10; and gendered subjectivity, 130, 139–40, 145; and medicina popular, 104; and MUP, 26, 79; and quinceñeras, 130, 132, 136–37, 138, 139, 140, 149, 152, 153; and the Virgin, 138. See also Liberation theology
Centro de la periferia, 3, 34
Church, Catholic, 10; Mexican, 70–71; and new, 10, 72–78; and religious agency, 75, 76, 78; and traditional, 10, 72–78, 80–91, 204n7
Citizenship, 13, 167
Clifford, James, 185
Cohen, Anthony, 48, 57, 67, 139
Colonia popular, 7, 19, 38; and colonos, 27; as a space of negotiation: 31, 38; as a spatial process, 3; and urban space, 42, 48–49. See also Neighborhood; Polanco
Confianza, 49
Connerton, Paul, 202n13
Coole, Diana, 195n3
CoReTT, 27, 30, 200n17

237

Craske, Nikki, 153, 159
Culture and Personality theory, 6, 7, 195n4
Curanderismo, 115–17, 206n3

Das, Veena, 8, 166
De la Peña, Guillermo, 20, 21, 22, 23, 24, 41, 58, 94
De la Torre, Renée, 20, 34, 41, 63, 80, 94, 130
Dethlefsen, Thorwald, 208n13, 209n18

Escobar Latapí, Agustín, 11, 22, 25, 199n12
Experience, 6; embodiment of, 155, 157, 201n5, 206n2, 212n3; gendering of, 136, 144–46

Fardon, Richard, 168
Ferguson, James, 2, 5, 12, 65–66
Fieldwork, problematization of, 2–3
Fiesta: and quinceñera, 4, 134–36, 139, 145–50
Finkler, Kaya, 208n12
Fortuny Loret de Mola, Patricia, 80
Foweraker, Joe, 25, 26, 80
Fox, Vicente, 14, 15
Fraccionamientos populares, 24

García Canclini, Nestor, 79, 84, 112
Gender, 157, 177, 178–79, 214n5; and Catholicism, 174–75; and motherhood, 157, 170–71; and self-knowledge, 173, 176; and womanhood, 173. *See also* Subjectivity; Womanhood
Giddens, Anthony, 57, 102
Gledhill, John, 8, 85, 197n12
Goddard, Victoria, 133, 144
González, Luis, 58, 63
González de la Rocha, Mercedes, 7, 11, 25, 28, 36, 37, 163, 164, 167
Good, Anthony, 212n5
Guadalajara: demographic expansion, 20; development of, 20, 23; economy, 9, 20, 22, 25; and mestizaje, 202n17; urbanization of, 22, 23, 24
Gupta, Akhil, 2, 11
Gutmann, Matthew, 7, 162, 167, 175, 196nn6,7
Gutiérrez, Natividad, 198n3

Hannerz, Ulf, 5
Harvey, Neil, 13

Higgins, Michael, 7, 196n5
Homeopathy 118–26; as divination, 124; and modernity, 125; principles 189–90; professionalisation of, 119–21; scientificity of, 120. *See also* Alternative medicine

Identity, 2, 57, 196n8; and Catholicism, 11; emergence of, 57; female, 5, 157–61, 177–79; and migration 57; process of, 7; and quinceñera, 132, 136, 139–44; ranchero, 57–62. *See also* Migration; Subjectivity; Womanhood
La ilusión, 4, 5, 129, 132, 212n2; and becoming a mujercita, 140–43; and suspension of disbelief, 143, 154
Inglis, Brian, 208n13

Jackson, Michael, 206n2
Jalisco, 22
Jehovah's Witnesses, 137
Jesuits, 72, 80–86. *See also* Comunidades Eclesiales de Base; Liberation theology

Kearney, Michael, 199n12

Lancaster, Roger, 175
Latin American Subaltern Studies group, 204n8
Lehmann, David, 76, 81
Levine, David, 78, 80, 158, 162
Lewis, Oscar, 6, 199n12
Liberation theology, 4, 70, 79, 81. *See also* Comunidades Eclesiales de Base; Jesuits
Localism, 5, 41, 65, 177; and prisms of belonging, 66
Logan, Kathleen, 7, 97, 101
Lomnitz, Larissa, 3, 7, 20, 131
Lomnitz-Adler, Claudio, 40, 132, 158; and intimate culture, 66, 201n2
Low, Setha, 54

Mahar, Cheleen, 40, 97, 126, 159
Martin, Joanne, 152, 159
Martín-Barbero, Jesús, 50
Massolo, Alejandra 157
Mattingly, Cheryl, 102
Medicina popular, 4, 12, 97, 102; and authenticity, 107; and causality of illness, 107–11; and healing, 112 –14;

and *nervios,* 110; and Vidasana group, 103–7, 209n20
Melhuus, Marit, 129, 138, 142, 157, 158, 160, 166, 178
Menéndez, Eduardo, 102, 109
Mestizaje, 197n3
Mexican health system, 98–101, 207n5
Mexico City, 20
Movimiento Familiar Cristiano, 86–89; and quinceñera, 148; and religious agency, 85, 90
Migration, 3–4, 9, 39, 52–54; and embodiment 54–55; and narratives, 52–53, 54, 55, 56, 57; and nortenización, 52; and subjectivity, 10; and taxonomy, 54; theories of, 7, 23, 40, 199n12; and urban space, 40. *See also* Prisms of belonging
Mirandé, Alfredo, 175
Modernity, 8, 51, 79, 185, 186; and alternative modernity 5, 11, 12, 70, 177, 182, 187; anxieties of, 94, 155; failure of, 13; and illness and healing, 112, 124–27, 187; and Mexican Catholicism, 10, 11
Modernization, 6, 14; critique of, 57; and urbanization, 186
Molyneux, Maxine, 158, 211n2
Monterrey, 20
Moore, Henrietta, 145, 212n3, 213n1
Mujercita. *See* Womanhood
Movimiento Urbano Popular, 26, 33; and Comunidades Eclesiales de Base, 26

Neighborhood: and rituals, 151; as space of negotiation, 31, 38; as a spatial process, 3; and urban space, 42, 48–49; and violence, 47, 48. *See also* Colonia popular; Polanco
Nervios, 110, 170
Nigenda, Gustavo, 99, 102, 207n5
Nostalgia, 62–63

Ong, Aihwa, 185

Pader, Ellen, 45
Parameshwar Gaonkar, Dilip, 12
Parkin, David, 76, 140, 145
Paz, Octavio, 160, 161
Polanco, 17, 18; churches in, 35, 71–72; demography of, 28; history of, 29; and housing, 42–43; and land disputes, 29–30; and mobilization, 33–34; multiple perceptions of, 37, 48–50; as urban process, 38. *See also* Colonia popular; Neighborhood
Posada Ocampo, Jesús, 204n6
Priesthood, 71–78
Prisms of belonging, 5, 9, 10, 11, 39, 65, 68–69, 183, 184; and gendered subjectivity, 165, 166, 178, 179; and localism, 41; and medicina popular, 105; and the rancho, 62; and religious discourse, 91, 92, 94; and rituals, 154, 155; and urban life, 55–56
El pueblo, 9; and identity, 62–65; as negotiated meaning, 51, 76; and representations, 12, 63, 65; as the popular subject, 69, 70, 80, 83, 95, 187, 203n1, 204n8

Quinceñera, 4; and family relations, 144, 146–53; and the female body, 142–43, 149–52; and gendered subjectivity, 128–32; the ritual of, 133–37, 146; and suspended disbelief, 143, 154, 160; and the time of la ilusión, 140–43. *See also* Comunidades Eclesiales de Base; Fiesta; La ilusión

Ramírez Saíz, Juan Manuel, 26, 33
Rancho, 9, 58; and identity, 57, 62; and masculinity, 60; livelihood in, 59, 61; and prisms of belonging, 62–65; and religiosity, 60–61
Redfield, Robert, 6, 115, 199n12
Regalado Santillán, Jorge, 26, 33
Rituals: and quinceñera, 133–37; and weddings, 134–35, 146. *See also* Fiesta
Rouse, and transnational migration, 23

Salinas de Gortari, Carlos 13, 196n9, 205n12
Scarry, Elaine, 8
Scheper-Hughes, Nancy 110, 206n2, 212n3
Scott, Joan, 5, 6
Selfhood, theories of, 6–9 195n3, 211n1
Stephen, Lynn, 26, 167
Stern, Steve, 165
Strathern, Marilyn, 142, 213n8
Subjectivity, 6, 51, 127, 157–59, 165n3; and embodiment, 9, 50, 54, 55; gendered, 139–41, 154, 167–68, 176–77, 212n3; and historical transformations, 7; and migration, 53; and narratives, 53–54;

Subjectivity *(continued)*
  and el pueblo (as the popular subject), 69, 70, 80, 83, 95, 187, 203n1; and religious discourses 70–77, 85, 94, 130; and the rural, 60, 64; and urban anthropology, 11; and urban space, 40, 45, 47, 50
Suffering, 157, 170–71, 173, 179, 184

Tianguis, 35
Trotter, 115
Tree of death 193
Tree of life, 192

Urbanization 19; and medical practices, 125; and modernization, 186; perceptions, 52; and urban desires, 50

Van Young, Eric, 202n17
Varley, Ann 23, 160, 165, 214n6
Vaughan, Mary Kay, 153
Vélez-Ibañez, Carlos, 7, 30, 162

Vernacular modernity. *See* Alternative modernity
Visweswaran, Kamala, 195n5
Void of Knowledge, 5, 8; and gendered subjectivity, 168–73

Ward, Peter, 24, 99
Williams, Raymond, 15, 37, 53, 92, 125; residual and emergent formations, 15, 70, 125, 155, 184, 186
Womanhood: and the body, 150, 154–55; and healing processes, 113–14; and livelihood, 46; and motherhood, 159–60; and mujercita, 140–41, 146–49, 153; and representations, 160–61, 168, 170–76; and rituals, 131, 133, 139–40; and second birth, 165; traditional, 161–63, 165. *See also* Gender; Subjectivity
Worsley, Peter, 98, 208n15

Zedillo, Ernesto, 13, 196n11

Compositor:	Binghamton Valley Composition
Text:	10/13 Galliard
Display:	Galliard
Printer and Binder:	Maple-Vail